African
Caribbean
Black People's
RESILIENCE
During COVID-19

Edited by

Delores V. Mullings, PhD

Olasumbo Adelakun, PhD

Jennifer Clarke, PhD

DEMETER

African, Caribbean, and Black People's Resilience During COVID-19

Edited by Delores V. Mullings, PhD, Olasumbo Adelakun, PhD, and Jennifer Clarke, PhD

Demeter Press
PO Box 197
Coe Hill, Ontario
Canada
K0L 1P0
Tel: 289-383-0134
Email: info@demeterpress.org
Website: www.demeterpress.org

Demeter Press logo based on the sculpture "Demeter" by Maria-Luise Bodirsky www.keramik-atelier.bodirsky.de

Printed and Bound in Canada

Cover artwork: Eboni-Ra Mullings
Typesetting: Michelle Pirovich
Proof reading: Jena Woodhouse

Library and Archives Canada Cataloguing in Publication
Title: African, Caribbean and Black people's resilience during COVID-19 / edited by Delores V. Mullings, PhD, Olasumbo Adelakun, PhD, Jennifer Clarke, PhD.
Names: Mullings, Delores V., editor. | Adelakun, Olasumbo, editor. | Clarke, Jennifer, editor.
Description: Includes bibliographical references.
Identifiers: Canadiana 20230531091 | ISBN 9781772584677 (softcover)
Subjects: LCSH: COVID-19 Pandemic, 2020—Literary collections. | LCSH: COVID-19 (Disease)—Social aspects. | LCSH: Black people—Social conditions. | LCSH: Resilience (Personality trait) | LCSH: Racism. | LCSH: Discrimination in medical care.
Classification: LCC RA644.C67 A37 2023 | DDC 305.896—dc23

 Funded by the Government of Canada · Canadä · The publisher gratefully acknowledges the support of the Government of Canada

To all the authors who have poured their hearts into this book and their unwavering support networks, this is a tribute to your immense perseverance and passion. Your commitment to sharing the stories of ACB individuals and communities globally during the unprecedented times of COVID-19 has created a powerful testament to resilience.

With your words, you have shed light on the strength, beauty, and extraordinary spirit of ACB people.

This book is also dedicated to the ACB communities—encompassing those who came before us, those who have left us, and those who move beside us today. We pay tribute to the trailblazers, whose actions prepared the way and whose struggles and victories shaped our own paths. We recognize the shoulders upon which we are positioned, acknowledging their profound impact on our journey.

To the past, present, and future generations of ACB individuals, this dedication symbolizes our collective strength and endurance. It is a reminder that we are part of a continuum, united by shared experiences and a common goal—to uplift, empower, and celebrate our rich histories and the beauty of our diverse communities.

This dedication will continue to serve as a reminder of our unity and our collective strength of spirit inclusive of our uniqueness, challenges, and differences.

Acknowledgments

In writing this book, we are humbled and inspired by the countless African, Caribbean, and Black (ACB) individuals around the world who have played significant roles directly or indirectly in shaping its narrative. Your resilience, strength, and steadfast spirits have left an indelible mark on these pages, and we are forever grateful for your influence.

To ACB individuals, families, and friends who have faced the risks of the pandemic head-on—working tirelessly on the frontlines of hospitals, care centres, long-term care facilities, nursing homes, food-service facilities, restaurants, sporting events, public transportation, supermarkets, and groceries stores—we extend our deepest gratitude. Your selflessness and sacrifice were a beacon of hope, providing care and support to those in need during those challenging times.

To those who experienced the devastating loss of loved ones, homes, jobs, and livelihoods, your unwavering spirit and determination have been a testament to the human capacity for resilience. Because of you, we are reminded of the strength of the human spirit in the face of hardship by the many stories of resilience and hope.

Our heartfelt appreciation to the unsung heroes of our communities, who despite daunting circumstances, came together in a time of collective grief and profound loss, seeking alternative ways to grieve, heal, and support one another; your strength and compassion have left an everlasting impact on this book, and your dedication is deeply admired.

This book serves as a tribute to each and every one of you—ACB individuals, families, friends, and communities—who have shaped its essence. Your stories, struggles, and triumphs is a model of strength, love, and unity that can emerge from even the most challenging of circumstances.

To all the reviewers, readers, and storytellers, behind the scenes administrators and supporters who embarked on this journey with us—thank you!

We want to express our deepest gratitude to all those who have contributed to this book, directly or indirectly. Your love, support, and encouragement have been invaluable, fuelling our passion and dedication to shed light on the experiences and narratives of ACB individuals. This book was possible because of your belief in the power of storytelling and amplifying our voices. It is important to continue uplifting and celebrating the immense beauty and resilience of ACB communities globally. In so doing, there is hope for change within our communities and a future that will shine even brighter.

With deepest gratitude.

A Note about Language and Terms

We use the term African, Caribbean, and Black (ACB) in this book to refer to Black people of African ancestry who reside either in the African diaspora or in continental Africa and have experienced the violence of enslavement, colonization, and institutional anti-Black racism at the intersections of, for example, gender, sexual orientation, religion, age, and country/region of residence. This term is also used interchangeably alone as a single term (e.g., Black) or together.

Some of the stories and narratives in this book are from its contributors' personal perspectives; as such, they are personal in nature, and we have striven to leave the essence of who the authors are and how they present themselves in terms of how they speak, write, and relate through their narratives and stories. This book is intended to appeal to various types of people from different backgrounds. Therefore, some of the language may seem contradictory to general editorial standards.

Contents

CONTENTS

Introduction

Why This Book

Delores V. Mullings, Olasumbo Adelakun, and
Jennifer Clarke

The United Nations (UN) declared 2015 to 2024 the International Decade for People of African Descent—a decision that recognizes that these populations represent a distinct group whose historical experience of enslavement and colonization continues to have lasting effects on their daily lives and that their human rights must be promoted and protected. COVID-19, as many authors note in their chapters, has affected Black life to such an extent that meaningful social, financial and economic gains have mostly been erased. It remains to be seen how governments around the world will address the significant negative impact COVID-19 has had on African, Caribbean, and Black (ACB) peoples. In addition, how will the UN declaration and recommendations for change be used to address the historical, current, and additional disadvantages, violence, and trauma Black people face? Within this framework, we as Black people control what is written about us and contribute to making our future better; to that end, we write our stories and centre our goals, aspirations, struggles, and triumphs.

This book is a necessity for people of African heritage, no matter where on the planet they physically and spiritually reside—be it in this universe, a parallel one, or in the afterlife. It is a collection of narratives and stories of Black life and the struggles and survival of our people—a representation of the essence of our resilience—under extreme circumstances during the COVID-19 pandemic. It also brings to light some of the opportunities and challenges that Black populations have faced globally during the pandemic. We wanted a book that people with different levels of education, mostly from grade eight to high school, could read and understand. We met that goal, as the collection contains only four academic chapters and 10 short chapters that tell personal stories of Black life during the pandemic.

The edited book contains ten pieces of poetry and seventeen chapters, including the introduction and epilogue, from six different countries: Canada, Jamaica, South Africa, England, Nigeria, and the US. Twenty-seven ACB authors contributed to this collection, ranging in age from twelve to eighty-four, and age is only one aspect of the nuances among this diverse group. The authors are unique and multilayered individuals whose intersecting social identities include work and educational status, gender and sexual orientation, health status and wellbeing, language, and geographic region, among others. They are retirees, informal caregivers, service workers, academics, professionals, and students. They are middle and working class. They live with (dis)abilities, including chronic pain, physical mobility, vision and hearing loss, and episodic disabilities, such as arthritis and diabetes. The book covers a range of topics and themes that include adjusting to school, caregiving, experiencing birth, death and dying of loved ones, arts and culture, LGBTQ+ support systems, small business, employment and entrepreneurial activities, food insecurity, farming, youth living in state care, long-term care residence, intimate partner violence, and navigating the tenure and promotion process. Most of the authors have personal experience with someone they love either dying from COVID-19, or from COVID-19-related complications, or someone narrowly escaping the jaws of COVID-19 death. Furthermore, during the pandemic, we all struggled with vicarious racial trauma with the media replaying videos of brutality and violence towards Black life, often leading to death and the pain of our relations.

Before the COVID-19 pandemic, Black bodies were already vulnerable to public death, and Black pain often trended on social media and was experienced in public spaces as entertainment—a consequence of systemic anti-Black racism. Systemic anti-Black racism manifests itself in many ways: police brutality, high rates of school suspension for Black children, overrepresentation in the child welfare system, low completion rates in postsecondary institutions, high unemployment and underemployment rates even for the educated, a concentration in the low-skilled, secondary market, lack of access to culturally responsive health and mental wellness care, high incarceration rates, scrutiny, stereotyping, targeting, over policing, criminalizing, and exclusion. African Americans sounded the alarm about the high rates of Black death resulting from COVID-19 infections. We saw Black death, loss, grief, and pain on the twenty-four-hour formal and informal news cycle.

At the same time, pandemic experts in Western countries predicted grave destruction and catastrophic COVID-19-related events in continental Africa. Despite significant disruptions, the catastrophic COVID-19 scenarios that many Western analysts predicted for the African continent have not materialized. After the first twenty-four months of the pandemic, the emerging pattern is one of resilience, not insecurity, chaos, or conflict.

Impact on Black People Globally

ACB people in the African diaspora began to draw attention to the impact of COVID-19 on Black people globally shortly after the pandemic was declared. At the same time, some governments, politicians, decision makers, and members of the general public in Western countries blamed Black people for their own vulnerabilities to COVID -19 without connecting those vulnerabilities to systemic anti-Black racism. As Black people tried to address the impacts of the pandemic, the world was assaulted with the public execution of George Floyd, an African American father, in May 2020 by a police officer and now convicted murderer. The Black Lives Matter (BLM) movement helped galvanize massive demonstrations opposing anti-Black racism and police brutality globally. While many people around the world can identify by face and name some Black people who were injured or died at the hands of police in the US, many would not recognize the name Chantelle Krupka, whom police shot and tasered in Peel on Mother's Day 2020, or the names Regis Korchinski-Paquet, Latjor Tuel, and D'Andre Campbell, who each died while interacting with Canadian police officers between 2020 and 2022.

We wanted to document and tell our own stories from across the globe of grief and loss, birth and death, caregiving, thriving and challenging institutional racism in our strength and glory regardless of what we call it. Black people globally have different experiences and should not be lumped into one group. Black people in the diaspora—the Caribbean, Latin America, Africa, Europe, North America, and Asia—may share a common historical background, but there is uniqueness within these different groups. While individuals born and raised on the continent have different experiences with colonization and the transatlantic enslavement industry, diasporic Africans are deeply scarred by intergenerational trauma and continue to live with its remnants. It was important to curate this collection to give Black people, wherever they live, the opportunity to speak their truths.

As we were finalizing the drafting of this book, the world watched as the Russia-Ukraine crisis ensued. Caught in the middle of this crisis were Black international students, who made their way to neighbouring countries to flee the war. Many of these Black students travelled for days, walked for hours, and queued at border crossings in freezing winter conditions only to be told priority would be given to Ukrainians to cross to safety. In the absence of immediate evacuation help from their different governments, many ACBs, primarily students were stranded. Black students in Ottawa and a community group in the UK started rescue efforts by raising funds to help ACB people who were stranded in Ukraine find space in bunkers and transportation to safety.

An example of this activism was a group of women who formed the Black Women for Black Lives group, which provided Africans and Caribbeans with information on the safest routes out of Ukraine to flee the war-ravaged country. This raises the question: have actions during the pandemic trampled some of the hard fought gains that ACB individuals and communities have achieved? History depicts how during the slave trade, enslaved Africans used hair braiding to relay messages, creating escape routes and maps to flee plantations and their captors. This irony is not lost on Black communities. The impact of the racial inequity on Black people that was seen during the COVID-19 pandemic has not been fully understood. We can only decipher some aspects now, but we really do not know the long-term health, financial, social, and emotional toll the pandemic has had on ACB people.

Black People's Resilience

Resilience indicates a positive adjustment or adaptation to threats, stress, tragedy, adversity, or trauma or the capacity to recover quickly from difficulties. It is often measured by outcomes. Historically, the lives of Black people globally have been described in terms of war, poverty, and disease, with no attention paid to their abilities and strength in overcoming these adversities. When going through unpleasant experiences, members of Black communities often rely on support from family members, friends, and peers to overcome adversity and focus on their wellbeing and health. For Black people, resilience is multilayered and complex, as in Justice Sonia Sotomayor's bootstrap analogy: "No matter how tall the heel on your boot is, the barrier is so high, you need a small lift to help you get over it" (Amzat et al.).

ACB health workers have played a fundamental role in COVID-19 responses locally and globally, including leading interventions to improve the resilience and responsiveness of health systems in sub-Saharan Africa. The African concept of social capital, Ubuntu, which focusses on a shared sense of responsibility, led communities to become frontline workers and advocates to communicate information while risking themselves during calls for social distancing measures. Ubuntu—coupled with resilience, determination, and past experience in controlling outbreaks—has enabled the continent to work faster, smarter, and better at responding to the pandemic (WHO). This social support existing within many Black communities is recognized as an important resource that creates survival capabilities and recovery strategies after adversities occur. With this support comes the ability to survive social, economic, and environmental challenges.

"Overcoming" and "bouncing back" are powerful words and phrases that have been applied consistently to describe how Black people cope with major and minor incidents of anti-Black racism and oppression; they are requirements for the survival of Black life. To understand resilience and strength among Black people, it is necessary to acknowledge their experiences and resistance against the legacy of anti-Black racism and discrimination, which continue to affect our daily lives even today. The reasons for Black resilience are complex, but they are often attributed to a history of overcoming adversity and to strong, supportive community ties.

Works Cited

Amzat, J., et al. "Coronavirus Outbreak in Nigeria: Burden and Socio-Medical Response during the First 100 Days." *PubMed Central*, 22 June 2020, https://www.ncbi.nlm.nih.gov/pmc/articles/PMC730 7993/. Accessed 28 Aug. 2023.

World Health Organization (WHO). "Africa on Track to Control COVID-19 Pandemic in 2022." *Africa Renewal*, 10 Feb. 2022, https://www.un.org/africarenewal/magazine/february-2022/africa-track-control-covid-19-pandemic-2022. Accessed 28 Aug. 2023.

PART I

Navigating and Resisting Challenges

Chapter 1.

COVID-19's Role in Disrupting the Myth of Resilience

Alyson Renaldo

The entity of resilience is one that is interwoven into many Black narratives of courage. Resilience, more than any other inspiring notion, has served our imagination and lived experiences alike. Be it in myth, legend, biography, or nonfiction, resilience is the (not-so-secret) weapon lurking near the end of a story, positioned as the impenetrable backdrop of a person's resolve. It is analogous to that final frontier of a person's strength that no amount of abuse or treachery can ever truly overtake. It is endlessly inspirational.

However, what exactly are we defining as resilience, and is it good? Is it nourishing? With this in mind, we turn to the following questions.

1. What passes for resilience within the African, Caribbean, and Black (ACB) experience?
2. Is our relationship to resilience appropriate?
3. What has the COVID-19 pandemic taught us about our relationship to resilience?

Before we can answer these questions and understand the special relationship between the ACB community and resilience, we must first look at what resilience is and how it has typically been defined. First, resilience is more felt than known; the description may feel a bit abstract and disconnected because we are trying to think about a thing we usually feel, sense, and cleave. For example, have you ever nodded your head in approval to the tempo of Bob Marley's "Buffalo Soldier," closed your eyes while listening to the lyrics of Johnson's "Lift Every Voice and Sing," thrown up the X-arms greeting like the fictional residents of Wakanda from *Black Panther* (Cooglar), or danced down the road to the Ultimate Rejects' feel good Soca hit "Full Extreme"—a tune that proudly asserts, "The city may burn down... we jamming still!"? If you have, then you have connected to artistic expressions of resilience; those are the spaces (that is, the inspiring feeling) to which this offering refers.

Second, the *Cambridge English Dictionary* defines resilience as "able to return quickly to a previous good condition after problems" ("Resilience"). If someone or something can return quickly to its previous good condition, that would suggest that little to no permanent disturbance has occurred—almost as though the harm never took place at all.

Finally, the actualization of what is felt and what is defined as resilience in ACB communities is a level of unspoken investment in the power of resilience. It fortifies the hope and commitment of the untainted parts of us that compel us to believe that in the struggle of life, ultimately, evil cannot ever fully overtake good.

Let us be clear: we are speaking about actual evil, as in terrible human actions, intentions, and the resulting damage from those actions. Some may be more familiar with the misuse of the word "evil," perhaps spoken from pulpits and political rallies, wherein any human experience beyond their own, is branded "evil." The latter is a misuse because the word is summoned to horrify listeners into obsessing over their proximity to an incalculable spiritual punishment or reward. We are discussing calculable (and calculating) actions with mortal consequences. Actions whose effects are so corrosive that they literally rip through fostered bonds of community, notions of ethical treatment, civilizations, and, perhaps most distressingly, the delicate bonds of compassion and love. These actions harbour such ill intent that many of us are loathed to truly understand why or how they were conceived in the first place.

For anyone who has borne witness to, or dealt with, the affects of unabashed cruelty, a part of their being is pushed to express themselves in response to the pain—that the resulting destruction they are witnessing cannot be the end of the story. No way. It just cannot be.

We will not accept it. Enter resilience—that indefatigable belief that not even evil and violence wrapped in greed, insecurity, and covetousness can overtake.

Why We Cherish Resilience

Resilience maintains the proverbial line in the sand. It has served as a line of protection against the annihilation of the mind, body, and personhood of ACB people during colonial schemes of kidnapping from West Africa, the Transatlantic Slave Trade and today's remaining structures of institutionalized racism. Resilience has most notably been an ACB bedrock in three ways:

1. It permits us to cleave to the ultimate emblem of courage whether we feel in the moment that we can manage or not. The idea that someone could dig down so deeply within their being and find what is needed to stay the danger before them is an enviable tool. Given the extreme evils that ACB communities have faced, the need to believe somewhere inside you that you can survive your circumstances cannot be overstated.

2. Resilience appears to be impervious to being co-opted by mechanisms of discrimination, oppression, and cruelty. Unlike other touchstones—such as democracy, freedom, and the people's will, which have fallen victim to agenda-laden distortions, resilience remains the property of the individual who faces danger head on, not of those who create the danger. Resilience calls upon every individual to remain resolute and to reveal and lay bare their reserve courage to overcome, to find more within and to be more. These are decisions that every individual makes— decisions that ultimately benefit their entire community. The opposite is true of purveyors of exploitation and theft. Exploitation can claim nothing beyond daring. Daring is not courage. Human-made malignancies lay bare their creator's personal lack and greed. Courage protects and reinforces; daring disrupts so it can be seen at any cost.

3. Resilience is malintent's vulnerability, evil's weakness. It stands as a counterpoint to deceit and cowardice. You can take almost anything from an individual or a collective by continually manufacturing tools of harm. Think of South Africa's apartheid,

gerrymandering in the US (a way governing parties try to cement themselves in power by tilting the political map steeply in their favour and away from the desires of the actual residents of the area [Wines]), Colombia's displacement of historically Black communities (Bledsoe), and global policing that disproportionately targets Black bodies, which apparently includes breathing, as evidenced by the public execution of George Floyd. Malintent can take lives, but it cannot take anyone's commitment to mount a resistance, girded by resilience, and to push back at the evil being launched at the good.

Locating Resilience in the Black Experience

Yes, the state of resilience has served us well, but what has been powering this resilience? The "what" powering our resilience is part of us. It is not an external force we summon. Nope. Resilience pulls from us; it is our internal life force. The stuff of resilience consists of whatever emotional, physical, and mental resources we give it, whatever can be syphoned from staying the course in that moment of peril. Amid the metaphors of its resilience being called and depended upon, we must be mindful that the "what" is us. Has that "what" been serviced? Are we making efforts to replenish the "what?" Let us continue this investigation.

The sophistication and deficit of summoning resilience is that it does not ask any questions about whether you are whole or healthy enough to confront the challenge you are asking your resilience to meet. Resilience hears "Keep us going—hold back this badness!" and complies— no questions asked. As resilience is part of you, it relies on your good judgment to care for and replenish its sources. The next time you call on it, resilience will simply pull from whatever is available. It is brilliant as a survival tool, but problematic as a mode of dealing with everyday life.

Admittedly, the effects of macro- and microaggressions created by institutionalized racism on ACB in the diaspora are constant, such that there is not always a discernible line between survival and living, which creates a chronic need for resilience. Sometimes we require every tool we can get to remain vigilant against racism, but if one of these tools of vigilance does not replenish our sources of resilience, what are we doing to ourselves? So far, we have more questions than answers here, but let us keep going.

The Myth of Resilience

Enter the mythology of resilience and the creation of the ACB twenty-four-hours-a-day, seven-days-a-week soldier, whose narrative suggests that the Buffalo Soldier within us is an inexhaustible source requiring little replenishment. This sentiment is evident in how we dialogue about our resilience. Need proof? You might have heard this brand of praise: "That guy's a soldier, son!" or "That girl can handle anything!" As our relationship to soldierdom is more felt than considered—a defence mechanism—our goal in identifying someone as a soldier is an effort to bestow the highest compliment to a person in times of struggle. Ironically, though, the soldier metaphor is inadequate.

Okay, let us first understand who and what an actual soldier is and does. Traditionally, in the Western world, soldiers may find themselves trained and paid to fight a war, or invasion. Soldiers may never engage in a traditional battle during their career, but if they do, that willingness to sacrifice is accorded societal appreciation. It is understood that that soldier's exposure to peril is for a finite duration of time. Once the tour of duty is completed, the soldier returns home to a society that holds some understanding of the scope of the sacrifice that was made (likely not an adequate understanding but some). At the very least, society understands that it should remain mindful of the taxing circumstances of a soldier's journey. Additionally, (within societies) benefits, resources, and medical personnel are made available specifically to treat visible or invisible wounds sustained due to combat experience. While these services may not be sufficient to fully address the needs of soldiers and veterans, military hospitals—such as the South African Military Health Service in Pretoria, South Africa, the Royal Centre for Defence Medicine in Birmingham, England, and the Sunnybrook Veterans Centre in Toronto, Canada—can be found in most in many parts of the world.

By contrast, the ACB person that we seek to compliment, by referring to them as a soldier, has been fighting a war that began generations before they drew their first breath—twenty-four hours a day, seven days a week. To be clear, this illustration relates more to ACB persons within the diaspora, given their historic enslavement experience. Their soldier duties are not a chosen career path but a burdensome, unspoken addition to their home, family life, and actual work life. The ACB soldier knows that imperialist aggressors have created a system of exploitation wrapped in a narrative of "it is your fault," which current national and international structures seem content to maintain. However, before this plight can truly saturate the soldier's understanding, they will be forced to suspend further consideration to dodge yet another of the othering bullets or protect newcomers entering the battlefield. Unlike actual soldiers, the ACB soldier experiences little collective empathy for their plight, except intermittently, when the public, many of whom bear a striking resemblance to the aggressors, feel some limited, philosophical proximity to the aggressors' agenda and wish in that moment to distance themselves from that legacy.

So why in the name of all that is reasonable does the ACB soldier not just give up? Because they have parents, children, partners, and friends whose wellness is at the forefront of every consideration. They cannot extinguish the hope that if they just soldier through, their lived experience can be better. They push onwards, therefore, with whatever they have that is not allocated to breathing or keeping their hearts beating: their resilience. This is not the landscape of an actual soldier. There is not a parallel to describe what has been asked of the Black diaspora over the past five hundred years for enslavement to now. Truthfully, what word could adequately define this fate? None. Therefore, the term soldier will remain our stand in.

From earlier discussions, recall that actual soldiers are offered some resources and support. Has anyone ever heard of the Buffalo Soldier Memorial Veterans Hospital near the former Maroon communities of Jamaica? What about the Transatlantic Slave Trade PTSD Trauma Ward of São Paulo, Brazil? The Institutional Racism Recovery Wing at the Mahogany Medical Centre for ACB Veterans in Surrey, England? Maybe the Neo-Colonial Trauma Response Units in West Africa? All right then, at least the state-of-the-art Survivors of Segregation VA Hospital down in Atlanta, Georgia, right? Spoiler alert: No one has heard of these resources. They do not exist.

We speak with admiration of an ACB soldier's frontline bravery—resilience—but rarely of their need for resources to support their recovery. There are few ACB persons, if any, who have not called upon resilience to reduce institutional racism. Plainly put, ACB people's relationship to resilience is a necessity.

The History that Necessitated the Overuse of Resilience

Resilience is a response to extremes. It is a call to battle, but no actual soldier has ever spent every day of their life on the battlefield. And even if such a thing were possible, their perception of living—of thriving—would be heavily mitigated (not to mention distorted) by excessive exposure to gore, violence, and death. A wartime soldier would consider it a good day if they saw only one bombing that day as opposed to the seventeen they witnessed two days earlier. They would be accustomed to perpetually functioning in a space of vile extremes—a place where anything less than horrendous is manageable. Proximity, however, to the horrendous should not be anyone's bedrock of perception, which in subtle and overt forms has been the reality of the Black diasporic person since 1502. "Horrendous" is also precisely the word to describe the proximity Black persons have had to the legacy of the transatlantic slave trade's iteration of the practice of slavery.

The unwillingness of the architects of the Transatlantic slave trade (and their beneficiaries and descendants) to make amends or even truly acknowledge the depths to which they have prolonged injury at every level of Black personhood has further fortified the Black community's relationship to the horrendous and to the need to hang on to their resilience. Can anyone truly return to a previous good condition when tethered to the unthinkable? Or do they merely look like they have? If in fact they do look like they have, then what are we witnessing and defining as their resilience?

The answer is what we are witnessing is courage. It is resolve—the decision to try to be as resilient as possible.

COVID-19's alarming impact on ACB persons has revealed the extent to which its diaspora has unconsciously relied on resilience to cope with institutionalized racism. To illustrate this point, there is a strange but oddly appropriate image that comes to mind that summarizes what ACB communities are continually called to do in response to racialization. It is an allegory that is likely rarely associated with this discussion. It is found in JRR Tolkien's masterpiece, *The Lord of the Rings*. Author John Tolkien was a South African-born English writer, professor, and drafted soldier who fought in World War I (Doughan 15).

In the epic story, the wizard Gandalf (I know, I know, but stay with me here) and his companions are on a quest to stop the powers of evil in the form of a ring from reasserting itself and its creator, Sauron. On their long journey to fulfil this quest, they find themselves in the Mines of Moria, the lair of an ancient demon, a Balrog. (Why this beast is so unpleasant and intent on harming a group that just happens to be passing through these mines, no one knows.) Gandalf holds off the large, fire-breathing, whip-wielding being, summoning all his courage and resilience while uttering the battle cry, "You shall not pass!" As the demon tries to attack him and his companions, Gandalf's stance throws the demon back, stumbling, falling into an endless pit. But before the beast perishes, it hurls the tip of its whip at the wizard's knees and drags him into nothingness with it. Before succumbing entirely to the whip's pull, Gandalf, clinging to a piece of rock, orders his traumatized companions to "fly [run away], you fools!" before disappearing below (Tolkien 430). His companions watch helplessly as the tip of that whip—that unrelenting agent of malintent—tears a hole into their purpose, community, and bonds of friendship. Without a second to grieve or process the magnitude of this damage, the troop presses forwards, bracing for more potential harm as they continue the quest thrust upon them (Tolkien 430).

Now substitute the fictional Gandalf for your ancestors, our grand-mother, the struggles our immigrant parents faced to create a dignified life for us. Then substitute the Balrog for the slave ships, the plantations, the US police officer's knee on George Floyd's neck, the disparity of access to resources between two citizens of the same wealthy country, whose only glaring difference is skin colour, and the talk of diversity and equity all around that oddly never results in any lasting systemic accountability from the speakers or any measurable reallocation of empirical resources to those about whom they speak. *The Lord of the Rings* may exist in the realm of fantasy fiction, but the parallels to this discussion do not. It is unlikely that Mr. Tolkien had the plight of the Black diasporic experience at the forefront of consideration when he penned this scene, but he was a soldier in, and bore witness to, carnage.

Black People's COVID-19 Response to the Resilience Myth

It is against this historical backdrop of racial injustice that the Black diaspora's perpetual calls to resilience were forged and likely where its celebration of survival was born. It is also the space in which we manoeuvre, to varying degrees, with pursuits of thriving ever contextualized by resilience and surviving, not wholeness.

If resilience is returning to a previously good condition, then the myth of resilience is believing that when we witness a person or community still standing and displaying courage in the face of harm, it means they have somehow returned to the previous good state. Spoiler alert: They have not. Fast forwards to the present day. In ACB communities, battle scars of resilience are proudly worn. Praise of our cunning is proudly spoken. Questions of replenishment are met with collective chuckles.

Enter the COVID-19 virus and the pandemic, which ripped through ACB communities in Canada and the entire world. It is a sophisticated, highly adaptive air-borne virus that happily exploits the low priority we have placed on replenishment—a virus that has zero interest in how or whether we choose to venerate depletion and even less interest in whether we choose to define long-held emotional, physical, and mental vulnerabilities as resilience. It wishes to live. Unlike the ACB soldier's battle, the virus's motives are clear. COVID-19 turned everything upside down and inside out. It disrupted everything, including the myth suggesting a benefit to the chronic use of resilience, although this disruption may be, in the most vulgar and harmful of means, a positive by-product.

This invisible virus now forces the question: Can we sustain the chronic use of resilience and expect to thrive? Given the disproportionate impact this virus has had on the Black community around the world, the question of "what is being used to maintain resilience?" ought no longer be a chuckle-worthy or philosophical question.

How, though, could a virus be any kind of threat to a people who have continually displayed amplified courage through generations of assault? Come on, really? Surely these soldiers can make their way through this, as they have so many times in the past. Scars are nothing but little bits of visual evidence of resilience—a return to a previously good state. Are they not? "Biochemically speaking," explains racialized biochemist and chemistry professor Dr. Mohamad Abbani, "when we see a physical scar, you are not seeing a return to anything but a replacement" (Personal interview).

Wait, what now?

Dr. Abbani continues:

> When cells that [made up that area before the injury] were harmed, they were not just harmed; they actually died. When you see someone with a scar, you are looking at a copy of the previous cells. They are similar but not the same. No matter what, some variation [of the original state of the cell] has occurred. Sometimes the variation can be advantageous or benign but not often. This is why reinjury to any region of the body can be detrimental because the more a space is disrupted and requires replacements, the farther away one is moving from the original genetic coding. When we witness scars, we are seeing more cells there. Copies, trying to remind us not to reinjure. (Personal interview)

The body is not conscious, yet even its mechanisms for healing in creating scar tissue seem to convey the message that we ought to avoid circumstances requiring perpetual resilience because damage and repairs are costly. Wounds permanently change something in you that cannot be returned. The cost is, in fact, quite high. What we still have as a community are largely untreated ACB soldiers. People who have been forced to rely on resilience in mythic proportions—the myth that resilience is an inexhaustible, deep space that needs only the seeker's resolve to wield it.

The generational proximity of the Black diaspora to the need for resilience has resulted in a distorted picture of what is occurring. We have been using a temporary survival device as a modality of living, forgetting that at its core resilience is a temporary coping mechanism. It is a mechanism of mental, emotional, and physical depletion, not an indicator of courage. Courage and resilience are not the same thing. An exhausted soldier can still be a courageous soldier. Our community is disproportionately impacted by COVID-19 virus as a result of some of those untreated wounds. Wounds that in modern times present themselves as sophisticated and subtle forms of illness. For example, we cannot see diabetes, high-blood pressure, despair, and lupus, yet their impact can be life altering and life threatening.

Dr. Abbani explains that:

One of the paths to developing diabetes is essentially a narrative of the breaking point of resiliency, if you wish to call it that. The body accommodates the overuse of the pancreas until it can no longer manage, at which point it forges entirely new paths to deal with the onslaught it is facing. The problem is that these new compromised paths may become part of that person's physiological makeup; they may also become part of the genetic coding now provided to that person's offspring. (Personal interview)

The book *Epigenetic Changes in Diabetes* expands this definition by stating that "Epigenetic changes often translate environmental stimuli to changes in gene expression" (Al-Haddad et al. 64). And as Dr. Abbani states, "High-blood pressure, asthma, and lupus, to name a few, can function in much the same way [environmentally]" (Personal interview). Communities that experience these types of autoimmune diseases have had to do so largely in response to environments and diets for which their bodies were not originally designed. "What people do not understand is that the process of physiological adaptivity is a slow one … adaptivity on the time scale of evolution cannot be captured in a few generations" (Abbani, Personal interview). It may take generations for the descendants of displaced persons to adjust.

Oh dear.

Furthermore, "resiliency is misinterpreted by the nervous system as a way of compensating for hidden pain," explains a racialized registered massage therapist, called Miranda. "I'm licensed to touch the body, not the mind, but many of us [massage therapists and manual therapists] are seeing the clear correlations between the two. Some of us are allowing our knowledge of that patient's trauma to inform how we treat, but until the licensing boards fully recognize and update our scope of practice to include trauma-informed treatment, it's best for me to remain anonymous."

"Sometimes what we are defining as resiliency," she continues, "is actually chronic disassociation. When people of colour enter my clinic, I immediately prepare myself to push harder, massage even deeper into their bodies because many don't feel a normal massage; there are entire areas of their bodies that are numb" (Personal interview with anonymous massage therapist).

Numb?

"Emotions influence how the nervous system is expressed. There are two modes: the sympathetic (fight or flight) and parasympathetic (rest and digest). It is really hard for the body to know when to turn on which mode because all of it depends on how trauma shows up in the body" (Personal interview with massage therapist).

What exactly is the nervous system?

The massage therapist explains:

> The nervous system includes the brain, the spinal cord, and all the nerves that come out of your spine. It is the electric system of your body. The nervous system is the highway for the connectivity of a person's mental, physical, and emotional wellbeing. If there are blockages, the nervous system compensates. Depending on the pressure, it can disassociate altogether. Given the strain of being a minority in white societies, disassociation is something I often see in my patients of colour. As a woman of colour, I also live it. I can recognize both collective and individual trauma, as it can be multilayered. I leverage my professional discipline to hold space [for the client], as much as I can.

The exposure of mythic resilience brought on by COVID-19 is positive because residual trends of resilience veneration and resistance to self-care are largely subconscious. Resilience in and of itself is a laudable tool. However, reliance on resilience as a modality of navigating everyday life is dangerous. Reliance on resilience by a community—by generations of a community—results in disproportionate vulnerabilities that have no viable means of defence.

My mother, for example, is retired. Her days of working full time and raising a family on her own are now well behind her. These days, her schedule is more open and relaxed. Recently, Mom was experiencing some soreness in her arm. As her retirement medical package covers massage therapy, she decided to go see a massage therapist. I later asked her how the appointment went. "Good," she explained, "the young man [massage therapist] asked me how often I went to massage therapy when I was working."

After a pause for effect, we both broke out into hysterical laughter. "Often?" I repeated, fanning the flames; the laughter ramped up all over again.

After the phone call with Mom ended, quiet reflection began. Why was the therapist's question so humorous to us? What was funny? The smile quickly dissolved from my face. It seems we were genuinely amused by the mere notion that Mom, or anyone with her profile (Black, single mother, immigrant, hardworking), would have thought to give mental attention to addressing nonlife-threatening/nonwork-inhibiting ailments of any sort. It was laughable, but really, it ought not be.

We laughed because mom's experience of life as a racialized person in a wealthy, Western nation is one of pushing through and getting by. None of the mechanisms of success or comforts available in her adopted home were made with her success in mind. Therefore, most of her lived experience here was spent trying to hold the figurative hole in Canada's cultural fence open long enough for her and me to safely crawl through and appropriate some of the nation's comforts for our use. Taking a break from prying open those steel fence links seems ridiculous on the face of it. Furthermore, spas, massages, etc. are for the "Karens" of the world, whose lives rest parasitically on the rest of ours. (Sidebar: The colloquial term "Karen" initially referred to a "barbed but humorous caricature of entitled white women" [Romano], but as the post-George Floyd discussion surrounding spaces of white supremacy intensified and widened, so too did the association of the name Karen with privilege and mechanisms of oppression.) They have time and ill-gotten resources to convince themselves that they need self-care and support to walk through all those open gates that lay before them—that the task of availing themselves of all that privilege is taxing. While many of us would like to have access to Karen's resources, few of us wish to be her or like her. She is a patron of the spa. She is a visual aid of the second and third reasons we cherish resilience. She is a vulgar, vapid counterpoint to anyone of depth (let alone resilience-based ACB soldiers), and her surfaced, trite reality cannot make claims to resilience or courage. Therefore, do we really wish to be guided by anything Karen is doing? Not even remotely. So, what ACB soldier would have interest in booking time at Karen's spa? None. There is more valour in remaining on the battlefield.

Understanding the Need for a Road Forward

"Self-care is not the spa," reveals racialized registered psychotherapist Gina Miranda: "Health means looking after all facets of self: energetic, social, mental, emotional, physical, and financial. For some of my clients of colour, I don't know that they notice COVID-19 in the same way [as others]. For them it's just another thing. Just one more speed bump in the face of so many pre-existing and additional challenges" (Personal interview).

The COVID-19 airborne virus, which was so deadly that it shut down the major social and commercial interactions of this planet, defined as "just another speed bump?" It is disturbing to even contemplate what she would define as an actual roadblock.

"Trauma lives in the body," Miranda continues. "All of our mental health symptoms, from depression to anxiety, live in the body. If we don't pause and consider the cost of our lived experience, it will catch up with us in either extreme mental disorder or physical complications" (Personal interview).

While preparing this piece, my mind was cast back to a recent conversation with a prominent Black Canadian academic. This is a woman who shares a similar profile to my mother, save for her age, meaning that later when this Black Canadian academic encountered that same hole in the nation's cultural fence, she was able to widen it even more, affording herself achievement of the highest rungs of education and its administration: "I am accustomed to pushing through. When I lost my son, I remember being preoccupied with making sure he was a donor to other babies and with making sure that people who needed them received all the stuff I had for his nursery" (Personal interview with anonymous academic).

Wait. What? When she lost...whom?! What?! The assertion went so fast that I was not even sure what had been heard because the academic's tone had not shifted from the last topic. I sat in front of her listening and watching in confusion. The topic was devastating, but the delivery was... resilient. It took two days for me to circle back and ask whether she had been able to truly deal with her loss and seek help for it. Was this the demeanour of a woman callously recalling trauma? Hardly. This was a window into the profile of a person for whom a deadly virus could be considered just another speed bump.

"Just because you are not aware of the stress that your body is under," adds Miranda, "doesn't mean that your body is not under stress. I'm a trauma therapist. I use EMDR [eye movement desensitization and reprocessing] and sensorimotor as treatment modalities. I don't want my clients to simply cope with their symptoms, I want them to resolve them" (Personal interview).

Coping. A synonym for chronic dependence upon resilience. My mother and I laughed that day at the massage therapist's assumption, but we certainly did not laugh when the nephrologist informed us that Mom would require a kidney transplant. You see, after years of pushing through, as did the Black Canadian academic, of prioritizing widening that fence over seeking out every medical resource to solve her chronic stomach aches, an infection had ravaged my mother's kidney function until there was none left. (Luckily, her daughter had a spare kidney, but that is another story.)

Moving Forward

No element of prioritizing self-care invokes laughter for my mother or me anymore, nor should it for anyone in the Black diaspora. Attending to the needs of our personal and collective landscape is a rising sentiment in our community. Yes, things are changing and progressing. There are likely many of generation Y and Z (those born from 1992 on) who would have had a prompt and detailed answer for my mother's massage therapist, accompanied by zero laughter. However, we must remain diligent in maintaining a collective consciousness about our wholeness. It can be tempting to resort to disconnection and reliance on resilience, as doing so can also mean a reprieve from disconnection—from the pernicious spectrum of institutionalized inequality that has necessitated it, whose tentacles maintain their hold the in present day.

The COVID-19 pandemic has given us the opportunity to reassess what we ought to prioritize as a community. Yes, it is true that through this global crisis, we can once again bear witness to our fundamental abilities of endurance through hardship. Our ability to endure will always be a point of pride, as it should. Recognizing, however, that chronic resilience is an avatar of vulnerability is crucial. If we are the stuff that can harness super-human levels of resilience, then let us commit to rerouting that resolve and commitment to selfcare, wholeness, and personal and collective nurturing.

We can do it. We must do it. It will not even require our resilience, but a reallocation of our focus to what is best for us. Let us now answer our initial questions:

1. What is passing for resilience within the ACB experience? Us. Our essential, individual, and collective life force.
2. Is our relationship to resilience appropriate? Um, absolutely not. No. It has been understandable but is no longer appropriate.
3. What has the COVID-19 pandemic taught us about our relationship to resilience? That we must actively and radically diversify our coping mechanisms. Now.

Make no illusion, the war against inequity and for basic human rights into which we were born is not over. It senselessly rages on. But maybe allowing our resilience full access to the pernicious fears of our aggressors can lessen its effects. Let us prioritize nutrition. Let us seek out spaces of healing therapists and friends who are invested in growth, not survival. Let us retire the use of resiliency wherever possible. Let us nurture ourselves and model that behaviour for all. Let us offer loving deposits, not survival techniques in the lives of those around you. Let us whisper behind one another's backs: "Yo, that gal is balanced for days!" "That dude spent some time working on himself; he is secure in these streets!" I know, I know, it may take a while for these axioms to catch on, but not as long as you might think. Just as soon as someone flings a Soca or Samba beat, Reggae rhythm, or a crisp West African drum beat under them, they will trend into anthems. Soon, we will all be feeling it, not thinking it, just as we did for other things. We will smile as our legacy of connectivity continues.

The COVID-19 pandemic has afforded us a startling reminder of the need to continually shift our collective gaze towards the dogged (healthy) pursuit of balance, thriving, joy, and fulfillment—which is every human's birth right, not to mention the truest defence against the real Balrogs of this world.

Works Cited

Anonymous Academic. Personal interview with Alyson Renaldo. 7 Aug. 2021.

"Resilience, N. (2)." *Cambridge Business English Dictionary.* Cambridge

University Press, 2021. dictionary.cambridge.org/dictionary/english/resilience. Accessed 5 Aug. 2023.

Abbani, Mohamad. Personal interview with Alyson Renaldo. 4 June 2021.

Al-Haddad R., et al. "Epigenetic Changes in Diabetes." *Neuroscience Letters* vol. 625, 2016, pp. 64-69.

Bledsoe, Adam. "Anti-Blackness Spread by Global Capital." Interview by Margaret Kimberly and Glen Ford. *Black Agenda Report.* Black Agenda Radio. 19 Oct. 2020.

Cooglar, Ryan, and Joe Robert Cole. *Black Panther.* Directed by Ryan Cooglar. Walt Disney Studios Motion Pictures, 2018.

Doughan, David. *J.R.R. Tolkien: A Biographical Sketch.* 19 May 2021, www.tolkiensociety.org/author/biography. Accessed 5 Aug. 2023.

Johnson, James Weldon. "Lift Every Voice and Sing." Performed by Melba Moore, *Soul Exposed.* Capital Records, 1990.

Marley, Robert Nestor. "Buffalo Soldier." *Legend: The Best of Bob Marley and the Wailers* (Remastered). The Island Def Jam Music, 2002.

Miranda, Gina. Personal interview with Alyson Renaldo. 7 July 2021.

Romano, Aja. "How 'Karen' Became a Symbol of Racism." *Vox.* 21 July 2020, www.vox.com/21317728/karen-meaning-meme-racist-coronavirus. Accessed 5 Aug. 2023.

Tolkien, J.R.R. *The Lord of the Rings.* Harper Collins Publishers, 1954.

Ultimate Rejects. "Full Extreme." Fox Fuse, 2016.

Wines, Michael. "What Is Gerrymandering? And How Does It Work?" *New York Times.* 27 June 2019, www.nytimes.com/2019/06/27/us/what-is-gerrymandering.html. Accessed 5 Aug. 2023.

Chapter 2.

Grieving during the COVID-19 Pandemic: Burial Rituals Among African Caribbean Mothers Living in Canada

Stephanie Fearon

Introduction

When I was ten years old, my great-grandfather died. For nine days, we celebrated his homegoing at our family's rural village, nestled in the brush of Saint Thomas, Jamaica's most eastern parish. I remember the early morning cries from goats being slaughtered on our ancestral lands. I recall the clamour of voices planning for and preparing curried meals with rice and peas and ground provisions. Aunty Etta, Grandpa's third-eldest daughter and loyal caregiver, declared, "We give thanks for Daddy's return to our Lord with fresh meat and food and community."

Neighbours and loved ones filed onto our family's homestead lugging sacks of yam, coco, and green banana. Most of them were from around the way. A few, clad in foreign outfits and perfumes, made the trek from England, the United States, and Canada. I watched a handful of men wield their machetes and slash through firewood foraged from the nearby bush. Meanwhile, my grandmother and her sisters transformed part of our yard into an outdoor kitchen. Aunty Elaine prodded and pushed breadfruit in the fire pit, as Aunty Bee and her two best friends took charge of the fried fish. I joined the other children and chased ground lizards around the naseberry tree, cooking pans, and piled wood.

At nightfall, the men huddled around the tables to drink one-hundred proof Jamaican white rum and play dominoes, a popular group game that many Caribbean peoples enjoy. We children settled on plastic stools with plates of food balanced on our laps. I relished the lingering taste of nutmeg and cinnamon from the chocolate tea we often drank. I listened to the women sing and recite Bible verses under the unlit, moonless sky. The men and children joined the women from our village and sang "O God, Our Help in Ages Past." Surely, I believed, our unified voices lifted Grandpa's spirit past the stars right to the front of heaven's gate. I admired the women and mothers in my family who led this extended wake. Their work, amid death, brought loved ones from across the diaspora together to celebrate Grandpa's life and to heal.

A paucity of literature investigates the effects of the pandemic on the burial rituals of Canada's African Caribbean communities. Little discussion centres on how they reimagine ways to collectively mourn during a pandemic. This autoethnographic essay weaves scholarship and personal reflections to present a harrowing account of the ways that African Jamaican mothers living in Canada have reconceptualized burial rituals during the COVID-19 pandemic. The essay draws on motherwork and Black diasporic scholarship as well as Black feminist–womanist storytelling traditions to share and analyze African Jamaican maternal stories of grief and innovation.

This essay begins by situating Jamaican burial practices within the ongoing legacy of Black existence in the diaspora. It continues with a presentation of the theories and frameworks guiding the study. Afterwards, a personal narrative grounds the exploration of grief and loss during COVID-19. This essay closes by exploring the conditions that are needed to sustain the leadership of African Jamaican mothers living in Canada and grieving during the pandemic.

African Caribbean Canadian Context

The enslavement of Africans and colonization in the diaspora have shaped burial rituals and their significance to African Caribbean burial processes. For African Jamaican communities, Nine Night is an extended wake where family and friends gather to celebrate Black life through communal acts of memory, grief, loss, and merrymaking. For nine days and nine nights, relatives, friends, and community members stand watch, ushering the deceased's spirit to its final resting place. Mothers and women enjoy a longstanding role as leaders in the creation and upholding of these distinct burial rituals where African religions and spiritual cultures blend with Christianity (Huggins and Hinkson 276). Their leadership in maintaining these burial traditions continues through migration journeys beyond the Caribbean and survives in African Jamaican communities in Canada and across the world.

Like Rinaldo Walcott (36), Christina Sharpe (5), Saidiya Hartman (*Lose Your Mother* 6), and Dionne Brand (26), and other African, Caribbean, and Black scholars, I take the stance that Atlantic chattel slavery and its afterlives are still unfolding in Canada. Hartman explains, "Black lives are still imperilled and devalued by a racial calculus and a political arithmetic that were entrenched centuries ago. This is the afterlife of slavery— skewed life chances, limited access to health and education, premature death, incarceration, impoverishment" (*Lose Your Mother* 6). Contemporary scholarship upholds my belief that slavery and its afterlives continue to inform the experiences of African Jamaican mothers in Canadian cities, such as Toronto (Onuora 38; Fearon 3). In these afterlives, anti-Black racism is endemic to Canadian institutions and profoundly shapes the health outcomes of African Jamaican mothers (Fearon 56).

The ongoing COVID-19 pandemic has further exposed the egregious effects of institutional discrimination on African, Caribbean, and Black communities in Toronto. In June 2020, Toronto Public Health's analysis of sociodemographic, disaggregated, individual-level data confirmed the overrepresentation of racialized groups in COVID-19 cases and hospitalizations. Data revealed that Black people of African and Caribbean descent comprised 26 per cent of COVID-19 cases in Toronto, despite representing merely 9 per cent of Toronto's population (McKenzie 1). Black Torontonian populations had COVID-19 case rates six to eleven times that of their white counterparts (McKenzie 1).

COVID-19 has resulted in a series of stay-at-home orders and social distancing measures, affecting African Caribbean funerary rituals that elicit large gatherings at the deceased's home.

Theoretical Framework: Black Feminist-Womanist Storytelling Traditions

A burgeoning body of scholarship emphasizes the importance of storytelling in African, Caribbean, and Black communities. Black storytelling is a deeply rooted practice that predates contemporary theoretical paradigms. African griots and enslaved Africans engaged in storytelling to order, make sense of, and give significance to, the past, present, and future (Sampson 9; Smitherman 150; Toliver 508). African and African diasporic communities continue to use storytelling to assert themselves, their ideas, and their dreams, especially in societies that seek their subjugation. In her ground-breaking text *Talkin and Testifyin: The Language of Black America*, Geneva Smitherman defines Black storytelling as a rhetorical strategy in which Black people condense broad, theoretical observations about life and relationships into concrete narratives, such as personal/self-stories, cultural stories, and metanarratives (150). Each retelling of a story, Smitherman explains, "recreates the spiritual reality for others who at the moment vicariously experience what the storyteller has gone through" (150). By sharing their lives through stories, African, African Caribbean, and Black storytellers reaffirm their humanity and agency to themselves and those listening.

Storytelling is a literacy strategy that also positions African, Caribbean, and Black women as trusted narrators of our own lives (Richardson 680). Black feminist-womanist storytelling involves collecting, sharing, analyzing, and theorizing African, African Caribbean, and Black women's stories (Baker-Bell 531; Toliver 509). It champions our words and narratives as sources of legitimate knowledge (Haddix 22). Informed by Black feminist-womanist epistemologies, Black feminist-womanist storytelling places our varied identities—such as race, gender, class, and citizenship—in conversation with one another through stories (Baker-Bell 532). Indeed, stories create space for us to examine the intersections of our oppression and envision possibilities (Butler 155; Glenn 137).

This essay is grounded in Black feminist-womanist storytelling—the theoretical framework that informed the stories I selected to share and the creative techniques in which they are presented. Collecting and writing the stories comprising this essay helped me further appreciate my identity as an African Jamaican mother living in Canada and deepened my understanding of grieving practices during the COVID-19 pandemic. Storytelling helped me prioritize my experiences, alongside those of other African Jamaican mothers, in discussions on leadership and burial traditions in Canada. Using Black feminist-womanist storytelling as a framework facilitated my journey towards self-healing and resistance. In their work on Black women's wellness and healing, Tamika Carey (27) and April Baker-Bell (532) demonstrate the liberating potential of documenting our stories. Carey maintains that writing "can become an instrument for healing ... or a means for Black women to enact their agency in resisting or repairing the conditions that wound them" (27). Much like other African, Caribbean, and Black women scholars, writing about my experiences through storytelling empowers me to reconcile past trauma, honour the dead, and imagine new ways to love myself and my community.

Methodology: Autoethnography

I used autoethnography as a research method to investigate my experiences and those of other African Jamaican and African Caribbean mothers grieving during the pandemic. Autoethnography helped me reveal and then grapple with intimate accounts of African Jamaican mothers' work in leading burial and funerary rituals in Canada. In her article, *For Loretta: A Black Woman Literacy Scholar's Journey to Prioritizing Self-Preservation and Black Feminist-Womanist Storytelling*, Baker-Bell (531) describes the fundamental features of autoethnography. By way of Tony Adams et al., she contends that autoethnography

uses the researcher's personal experience to detail and critique beliefs, practices, and experiences; acknowledges and esteems the researcher's relationships with others; uses deep and careful self-reflection/reflexivity to identify and interrogate intersections between self and society, the particular, the general, the personal, and the political; shows "people in the process of figuring out what to do, how to live, and the meaning of their struggles";

balances intellectual and methodological rigour, emotion, and creativity; and strives for social justice and making life better. (531)

My engagement with autoethnography required me to occupy multiple positions simultaneously within the research process: participant, researcher, and audience. Ultimately, it enabled me to deeply reflect on varying perspectives and the leadership of African Caribbean mothers and women living in Canada during the COVID-19 pandemic.

Research Questions

Autoethnography also equipped me with the tools to ask myself the following questions: How did I uphold African Caribbean grieving processes in Canada during the COVID-19 pandemic? In what ways did I provide leadership while experiencing my own grief and loss? How did these experiences relate to, or differ from, those of other African Caribbean mothers living in Canada during the pandemic? What supports do African Caribbean mothers living in Canada need to further honour their burial and grieving practices? Much like Baker-Bell (532), I relied on personal memory, journal writings, old text messages, social media interactions, and conversations with family members and friends to explore my research questions. These sources furnished pertinent information necessary to tell my stories.

Story Structure: Call and Response

This essay contributes to literature on Black motherhood and womanhood during the pandemic by presenting study findings in the form of an autoethnographic story. The story, titled "Conversations with a Rose," captures a series of personal text messages between the main character, Yasmin, and her terminally ill friend, Rose. The text messages in the story represent my WhatsApp messages and experiences of grief with a terminally ill friend during the pandemic. I documented my reflections on our conversations about Black Caribbean mothers grieving in Toronto in my diary. Accordingly, the study findings are a metanarrative of collective and personal journeys with life and death.

As the pandemic rages, and the government orders a province-wide lockdown, the two friends in the story swap text messages capturing their joy, hope, and grief. In "Conversations with a Rose," readers accompany the story's characters on a journey to rethink friendship, motherhood, womanhood, and burial traditions during a time when health and government officials mandate social distance mandates and isolation orders.

I included breaks in the stream of text messages exchanged between the two characters. At times, there are weeks or months where the two friends do not communicate. It is during these moments that readers are invited to participate in an improvised call-in-response where their own personal narratives are placed in dialogue with the voices of the characters. I welcome readers to engage in the call-in-response in ways that are authentic to them. Readers can meditate on the silences separately from the story or alongside. This invitation offers readers additional ways of seeing, interpreting, and, in some instances, relating to the loss experienced by African Jamaican mothers navigating a pandemic in Canada. Essentially, the story's structure encourages readers to consider the ways that multiple stories are layered to reveal African Jamaican mothers' grief and burial traditions during the pandemic.

Findings: Conversations with a Rose

January 9, 2019

Yasmin: Baby boy is here! He surprised us and came a month early.

Rose: Congratulations Yasmin. 🙏🥹.

Yasmin: Thank you. Thank you.

Rose: I am very happy for you.

January 17, 2019

Y: Good morning, Rose. I'm looking for a good new home for my cat Felix. I'm wondering if u would b interested in adopting him.

R: Hi Yasmin. I am afraid of cats. Would love to but can't help. I am still in hospital.

Y: U r still in the hospital?!

R: Yes, my dear I'm at Humber River. Today I am at Sunnybrook for testing.

Y: I'm so sorry to hear that you are still in the hospital. I pray for your healing.

R: Thanks Yasmin. I will let you know my next steps.

February 16, 2019

Y: Hey Rose! How r u doing? Thinking about u.

R: Hi Yasmin. I am doing great very hopeful. Rehab is going good. Thank you.

Y: I need to come and visit. Things are so hard with a new baby.

February 17, 2019

Y: Hey Rose! How r u doing today? Sending you love.

February 19, 2019

Y: Good morning, Rose! Baby boy and I wish u a fabulous day. How are things going?

R: The rehab is great. It's a lot on my joints but it is necessary. I enjoy the challenge. I need to be mobile. I will be going home on March 11.

Y: Did the testing lead to some diagnosis? Home as in JAMAICA or home as in ur apartment?

R: Yes, Dr. Burke says my symptoms mirror that of ALS patients. I am waiting on the dyed MRI and the arthritis test results. Whatever diagnosis I am given it's going to be a mental journey. No not going home to Jamaica yet. I wish.

Y: Jamaica is the next goal. Regardless of diagnosis, you will overcome! I'm rooting for u!

R: Yes. My friends in Jamaica are on standby with a ticket whenever I am ready.

Y: I'm so glad u went on leave from work and are now focused on u!

R: Yep. It was the best move. Thank you. I need all the positive energy.

March 17, 2019

Y: Good afternoon! I'm just checking in. How r u doing?

R: Hi my dear I am okay. Going home tomorrow.

April 26, 2019

Y: Happy belated birthday! Wish I could come and visit. Just waiting for baby to get bigger so I can leave him with my aunt.

August 28, 2019

Y: How r u doing?

R: I am doing okay. I was told at the pain clinic that I have massive nerve damage and arthritis. We have to treat the pain first. I am doing test after test. Should know soon what I have. Sometimes the pain is unbearable. This too shall pass.

Y: U need to write a book abt ur life. Write ur testimony.

August 29, 2019

R: You touch my soul. Thank you for being around. How is baby boy doing?

Y: Baby is getting big. How r u?

R: My dear the more they give me pain meds the more my body rejects. ALS does not come with pain. So they sent me to the pain clinic. I have nerve damage and arthritis now. I will be tested for other types of arthritis.

Y: They still not sure about what exactly is ur illness?

R: No one knows for sure. My son goes with me and asks all the questions.

Y: I'm praying for you.

R: The biggest problem now is the pain. I did three MRIs and the EMG test. The neurologist told me I have ALS. I asked him what did the test show. He keeps saying my symptoms mirror ALS. I asked him what if both patients had a headache would you treat them the same. He had no answer.

Y: These doctors don't know what they r doing. And u have pain...and pain isn't a symptom of ALS.

R: They are never sure. They see a Black woman and just put us into a box. Everything is a battle. But God will prevail.

November 11, 2019

Y: Congrats on being a soon to be grandma!

December 13, 2019

Y: Rose congrats on the granddaughter. Your son posted the pics on Facebook. She's beautiful.

R: Thank you. Never thought I would be here.

December 14, 2019

Y: How r u doing today? I'm thinking about u.

R: Thank you. Less pain today. I feel good but a bit tired.

Y: I'm glad u r not in too much pain today.

R: I am too. Thank God I have my granddaughter to keep my mind off myself. I see her on the video. It's the best!

December 26, 2019

Y: Merry Christmas Rose! How are you doing this morning?

R: Thank you. Merry Christmas Yasmin. I am good.

February 10, 2020

Y: Thinking of u 👶👶

R: Thank you. How are you and baby boy doing? 🖤👶😊

Y: Baby is getting big. He turned one in January.

R: I am good and hopeful. The horrible pain is gone 🙏. Now I am sorting out my diet with the help of a Jamaican friend here. I used to babysit her when she was younger. And now she's like a mother to me! Telling me what to eat and when to eat. She even prepares the food and drops it off at the hospice for me every week. God is good.

February 14, 2020

R: Happy valentine's day!

April 11, 2020

R: Hi good morning Yasmin. How r u and baby?

Y: We r doing well. Just keeping self isolated. We can't risk catching COVID. Wish I could come and visit. Only God knows when COVID will be over.

April 22, 2020

Y: Sending you a video clip of baby boy. Hope this brightens up your day!

R: Hi. Oh such a delight. Thank you Yasmin 😊🙏🤍🤍

Y: You are always in my heart 👩‍👧👩‍👧🤍🤍🤍

April 24, 2020

R: Aww thank you. I will always remember our time walking and talking. Life has been good. No regrets 🤍🤍🤍😊🤍😊

Y: Those moments of us together r the highlights of my life.

R: Yes, our memories r so good 😊

June 5, 2020

Y: Hey Rose! Just checking in on u. How r u doing?

July 12, 2020

Y: Good afternoon Rose. Just checking in. I hope you are having a great day.

July 29, 2020

Y: Hello Rose. Sending u love. I'm always and forever thinking of u.

August 6, 2020

R: Good morning Yasmin.

Y: Morning Rose 😊🤍

R: I'm good fingers are not too strong love 🤍. How r u and baby?

Y: I'm so happy to hear from you.

August 29, 2020

Y: Wishing u a wonderful day. Thinking of you always.

January 1, 2021

Y: Good morning. Happy new year!

R: Happy new year!

January 10, 2021

Y: What have you been up to?

R: Watching Netflix. I'm watching Girlfriends.

January 14, 2021

Y: Sending you a pic of baby boy!

January 15, 2021

R: Wow he's getting so big.

January 25, 2021

Y: Morning!

February 1, 2021

Y: How r u doing?

February 10, 2021

Y: Thinking of u

February 20, 2021

Y: Morning! Hope u r having a good day 🩶

R: Hi, this is Rose's daughter. On Thursday, February 25, 2021, our dear mother, Rose, passed away. She was a loving mother, aunty, sister, cousin, and friend. Rose will be missed by all who had the pleasure of knowing her.

February 26, 2021

Y: I miss you. Me and some of the mothers organized nine nights for u. We're doing it on Zoom so that ur friends and family from Toronto and Jamaica can attend. Ur mom even hops on Zoom...all the way from England and at her age. Took a bit of coaching, but she did it. Look at God! We're singing all ur favourite songs. COVID can't stop us from gathering to celebrate u!

February 28, 2021

Y: We're still meeting every night. Ur brother spilled all ur secrets LOL. Ur mom said u love jerk chicken. So we're eating jerk chicken every night until ur spirit is at rest.

March 6, 2021

Y: The tears just won't stop. I miss u so much. Kevin drove up to ur village in Jamaica. And read out...more like yelled out...2 Corinthians 4: 17-18. He did it all on Zoom. We all laughed. God knows u love that passage.

March 7, 2021

Y: May ur soul be at rest. No more pain.

September 28, 2021

Y: I miss u. Rest well in the arms of our Lord. I love u.

Discussion: Nine Night as Wake Work

Christina Sharpe's work, *In the Wake: On Blackness and Being*, offers various definitions of wake—a state of wakefulness, a watch or vigil for the dead, the track left on the water's surface by a ship, a disturbed flow (10). Sharpe defines being in the wake as seeing, inhibiting, and imagining life in the wake of slavery (18). Sharpe's theory of the wake also encompasses an exploration of wake work. Performing wake work, Sharpe explains, requires imagining new ways to live and survive in the wake of slavery's afterlives. In the face of Black death, wake work encapsulates "the ways we resist, rupture and disrupt that immanence and imminence aesthetically and materially" (13).

I use Christina Sharpe's theory and praxis of the wake to unpack "the modalities of Black life lived in, as, under, and despite Black death" (20). "Conversations with a Rose" presents Yasmin and other African Jamaican mothers as performing wake work. Typically, discussions on Nine Night centre the histories, spirits, and afterlives following death. However, the story positions Yasmin's wake work as occurring prior to and continuing after the death of her friend. Through the series of text messages exchanged between the two African Jamaican mothers, readers witness the central role of love in the practice of wake work. Yasmin demonstrates that in the midst of Black death during a pandemic, African Jamaican mothers leverage technologies—such as texting, teleconferencing, and video chatting—to nurture and care for themselves and one another. Given this, African Jamaican mothers' practice of checking in, praying, and preparing food for one another, in addition to Nine Night, represent rituals that honour the living and the deceased. These practices of collective love are vital for the mental, emotional, and ultimately physical survival of African Jamaican mothers and their community, especially during the COVID-19 pandemic.

Nine Night as Community and Survival during the Pandemic

In the article *The Repast: Self and Collective Love in the Face of Black Death*, Haile Eshe Cole investigates the repast as a form of collective love (217). Echoing Cole, I underscore the critical role of community support in Jamaican Canadian burial traditions. The offering of food, fellowship, and time spent are key components to surviving the experiences of Black death in Canada. "Conversations with a Rose" shows that the community's watch over a person's spirit commences long before the loss of life. For example, Yasmin prays for Rose's health while other African Jamaican mothers cook for their friend. An extensive body of research examines the roles of families, extended networks, and fictive kin in African, African Caribbean, and Black communities (Fearon 47; Stack 9). This work further illuminates the significance of social networks in supporting African Jamaican mothers in Canada during a pandemic. I argue that collective love, which is at the root of these relationships, is a radical expression of justice, especially within contexts that seek to dehumanize Black mothers.

"Conversations with a Rose" also highlights the leadership role of African Jamaican mothers and women in leading burial traditions during a pandemic. The story captures African Jamaican mothers leveraging technologies to perform burial rituals with members of their community dispersed throughout the diaspora. Much literature exists about the connections between Black motherhood and loss. However, the scholarship revolves around discussions of Black mothers' loss of their children. Cole warns against presenting Black motherhood as synonymous with loss (218). Although "Conversations with a Rose" does explore the violence and loss experienced by African Jamaican women and mothers in Canada, it is not presented as the signpost of their motherhood and womanhood. Instead, the characters of Rose, Yasmin, and the other African Jamaican mothers are presented as pillars in their community—the carriers of love both in life and death. Through their caretaking and their leadership, the African Jamaican mothers in the story help their communities live and mourn.

Conclusion

In Canada, a paucity of literature investigates the impact of the pandemic on the burial and bereavement rituals of Canada's largest Black immigrant population: the African Caribbean community (Statistics Canada 1). This chapter adds to the scholarship by illustrating the creative ways that African Jamaican mothers exist, resist, and persist during the COVID-19 pandemic. In this essay, I used Black feminist-womanist storytelling to weave together personal stories of loss during the pandemic with current literature on Black life and motherhood. This research is significant, as scholarship that centres African Caribbean mothers' experiences with loss are limited in Canada. This work, accordingly, presents a more detailed narrative of African Jamaican mothers' labour and leadership within their communities in Canada.

This chapter puts forward recommendations to sustain African Caribbean mothers' wake work during the pandemic. Institutions must honour the significant roles that kin and fictive kin play in African Jamaican mothers' support networks. Hospitals and hospices should prioritize establishing systems and technologies that nurture relationships between African Caribbean mothers and their communities. African Caribbean mothers should have access to, and engage in, video chat technologies and rich remote programming that nurture their relationships through all phases of a life-limiting illness. I urge Canadian institutions to reimagine high-quality hospice care to involve partnerships with members of African Caribbean mothers' support networks and local cultural organizations. Such partnerships facilitate African Caribbean women and mothers' virtual participation in familial, local, and international events of cultural and personal significance.

African Caribbean women and mothers must help lead the discussions about how Canadian institutions can value Black existence during life and after death. This collaboration between African

Caribbean mothers, hospice residences, and palliative care institutions would further patients' advocacy for access to health professionals who provide culturally responsive services. These services might include social work, spiritual care, speech language pathology, physiotherapy, and nutrition.

COVID-19 continues to rage across the world. In memory of Rose and all the African Caribbean mothers who have lost life during the pandemic in Canada, I close this essay by calling on government officials and scholars alike to preserve Black existence, even amid death. Let us heed Hartman's advice and honour the lives and deaths of Black mothers by "grasping their beautiful struggle to survive, glimpsing their alternative modes of life, [and] illuminating their mutual aid and communal wealth" (*Wayward Lives* 38).To begin, researchers, government officials, and society at large must revere African Caribbean mothers and the women they love as thinkers, leaders, and cultural bearers worthy of living and dying with dignity.

Works Cited

Adams, Tony E., et al. *Handbook of Autoethnography*. Routledge, 2016.

Baker-Bell, April. "For Loretta: A Black Woman Literacy Scholar's Journey to Prioritizing Self-Preservation and Black Feminist-Womanist Storytelling." *Journal of Literacy Research*, vol. 49, no. 4, SAGE Publications, 2017, pp. 531-32.

Brand, Dionne. *A Map to the Door of No Return: Notes to Belonging*. Vintage Canada edition, Vintage Canada, 2002.

Butler, Tamara T. "#Say[ing]HerName as Critical Demand: English Education in the Age of Erasure." *English Education*, vol. 49, no. 2, National Council of Teachers of English, 2017, pp. 155.

Carey, Tamika L. *Rhetorical Healing: The Reeducation of Contemporary Black Womanhood*. State University of New York Press, 2016.

Cole, Haile Eshe. "The Repast: Self and Collective Love in the Face of Black Death." *Women, Gender, and Families of Color*, vol. 7, no. 2, University of Illinois Press, 2019, pp. 217-18.

Statistics Canada. *Diversity of the Black Population in Canada: An Overview*. *Statistics Canada*, 2019. www150.statcan.gc.ca/n1/pub/89-657-x/89-657-x2019002-eng.htm. Accessed 7 Aug. 2023.

Fearon, Stephanie. *For Our Children: Black Motherwork and Schooling.* 2020. University of Toronto, PhD dissertation.

Glenn, C. "Stepping in and Stepping out: Examining the Way Anticipatory Career Socialization Impacts Identity Negotiation of African American Women in Academia." *Presumed Incompetent: The Intersections of Race and Class for Women in Academia,* edited by G. Gutiérrez y Muhs, et al., 2012, pp. 137.

Haddix, Marcelle. *Cultivating Racial and Linguistic Diversity in Literacy Teacher Education: Teachers Like Me.* Routledge, 2016.

Hartman, Saidiya V. *Lose Your Mother: A Journey Along the Atlantic Slave Route.* Farrar, Straus & Giroux, 2008.

Hartman, Saidiya V. *Wayward Lives, Beautiful Experiments: Intimate Histories of Social Upheaval.* W.W. Norton & Company, 2019.

Huggins, Camille L., and Glenda M. Hinkson. "Contemporary Burial Practices in Three Caribbean Islands Among Christians of African Descent." *Omega: Journal of Death and Dying,* vol. 80, no. 2, SAGE Publications, 2019, p. 276.

McKenzie, Kwame. "Socio-Demographic Data Collection and Equity in Covid-19 in Toronto." *eClinicalMedicine,* vol. 34, Elsevier Ltd., 2021, p. 1.

Onuora, Adwoa Ntozake. (2021). *Anansesem (Storytelling Nights): African Maternal Pedagogies.* [Doctoral dissertation, University of Toronto]. ProQuest Dissertations.

Richardson, Elaine. "'To Protect and Serve': African American Female Literacies." *College Composition and Communication,* vol. 53, no. 4, 2002, pp. 675-704.

Sampson, M. "Going Live: The Making of Digital Griots and Cyber Assemblies." *Practical Matters,* vol. 12, 2019, pp. 9.

Sharpe, Christina Elizabeth. *In the Wake: On Blackness and Being.* Duke University Press, 2016.

Smitherman, Geneva. *Talkin and Testifyin: The Language of Black America.* Houghton Mifflin, 1977.

Stack, Carol B. *All Our Kin.* Basic Books, 1997.

Toliver, S.R. "Can I Get a Witness? Speculative Fiction as Testimony and Counterstory." *Journal of Literacy Research,* vol. 52, no. 4, SAGE

Publications, 2020, pp. 508-09.

Walcott, Rinaldo. *The Long Emancipation: Moving Toward Black Freedom.* Duke University Press, 2021.

Chapter 3.

Navigating COVID-19 Nursing Home Care Restrictions: Who Is Going to Visit Mama?

Delores V. Mullings, Vinnette Thompson, Marcia McLaughlin, Joyce Mullings, and Eboni-Rai Mullings

Introduction

Many older adults lived in nursing homes prior to the COVID-19 pandemic. They enjoyed the company of their families, friends, and church brethren regularly. However, during the pandemic, the government implemented measures—such as social distancing, self-isolation, and visitation restrictions—that reduced and eliminated opportunities for social contact among long-term care residents and their loved ones. Whereas parts of Canada, such as the Atlantic region, have had less restrictive public health measures, Ontario has been in various levels of continuous lockdown for most of the past eighteen months. This has been a challenging time for many families and especially for elders who live away from their families. Using photovoice, dialogue, narrative, and poetry, this chapter shares the experiences and perspectives of four women and the strategies they used to keep connected, deal with fear, and remain positive during the COVID-19 pandemic.

Family Background

This chapter focusses on the interactions and activities among some members of the immediate family, including Maddah Joyce Buchanan Mullings, an elder, and primarily her daughters. She is referred to by other names—Mom, Mama, Sister Mullings, Maddah Mullings, Sister Joyce, Miss Joyce, and Maddah Joyce—depending on the person's relationship with her. Delores calls her Sister Mullings and Maddah Mullings, whereas Vinnette and Marcia call her Mama and Mom, respectively. The workers refer to her as Sister Joyce, Miss Joyce, and Maddah Joyce. We will use these names interchangeably according to the speaker in this narrative. Sister Mullings is the mother of four children: one boy and three girls. She currently resides in a nursing home. Like many Jamaicans of African descent who migrated to Canada between 1911 and 1989, she is now old. Folks of this generation have spent most of their lives in Canada and have grown old in a place that many thought would only be a steppingstone to a better life in their countries of birth. Aunty Hanna Mullings, now deceased, came to Canada as a domestic worker in 1967. By 1970, she had earned her nurse's aide certificate (now known as a personal support worker [PSW] certificate), freed herself from the Caribbean Domestic Workers Scheme, and sponsored her brother, Papa Bertie, who came to Canada in 1971. In 1973, Papa Bertie sponsored Sister Mullings, and by 1974, they sponsored the four children they had together (Marcia, Delores, Vinnette, and Elvis) and one of Papa Bertie's children (Keith) from another relationship whom Sister Mullings adopted. Aunty Hanna parented Delores along with Angela, another niece whom she adopted. The other children lived with Papa Bertie and Sister Mullings.

After her retirement, Aunty Hanna lived between Jamaica and Canada as she had envisioned when she first came to Canada. She experienced life in a nursing home as a worker but never as a resident. Maddah Mullings had hoped to have a similar life, but it was not to be. Sister Mullings and Papa Bertie separated and then divorced; they each live separate lives now. As Sister Mullings had never lived alone in her life, she found it difficult to adjust, and so she shared a home with Renee, her eldest granddaughter. Within two years, she suffered a stroke and needed more care than Renee could provide. During her recovery, she lived with her youngest daughter, Vinnette, and her family and later with Marcia, the eldest.

When Maddah Mullings's health improved, she lived by herself with support from her family and formal community support. When her health got worse and she was unable to care for herself, Sister Mullings left her apartment to live with Delores and her husband. Sister Mullings had two more strokes and other serious health conditions. With Sister Mullings long history of health concerns, Delores struggled to care for her even with community support. Other family members' homes were no longer options because they were not suitably adapted. The family began to think about and plan for her long-term needs.

Sister Mullings initially did not want to live in a nursing home because of her fear of living among strangers, missing her family, feeling lonely, racism, and being in an environment that lacked Caribbean culture. She agreed that her healthcare needs were more than her family could manage, and she became a resident at a nursing home one year prior to the onset of the COVID-19 pandemic. The family, including blood relatives and church brethren, settled into a routine filled with in-person visits, socializing, and caregiving. This ended abruptly in March 2020, just a few weeks after the family had a big surprise birthday celebration for Sister Mullings. Since then, the family has been trying to work within pandemic measures while keeping in touch and continuing to care for her, with telephone and social media (e.g., Signal) as major communication tools in their roles as daughters and essential caregivers.

Do Pictures Tell a Whole Story?

Lifeline: Telephones

These two telephones (Figure 1 and Figure 2) represent the lifelines between Maddah Mullings and her three daughters—Vinnette, Marcia, and Delores—during COVID-19. The family managed to stay connected during the pandemic through these phones despite early challenges, and Maddah Mullings showed her character—this thing we call resilience—in staying positive even when she could not see or hear any of her family members. Fearing for her safety, her daughters spoke regularly and prayed for the best. The first phone (Figure 1) is black, easy to grip and hold, strong, and simple. There is a bright, colourful square with a range of orange to purple colours in the middle.

The large, white font showing the time of day is easy to read. A dark circle, the camera, is at the top centre, and there is a talk bubble at the bottom centre of the phone. Maddah Joyce had used a phone like this one for many years and was comfortable with it.

During the first part of the pandemic, public health measures forced nursing homes to lock their doors to visitors, so our families were unable to visit with Maddah Joyce. Family members, especially the three sisters, spoke with their mother many times per day using this phone to keep her company, comfort her, and help reduce her isolation. The phone was comfortable to handle and simple to use. It was literally a lifeline between Mom and us. We wanted to have live video conversations with Mama to see whether she looked cared for and whether her room was clean. With Mama's agreement, phone number two was purchased.

The second phone (Figure 2) has a thin, black outline within a sleek, small, smooth, colourful, and creative body. The colour ranges from light blue to dark purple with vague pictures in the centre. A thin, faded-blue circle about the size of a Canadian twenty-five-cent piece shows the time and date. Three very small white shapes are in the upper-right-hand corner. All these shapes and fonts were difficult for Maddah Joyce to see, and the learning curve to use this phone proved challenging, but she was determined, saying, "mi waan fi learn how fi use dis fone fah mi like it." We felt it important to not only encourage her but also coach her about how to use the phone. She was unable to use the talking function, so she could not answer the phone or make calls. This was a disaster, as we went from daily communication to days without speaking with Mama. It was important that she made her own choice about keeping or changing the phone. It was difficult to lose communication with her, but we did not pressure her into a decision. We wanted to make the decision for her, but we honoured and respected her wishes.

We were relieved when Sister Mullings reluctantly asked to return to the old flip-style phone that she had successfully used for many years. She felt that she would manage that type of phone more easily. To our dismay, the new Alcatel flip phone was worse. Mama was unable to speak with anyone by phone for days yet again. We later found out that this phone has frequent technical difficulties that cause it to disrupt and block the cell signal, resulting in no dial tone. We went back to the smartphone, and with help from all her children, her PSW, the nurses, and recreation workers, she now makes and answers calls without issue. This elder's perseverance to rise above difficulties and succeed was remarkable. Her determination also reminds us not to put our own limiting ideas on elders. Who would have thought that at eighty-three, Mama would have developed the skills to use a smartphone? She believed in herself and so did we.

Figure. 1. The first phone (Motorola). Figure 2. The second phone (Motorola)

PSWs: Unsung Sheroes

PSW are the backbone of nursing home care for elders. At Sister Mullings's nursing home during the COVID-19 pandemic, it was clear that most PSWs there were Black. They have been on the frontlines fighting COVID-19 in their work for and with older adults in nursing homes. The PSWs of Caribbean background refer to Sister Mullings as

Sistah Joyce and Miss Joyce, so we will use these terms in this section. The PSWs became a substitute family for Sistah Joyce when her family was unable to visit her, spend time with her, and physically help care for her. They took on extra work, such as combing her hair, helping her fix and charge her cell phones, loaning her their phones to contact her children and reheating the cultural foods that she received from them, and encouraging her in times of loneliness. PSWs are sheroes that are not recognized for their importance in the healthcare industry and specifically for their contribution in caring for elders like Sistah Joyce.

The woman in the photo (Figure 3) wears the blue-green uniform of the PSW with a dark green tie head (head scarf) and a blue nonmedical mask. She is one of the many PSWs who cares for Sistah Joyce. She is patient, kind, and gentle with a soft touch and smooth melodic voice. She has soft, smiling eyes, but they are hidden behind the mask. Like other PSWs, she is an unrecognized shero.

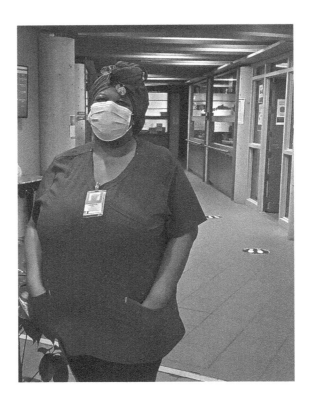

Figure 3. Coretta, one of Sistah Joyce's PSWs, Photo credit, Delores V. Mullings

Unrecognized Sheroes

The daily grind of work is etched on their faces
Tired backs, legs, and hands are evident
They guard the frontlines morning, noon, and night
Are scheduled for long tiring hours
Called in as substitutes last minute
When someone is unable to carry on
But we don't think much of their value
Afterall, they are just personal support workers
Not as important as nurses
Falling short of doctors' worth
Yet doing the dirtiest work
And the heaviest lifting in their roles
Cleaning residents' sick and dying bodies
Bringing food, removing plates and soiled beddings
Making beds and washing personal items
Yet they remain invisible under the daylight glare
To the general society, they are shadow people
But the residents and their families see and know all

Poem by Delores V. Mullings and Marcia McLaughlin

African Caribbean and Black families have a reciprocal care ethos where elders support the family in the best way that they can, and younger people help care for elders. Such is the case within Sistah Joyce's family. The reciprocal care is seen with the elder and her children.

We thank the staff for helping our mother through this hard time and working with her.

Siblings: Essential Caregivers

This section includes different dialogues between and among four women in response to questions posed about their feelings and perceptions during the lockdown, how they supported their elder in the nursing home, and how the elder received and provided support.

They discuss their feelings about the pandemic lockdown and why they decided to participate as essential caregivers, and they share some of the activities that they do in the essential caregiver role.

When the nursing home announced that two people from the family could be essential caregivers, the sisters discussed and agreed that Vinnette and Marcia would serve in the role. Three of the siblings live within proximity to Mom's residence, and Delores lives outside of the province. Although the sisters had to take a COVID-19 test weekly and sometimes twice per week, they did not mind the inconvenience, as that was the only way they could see their mom. Vinnette attends at least once per week, and Marcia biweekly when she is healthy, and while Marcia and Vinnette are the essential caregivers for the family, Elvis sometimes helps with phone technology. The sisters speak with their mom daily. Delores makes and coordinates all Sister Mullings' appointments, manages her finances, and communicates with the nursing home staff, medical specialists, recreational staff, and any other business, including Revenue Canada and telephone companies.

Maddah Mullings' Story

I was feeling a little bit scared because I didn't know if COVID-19 was going to come to the nursing home and attack the people and kill them. I didn't know if I was going to die—if the COVID-19 would kill me. It kill out whole heap ah people, killing people round the world, and in de nursing home. I was scared only for a short time. Mi belief in God keep me going. I pray to God to save me and my family and many people.

When COVID-19 came to my nursing home, I didn't feel any way. When I heard that it came to the third floor, sixth and seventh floor, I pray that it stays away from my floor. I pray every day many times a day. During the middle of the day sometimes, I just talk to God and keep asking him to let it bypass me, my family, and the people living in the nursing home. I told the Lord to make sure to flush it out like water in a garden.

After a while, we had to lock up in our rooms, and even before they told us to stay in our rooms, I never put my foot out there in the common areas. Vinnette told me to stay in my room and stay away from mingling with other people before that, soh me was in my room for a long time.

I was worried a little bit when I couldn't see my family. I wasn't fretting though. I was wondering if they were going to get sick. I was lonely sometimes when my family wasn't coming to see me, so I miss them a likkle. I talked with my family every day, so I don't feel too dreadful bad. I know that they can't come because of this COVID-19.

Mi tell mi family noh fi come and visit during COVID-19 outbreaks in de nursing home because I don't want dem fi catch it. I also was giving advice to my family about how to keep themselves safe from COVID-19. Dem tell me fi focus pon miself because me older an live ina nursing home soh mi haffi be careful.

I really like when my family come and visit; sometimes my daughters come alone and sometimes they come with my grandchildren and great-grandchildren. I love when my family come to visit. I want people to see that I have family coming to visit me yuh know. When the nurses and PSWs tell me that my family is coming to visit me, I feel happy and proud.

My faith in God was the big ting that pulled me through. I said to God, "I know that there is nothing too big for you and nothing that you can't do. Please don't let COVID catch me, my family or the people in the nursing home." I used to call my family names and count them when I pray. I pray for my family first and then everyone else. Thank God for everything.

Prayer Warrior

Our mother is the best mother ever
We call her warrior mama
Long before we knew what it meant
Even if she needs a bit of help now and then
She continues to help her family thrive
She gives good advice
Tries to give us money
Protects us from spiritual harm
by praying for us
Yes, she knows how to pray
We call her a prayer warrior
She backs that up with daily Bible reading

Her strong faith in God is endless
Warrior Maddah Mullings is on the case
And COVID-19 is no match for her.

Poem by Delores V. Mullings and Marcia McLaughlin

Marcia's Story

It was very sad. Very hard for me to place our mother in a long-term care home because we could no longer manage her because her health was getting weak. I decided to become an essential caregiver for my mom because I got to see her in person, often for a short time, and I could take care of her. My health was poor during the first wave of the COVID-19 pandemic, but it didn't matter how sick I was: I needed to see Mama. I was worried about my Mama's safety and if she was being looked after properly. So, when the opportunity came to be an essential caregiver, I didn't hesitate to step up. I was glad because I could see Mama and help take care of her. When I visit her, I tidy up her room, put things where she can reach them easily, read for her, do puzzles with her, play music for her, let her talk to other family members by video who cannot visit her because of the COVID-19. I cook her favourite foods and bring them to her. She loves her homemade Jamaican meals. I like to bring our food for her because she does not get any Jamaican food in the nursing home. Sometimes, I braid her hair, arrange her closet, do her nails, and talk about old-time things. I bring home her laundry and buy her new clothes. Being an essential caregiver for Mama is very good. It makes me very happy that I can be around my mom even though it is for a short time. At first, essential caregivers could not leave the room when we visited, but it was okay for me. Sometimes when I talk with Mama, she tells me she longs to see her family. That makes me feel sad for her, and I feel helpless because I can't do anything about it.

We were worried about our mother, so we were even thinking of how or what to do for her during lockdown. It was hard for me to be locked in, but I think it was even harder for Mama. When she fell in the bathroom, we could not go to the long-term care home or the hospital to visit her; that was very hurtful for me because we were not there to help her. Our brother, Elvis, picked her up from the hospital, and I know she was happy to see one of her children.

Vinnette's Story

I chose to become an essential caregiver for Mom because it was the only way to see her. The residents were not allowed regular visitors for fear of spreading the virus. Although it was for only 1.5 hours, two times per week, it was better than no visits at all. Doing the PCR COVID-19 test was painful at times, but for mama it was nothing. Each time I visited with Mom, I felt good to see her and I felt happy that my work schedule was flexible enough to give me the chance to see her.

I also became an essential caregiver because I was worried about Mama's safety and did not trust that she would be cared for properly. I was worried; there were so many negative news reports about people in long-term care homes. The reports about deaths, lack of staff, number of positive COVID-19 tests, and a lot of other things. I was also concerned about her being in her room. This was heartbreaking for me, as I could only sit at home and listen and hope for good news. She was not able to socialize with any of the other residents, and her only contact with the outside was with workers for a few minutes. Mom has fallen many times, and during the lockdown, I often wondered what would happen to her if she fell, and she did not have any support to help her get up or the workers were there to see that she was okay. Praying to God, our Father above, was the only thing we could do, so we prayed every single day for Mama's safety.

I work in an exclusive retirement home as a chef, so I was able to see first-hand how lonely the residents were when they were unable to see their families and unable to have a normal life. I saw how much their mental health deteriorated with the social distancing and isolation from their families. And that worried me a great deal, but my Mama is a very resilient person. She did not give up. She kept praying for herself, her family, and the whole world.

When I visit, we talk about everything, I read to her, take her laundry, arrange her room so it's neat and clutter free. I bring her care packages that include homecooked Jamaican meals, personal items, fresh tropical fruits that she does not get in the home (e.g., mangoes), and meal replacements. I want to make sure that if she does not like or want the food that the nursing home gives her, she has options. I really miss spending time with my Mom. Delores lives in another province and is unable to spend personal time with her regularly, so I video call her on all of my visits so that they can connect.

Vinnette and Delores: Window Visit

Vinnette: Sis yuh membah wen we went down to the nursing home one day in May 2020 fi visit Mama? Boy I was so excited to see har.

Delores: Yep, I sure do. Me did mek de appointment wid the people ah de nurses' station. It was a window visit. De worker dem bring har to de window. Yuh jumped out ah de car before me stop. I teared up and cried a likkle. I was so happy to see her. She was wearing her cream-colour hat.

Vinnette: Right, wid har pretty multicolour frock.

Delores: Remember how she was waving frantically and smiling? Even de PSW was smiling and waving.

Vinnette: A lot of other residents were standing at the window, and we waved at them, too. They also seemed happy to be seeing people even if it was from afar, and they didn't know us.

Looking Forward

Marcia: Mama, I'm videotaping you now. Say something to FamJam. FamJam, Mama is here and is going to speak to you now.

Mama: Hello FamJam. I miss you all very much. May God keep you safe. I pray for everyone all the time. I pray for the COVID-19 disease to go away. I wish I could see you all, but I am okay. I feel fine. I am not lonely so noh fret. I read my Bible all the time. God keep you and God bless you all. I love my family very much. I love you Ebi, Tony, Renee, Melissa, Kisha, and everyone. Tell everyone I love dem. Ah right massa bye. Mi gawn.

Along with many Canadians, the pandemic has frustrated and at times made people feel immobile, especially families with loved ones residing in nursing homes. From the dialogue and narrative among the women in this chapter, the family struggles to cope with COVID-19 measures. During the struggles, no one is thinking about resilience. They worry for and about each other. Although the elder, Maddah Joyce, was fighting loneliness at the height of the lockdown, she was protecting her family by asking them not to visit her during outbreaks at her residence. She also offered financial support to some family members who had lost their jobs, but given her situation living on fixed income, the family declined her monetary gifts. She, however, supported her family in ways that she could control by praying for their health and wellbeing. She prayed for herself, her family, the nursing home residents, and others around the world. Maddah Joyce continues to keep the faith in her fight against the COVID-19 pandemic. She is supported by PSWs, the majority of whom are African, Caribbean, Black (ACB) Canadians, and her family, especially her three daughters.

The telephone is the major source of communication between and among the family. Sister Mullings showed her resilience in learning to use a smartphone, which she uses to stay in touch with her family and church brethren. The sisters also keep in touch by telephone and social media. Family members send and receive recorded messages on the family's private social media account, so everyone gets updates about what is happening with her. Sisters Marcia and Vinnette share similar worries about their mom's care, safety, and wellbeing. Both do similar things in their essential caregiver role, including reading, doing laundry, and offering care packages with Jamaican foods and meal supplements. Like their mother, both sisters are strong in their faith in God and use prayer to help them cope during COVID-19. Sister Mullings is known within the family as a prayer warrior. The situation with COVID-19 changes constantly; the family does not know what will happen in the coming weeks or months, but they are prepared to continue staying close and supporting each for the duration of the pandemic.

Further Development

Sistah Mullings contracted COVID-19 in January 2022. Within days, Delores, who had visited Mama two days earlier, came down with a severe bout of it as well. Vinnette went to the nursing home daily for almost three weeks nonstop to care for her physically, spiritually, and emotionally. She was unable to walk, sit up, feed herself, or hold even basic conversation. By the grace of God, Mom survived, and we are all glad that she is still here with us. COVID-19 has ravaged her mind and body. She can walk now with her walker again, but her body and mind remain in serious peril. Vinnette contracted COVID-19 in early February and is still trying to regain her health as of March. Maddah

Mullings was never able to walk for more than a few steps and though she regained some aspects of her life, she now lives with dementia and muscle atrophy in her legs so she requires significant personal support to complete activities of daily living, like dressing herself.

Chapter 4.

Where Did Daddy Go? Reflections of an Adult Daughter of a Father with Dementia during COVID-19

Ngozi Iroanyah

I ask this question metaphorically. My father has rarely left our home in the past two years. At the beginning of the pandemic, he was still walking, talking, smiling. He was still laughing at random moments. He was wandering into the kitchen to watch me wash the dishes and commenting, smiling, or laughing in Igbo with what I can only assume were fragmented memories of his early life in Nigeria. I would always look at him and smile in return. I would give anything to have that time back.

My father was able to sit at the kitchen table on a chair and partially feed himself. My stepmom would relish when I came over to help her shoulder some of the care duties. It was a relief for her. My father was always happy to see me even if it took him a while to remember who I was. He would always greet this stranger with a smile and would give me an even bigger one when he could put my face to my voice. At first, I was almost gutted that he couldn't initially remember me, but I would give anything to have that time back.

My father was still able to go to the day programs and socialize with the staff and other clients there. He had some friends he would hang out with, as I was told by the day program staff. Those hours away from my family gave us respite and confidence knowing he was safe; they gave him a chance to develop new social skills and to move about and explore outside of his home. I would give anything to have that time back.

I don't know exactly when it happened during the pandemic and the lockdowns. When he sort of... stopped. I suppose it was gradually, little by little. I was living in Toronto during the first year and a half, dealing with my own life and struggling to cope with the ever-changing uncertainty and fear of COVID. I saw him and my stepmom often though. I am the primary guardian for all his affairs, so I was constantly maintaining and updating his insurance, retirement matters, taxes, etc., and by default, my stepmom's, too. It wasn't easy, but knowing that I was taking care of them made it worth it for me.

Then I noticed changes. He could no longer walk as easily. His gait turned into a shuffle, then into assisted mobility, then more stationary positions. He smiled and spoke less often. He needed more help with eating his meals. I decided to move back to Mississauga a year and a half after COVID first started, across the street from my dad and stepmom. It was time. And right on time because not long after I moved across the street, my stepmother called me late one night in a panic. She tried to lift dad out of his chair after he had dinner but could not manage him alone. He fell. In response to her call, I ran over. Dad was sitting on the floor smiling to himself completely unaware of what had happened. In contrast, my stepmother was a wreck. I helped her pick him up, clean him, change him, and put him to bed. I would give anything to have that time back.

I called Dad's caseworker, who came over to do another assessment. I asked her if her other clients' behaviours were like my father's. She emphatically answered: "Yes, some are even worse." The COVID-19 lockdowns, isolation, and restrictions on personal support workers' (PSW) hours and family gatherings meant that my dad had less socialization and stimulation that was especially needed for people living with dementia; it also meant little or no respite for us, and other family members. She said a lot of people on her caseload were deteriorating. I asked her for more PSW hours, more nurses, or something to help my dad and our family. Feelings of helplessness were growing inside me. My dad had a bed sore on his heel that was quite significant, but we couldn't get a doctor's appointment for him because medical offices were only taking certain patients during the lockdowns. We learned to be make-shift nurses and doctors for my dad; we learned to care for his wound ourselves mostly and then with the home care-nurse's help. The sore took a few months to heal, but it healed nicely with our attentive care and love. I would give anything to have that time back.

We watched my dad transition to a place that we didn't know, couldn't go, and where we couldn't reach him. He was at that stage for sure. He seemed more despondent, not continent, but still responsive to our voices and touch. That was the consolation. It was enough. It had to be. We continued to pour our love into him, and he reciprocated, although to the onlooker, his love wouldn't be obvious. He could not easily get in and out of bed by himself or with support. He could no longer sit on a chair for a long time. It was apparent that my father needed assistive devices to have a better quality of life. We got him a hospital bed and a wheelchair. We got him everything he needed that was within our power.

Then another major transition took place: Dad was discharged from the day program that he attended because as a prerequisite for participating, he had to be able to bear weight on his legs. So, when the day program reopened, he was not allowed to go. With that, Dad no longer had any outside socialization. All his socialization came from our family.

My dad is in palliative care now, with no confirmed time and date. I am there most days, helping him to eat by feeding him and dressing his new bed sores, spending as much time as possible with him. I only have this time with him left.

Chapter 5.

Seeking Tenure in the United States: Confessions of a Black Dance Professor during COVID-19

Gregory King

The Tenure Process Takes a Toll

Kerry Ann Rockquemore and Tracey Laszloffy explain that "the tenure track will be one of the most difficult and demanding stages of your academic career because of the high-performance expectations, minimal direct feedback, and explicit time constraints of your tenure clock" (12). But in addition to conducting creative and scholastic research, teaching, and performing institutional and community service towards tenure and promotion, academics must prove that they have performed said tasks, working assiduously to package that proof. That packaged proof—the tenure dossier—is then shared with various committees, placed on display (Monzó 313) for the department chair, school director, dean, and provost in hopes that it garners their support in the academic's trajectory towards reappointment, tenure, and promotion. As Lilia Monzó declares, "In many ways, the tenure process is an evaluation of who we are as humans" (313). This evaluation is part of the tenure process at most postsecondary institutions—a process in which colleagues are tasked with reviewing pretenured faculty's progress, offering advice, and working with the faculty being evaluated on a suitable, effective plan for realignment with their school, college, or department's tenure and promotion expectations.

But my pretenure reappointment process—and those of a large percentage of faculty of colour in academia—was anything but smooth. It was padded with discordance, the questioning of my work, and the undermining of my contribution to the institution, almost to the point of erasure. Monzó explains her own experience of going through the tenure process; after her fourth year, her colleagues reviewed her work and focussed solely on what was lacking without noting anything positive about her work or her potential (313). And Monzó's experience is not singular. My evaluations had been similar; my work was generally downplayed, and its deficiencies were highlighted.

During my third-year review, my division coordinator opted not to share concerns with me prior to discussing them with members of the faculty advisory committee—the initial committee charged with reviewing my work and making recommendations to the director. Constructed narratives were brought before the committee, which resulted in them framing me as "noncollegial"— a word repeated throughout the evaluation of my reappointment file. But "collegiality" is simply used as a tool for racism and discrimination, influencing the workplace environment (Frazier 6). Research has shown that unwritten expectations surrounding collegiality can be difficult to negotiate for faculty of colour and can often lead to exclusion from support and to workplace isolation (Frazier 6). But Rockquemore and Laszloffy consider this a double standard, where what is considered acceptable conduct is different for Black faculty versus their white counterparts (21). This kind of double standard, Rockquemore and Laszloffy explain, has a long history in the US where white dominance has been aggressively maintained "by limiting, controlling, and containing black people" (21). Furthermore, the "white power structure has been threatened whenever black people have dared to display boldness, acted decisively on behalf of their interests, asserted themselves with authority and confidence, and refused to acquiesce to attempts to control them" (21).

Black faculty who engage in ways that communicate a sense of boldness and authority are often labeled "arrogant," "aggressive," and "threatening." White faculty, especially white men, who exhibit similar behaviours are labeled "self-confident," "goal oriented," and "having leadership traits" (Rockquemore and Laszloffy 23). Although I was not present when the faculty advisory committee met to discuss my file and reappointment, I deduced what took place, based on my experiences; specifically, my experiences with the three female committee members who work in my division. When I reviewed the committee's recommendations, they all voted "no" to my reappointment. All! This was the weight I bore navigating the tenure and promotion process. And in my fifth year, the year my file was to be submitted for evaluation in consideration for tenure and promotion, the coronavirus (COVID-19) was declared a global health pandemic.

The Onset of a Global Pandemic

When the pandemic was declared, most major educational institutions across the US were directed to move in-person classes to remote online learning platforms. At Kent State University (the university where I was working to secure tenure and promotion), some faculty had as few as three days to transfer all in-person classes to a virtual platform. A lot of care was taken to ensure that students were supported: Mental health resources were made readily available and extensions on assignments were offered to those who would benefit from this safety net, along with the option of securing a Pass or Fail for courses in which they were registered, so as not to negatively affect their grade point averages. But I questioned what more could have been done to support faculty, specifically Black faculty. Professors of dance studies were hampered with the thought of taking studio-based technique classes online. For me, this mandate was accompanied by additional concerns as I stewed over whether a global pandemic—which made it highly unlikely that I could teach nationally, attend guest artists residencies, and conferences, which provide the work used to assess artists in the academy—would negatively affect my tenure and promotion award.

As a pretenured Black faculty member who experienced bias throughout my reappointment processes, I became fretful, knowing I would be unable to continue participating in activities that would augment my tenure dossier. And while my institution offered tenure-track faculty a courtesy extension on their probationary period leading to their mandatory tenure review because of COVID-19, I wrestled with this offer. I thought about my past experiences and not wanting to relive the trauma of withstanding an additional review process should I accept the pause on my tenure clock. This gesture from my institution, an articulation filled with good intentions, did little to provide any comfort as I continued to feel uneasy. I was positioned at the mercy of those who embody privilege; those who may prefer my privation as they decide whether I belonged.

All of these thoughts were front and centre, percolating in my mind as I contemplated safety around COVID-19, COVID-19 and racism, COVID-19 and higher education, racism in higher education, COVID-19 and the curriculum, and COVID-19 and those who are systemically marginalized, struggling to make sense of it all.

COVID-19 and the Systemically Marginalized

A 2020 commonwealth fund survey disclosed how COVID-19 exposed long-standing inequities by race, ethnicity, and income (Getachew). Two major highlights from the survey are as follows:

1. More than half of Black survey respondents reported experiencing an economic challenge because of the pandemic.
2. Both Black and Latino respondents reported pandemic-related mental health concerns.

Additionally, data from the US Census Bureau found that 41 per cent of US adults reported symptoms of anxiety and depressive disorders compared with 11 per cent in 2019, with Black and Latinos more likely to report symptoms (Getachew). What this study did not show was that in addition to carrying the weight of the fear of the virus, Black folks were being violated by the racial injustice that remains pervasive across the US.

COVID-19 and the Curriculum

I teach to share, so students may understand the knowledge being shared. Christine Sleeter and Jamy Stillman have shown that curriculum in the US exists as a rubric for both what schools should do, helping them situate their values in their learning, and how young people should view society (279). But the curriculum did not have

COVID-19 in mind.

COVID-19 made me scrutinize course content, course management, and the needs of the students and teachers. The dance faculty at Kent State had days to transfer their studio-based technique classes to virtual dance classes and few or no conversations around the conditions under which faculty were being asked to teach and under which students were going to be asked to learn. The pandemic created some issues like shifting the labour of education from school to individuals, biased assessments when exams were cancelled and students were graded based on partial work completed, and the sheer unreadiness for remote education. And although some of these were new worries, the pandemic illuminated burdens and inequities that already existed. As Sleeter and Stillman have argued, "In a society, groups struggle for the means to control the consciousness of people" (Sleeter and Stillman 279). The curriculum steers what is being taught in classrooms and the educational aims of an institution (Le Coq 21). It advances learning, but there were no stated guidelines for how faculty and students would function in a global pandemic and remotely. I questioned and grappled with how dancers would participate remotely. I know of and have used videos while teaching the Horton technique in virtual settings. Knowing this approach was not optimal for engaging in movement-based courses, I unreservedly tried to support the students' learning unconventionally.

In the face of COVID-19, and in addition to considering new methods of engagement, I employed diverse attitudes towards assessment. Technologies have been the driving force of globalization (Škare and Soriano 232) and COVID-19 shed light on some of the problems facing marginalized communities, especially those affected by a lack of said technology. If you have no access to what technology allows, you stand the chance of being excluded from a universal progression.

This was all compounded by the reality that some students did not have access to spaces conducive to dance training. Some lived in rural areas with poor internet connections, whereas others were quarantining in homes where they were responsible for assisting their families (e.g., children homeschooling, elder care, and home chores). Although administrators and faculty had the best of intentions in helping students continue with their studies, it appears that best practices in education through an equity and human rights lens may not have been thoroughly considered, given the swiftness with which we were asked to move from in-person to virtual classes.

Equity: Missing in Higher Education

Being a dance professor heightened the challenges of microaggressions, discrimination, and racial violence that I experienced, especially given that the arts are not as revered as disciplines in the science, technology, engineering, and mathematics (STEM) fields. COVID-19 intensified that discourse and further motivated feelings of discomfort because in preparing to be evaluated for tenure and promotion, I had grown accustomed to overproducing; I thought that was the only measure of my value to the institution while secretly wondering whether dance as a major was at risk of being expurgated.

When classes went remote, I worried my work would not be seen or valued. I knew that dance artists were out of work, had to manage their savings, and were forced to be grateful for the meagre federal offerings they received. I had been submitting yearly documentation of my progress towards tenure and promotion. But would a year of being unable to actively engage in research and creative activities grant my white colleagues' permission to disapprovingly assess me? Would it allow a process already buoyed by biases continue to allow Black faculty to be at the mercy of the acerbic pen of white members of the tenure and promotion committees? How would they know I was doing all that I needed to do and that I was deserving of tenure and promotion? Yes, COVID-19 gave me time to perilously ponder my trajectory in the academy. And there were days my ponder turned to panic; I never had a moment for my mind to be at peace.

When I started teaching online, some students were engaged but others proved noncommittal. Still, I kept trying. And trying. I had to consider new methods of engaging and employ diverse attitudes towards assessment, as the importance of live class experiences had been temporarily replaced by technology.

But online education is nothing new; in fact, it has revolutionized the way we approach education over the past few decades as it has grown increasingly popular. Compared to fall 2019 when only 36% of students enrolled in distance learning, the pandemic restricted in-person learning, causing over 75% of all postsecondary students in the

US to take online classes in fall 2020 (Hamilton). And while some classes in the dance curriculum—like dance history, dance mechanics, anatomy, and dance composition—shifted more easily to online platforms, professors of movement-based courses had to modify approaches to teaching course content, rethink assignments, and adapt assessments because of the decreased effectiveness of conveying to young dancers the rigor of embodied practices.

Virtual dance classes are also not new, and resources were made available to assist in moving dance-based pedagogy courses online. But COVID-19 took away my ability to be physically present in the space where I would demonstrate phrases, offer specific instructions, directly touch dancers' bodies (with permission) in a way that allowed them to become more kinaesthetically aware, and vocalize through rhythmic intonations and physical hints my expectations for the accompanist. Knowing I was unable to perform these tasks during social distancing, I asked four questions: (1) Were dance professors indirectly being asked to give into virtual dance classes as a possible new norm? (2) Would institutions ever accept the difficulty of taking some disciplines remotely? (3) Why are so many dance educators working industriously to create content for virtual dance experiences (I asked this while legitimately trying to remove my personal consternation with virtual dance classes)? (4) When would institutions stop failing Black faculty who continue to show up and contribute to the academy in tireless ways? I was also expected to be resilient and thrive in a climate of unjust scrutiny, microaggressions, and racial violence while working to secure tenure during a pandemic. I know the educators' expectations were absurd—having to cater to students at the risk of losing ourselves —but the expectations of a Black professor during COVID-19 who was also dealing with racism were enormously challenging. And dance as discipline magnified that challenge.

I wanted administrators to at least pretend that maybe they were inadvertently undermining the value of the arts as a discipline and the value of their Black educators. Maybe the academy should do more to actively and intentionally institute policies and protocols that are pro-arts (not anti-other disciplines) and pro-Black (not anti-white). With this in mind, I would suggest highlighting the seemingly (un)complicated reality that in-person interactions in dance education are a necessary part of the training and that the experiences of Black faculty need to be documented, shared, and addressed.

My trepidation compels me to consider how much of my tenure fetish was encouraged by my desire to have the academy validate my dancing spirit and to have that validation supported by more aggressively shifting the curriculum from one based on educating students in four specific disciplines—STEM—to educating them in five: science, technology, engineering, arts, and mathematics (STEAM). In short, administrators in higher education must advocate for the arts with the same effort as they do other disciplines. And no, the pandemic did not eliminate my knowledge that colleagues who served as evaluators of my file wore their biases visibly. It makes me wonder whether code words like "collegial," "professional," and "good fit" will continue to be used in evaluating pre-tenured faculty, as senior faculty worked to eliminate probationary faculty whose appearances, behaviours, or communication styles differ from the academy's white majority. Here is my charge: White faculty need to check their microaggressions because what they are indirectly saying is "We want diversity and equity, but we are not ready for change."

The Resilience and Resourcefulness of Some Dance Professors

To add complexity to the pandemic and my tenure process, in the US, 2020 saw protests erupt in response to the killing of unarmed Black men and women at the hands of police. This social unrest occurred in the wake of the murder of George Floyd, an African American man killed during an arrest after a store clerk alleged he had passed a counterfeit twenty-dollar bill in Minneapolis—and the killing of Breonna Taylor, a twenty-six-year-old African American woman who was fatally shot in her Louisville, Kentucky, apartment on March 13, 2020, after three white, plainclothes officers forced entry into her apartment. Their killings garnered international attention and galvanized communities.

Young people took to the streets following these senseless killings, calling for justice. And social movements exist to bring about or resist change, reflecting the people's voice. Similarly, the curriculum must more appropriately and accurately reflect the appeals of those we teach—Black students in need of equity, disabled students in need of better access, queer students in need of inclusion, immigrant students in need a metaphoric educational home, and white students in need of more nuanced history lessons. There is an aloneness to being a Black professor in a predominantly white institution. There is also an aloneness to the perils of negotiating racial injustice. I felt I existed in a vacuum as a Black faculty member during the pandemic. And the climate of social unrest intensified those feelings. I kept working, teaching online classes, advising students who were in a kind of mental peril, and preparing to submit five years' worth of proof showing that I belonged in an establishment curated by whiteness. The pandemic eroded what little normalcy I found living in that vacuum and made me question that normalcy. But even in the questioning, resilience won.

In a year of isolation, while battling injustice amid racial inequity, I saw Black people winning. Our presence was seen, our voices were heard, and our creativity was illuming. This was my proximity to resilience. Teaching while fighting, I lived with the unknowns of my tenure application or when another Black person would become the next hashtag. I cannot say I always celebrated my Blackness during COVID-19 and the year of social reckoning, but I saw my wounds, and in so doing made time to heal while teaching. I taught online, but I avoided teaching movement-based practices virtually. I would cringe at the thought of having a computer between me and a community of movers eager to be shaped by experiential learning.

Equally, I recoiled at the thought of teaching—sweating and panting while wearing a mask, a shield, while constantly maintaining my six feet of distance. Dancing in a virtual age frightened me because I no longer had the things that dance afforded me: the convergence of bodies in time and space. How could we put dance in a virtual space without its feeling artificial? All the aforementioned things I was unwilling to let go or lose. I adore the corporeal information that dancers exchange, and I love seeing bodies of all shapes and sizes moving to rhythms both familiar and unknown, trying to catch their next breath. I embraced the moments that bridged practice with performance, but I fretted that a part of that equation had been removed, leaving a void. It was our resilience that encouraged a reality born out of necessity. And for some Black folks, necessity produces inspiration, which is a pool in which Black creatives continue to swim.

Even with the return of live, in-person performances, COVID-19's long-term effect on the performing arts is unknown. Artists of all ethnic origins and arts organizations are working to figure out what is next for them and for the field. And while I was on my own journey, I gave into the realities of all my worries and fears to own the moment. I had invested in dance as a career, and life as a dance artist has taught me to be a creative problem solver, to set aside time to take daily inventory of self, and to consider family, friends, and all the people around me—everything needed to revive an economy drowning in the ruins of a pandemic and a society contending with police brutality and racism. As a dance professor, I found myself comforting unsure dancers and telling them that even if they never perform in a major dance company, the skills they learned from being in a dance class will contribute to their resilience.

Resilience can be bred from creativity. And surviving a pandemic, while battling social unrest, taught me that creativity was limitless.

My feelings of survival and resilience are tied to whiteness by a not-so-invisible string. I pondered how my white colleagues were fairing with isolation, a pandemic, their own tenure journeys, and fighting racial injustice. I wondered whether they had to protect themselves from being outside, from police brutality, and from unexpected deaths. The nature of Black folks in the US forces us to be hardwired to deal with adversity. My Blackness gave me ammunition to deal with questions of uncertainty, the mistrust of law enforcement, and the hardship of negotiating safety in white spaces. But adversity for Black folks is not new, and neither is our resilience. The aloneness of COVID-19 feels temporary, but the aloneness of racial injustice is more permanent.

During my time of quarantining, I was able to be more creative about how I rendered dance. I thought about the discipline and contended with how to reimagine how dance was taught, performed, and produced inside and outside the academy. What if the experience of being a part of the community component of embodied practices empowered dancers to use that experience to re-envision what community could be? Quarantining during COVID-19 granted me space to question how racial inequities, social justice, and ideas around movement intersected.

While the pandemic made me further question my journey towards tenure and promotion, it also reminded me of the communities of Black love and Black access that I enjoy. And as Black dancers continue to share cartographies of movement ideals, we stay energized and stimulate the narratives of Black dance professors who kept teaching, albeit virtually, during COVID-19 and who continue to be resplendently resourceful in the academy and beyond. These were perfect examples of how COVID-19 may have offered Black educators, like me, the chance to curate and harness our pedagogical powers.

I practice self-care by writing and by dancing. When my body swallows movement, I feel full in the aftermath. Throughout the pandemic I continued to find ways to move, dancing to maintain some sense of normalcy and holding on to my sanity. I am reminded of my resilience when I call on my village of warriors—my Black friends—to talk, vent, scream, cry, and laugh. I have reconstituted how my body lends itself to spaces and how spaces can allow freedom. Being Black, this freedom forbids defeatism, which is the antithesis to Black culture, to dance culture, to Black dance culture. What is a world with no art? We need people championing that cause, and dance is one of the most effective ways to show care and to demonstrate love.

On March 15, 2021, I was awarded tenure in the School of Theatre and Dance at Kent State University. On April 5 of the same year, I was promoted to associate professor.

Works Cited

Frazier, Kimberly N. "Academic Bullying: A Barrier to Tenure and Promotion for African American Faculty." *Florida Journal for Educational Administration & Policy,* Fall 2011, vol. 5, no. 1, 2011, pp. 1-13.

Yaphet Getachew et al., *Beyond the Case Count: The Wild-Ranging Disparities of COVID-19 in the United States* (Commonwealth Fund, Sept. 2020). https://doi.org/10.26099/gjcn-1z31. Accessed 19 Aug. 2023.

Hamilton, Ilana. "By The Numbers: The Rise of Online Learning in the U.S." *Forbes Advisor,* 24 May 2023, www.forbes.com/advisor/education/online-learning-stats. Accessed 19 Aug. 2023.

Le Coq, J. P. "The Essence of the Curriculum." *The Journal of Higher Education,* vol. 12, no. 1, Ohio State University Press, 1941, pp. 21-25.

Monzó, Lilia. D. "Humanizing the Tenure Process: Toward a Pedagogy of Heart." *Dignity of the Calling: Educators Share the Beginnings of Their Journey,* edited by Andrew T. Kemp, Information Age Publishing, 2018, pp. 313-322.

Rockquemore, Kerry Ann, and Tracey Laszloffy. *The Black Academic's Guide to Winning Tenure—Without Losing Your Soul.* Lynne Rienner Publishers, 2008.

School of Theatre and Dance. *School of Theatre and Dance Handbook, Sept. 2020,* https://www-s3- live.kent.edu/s3fs-root/s3fs-public/file/School%20of%20Theatre%20and%20Dance%20Handbook%20 2020_0.pdf?VersionId=9ED7m_hlAeb7ywg_mY_Nz0cYglG qmCYi. Accessed 7 Aug. 2023.

Škare, Marinko, and Domingo Ribeiro Soriano. "How Globalization Is Changing Digital Technology Adoption: An International Perspective." *Journal of Innovation & Knowledge,* vol. 6, no. 4, Elsevier BV, Oct. 2021, pp. 222–33. https://doi.org/10.1016/j.jik.2021.04.001. Accessed 19 Aug. 2023.

Sleeter, Christine, and Jamy Stillman. "Standardizing Knowledge in a Multicultural Society." *Curriculum Inquiry,* vol. 35, no. 1, 2005, pp. 27-46.

Riley, Susan. "What Is STEAM Education?" *The Institute for Arts Integration and STEAM,* Mar. 2023, artsintegration.com/what-is-steam-education-in-k-12-schools. Accessed 7 Aug. 2023.

PART II

Individual and Collective Activism

Chapter 6.

Black Queer Identities and Pandemic Survival Experiences in Canada

Delores V. Mullings, Wesley Crichlow,
Bukola Oladinni Salami, and Eboni-Rai Mullings

COVID-19 has affected Black people and all aspects of Black life in many ways; this is especially true among LGBTQ+ people. How have Black queer people managed during this pandemic and what does resilience look like for them? Many continue to experience exclusion and systemic marginalization and have suffered greatly from isolation and other social ills, such as homophobia and transphobia. For others, the story is different. This chapter offers a glimpse into what life has been like for some Black queer people during the COVID-19 pandemic. It includes uplifting stories that provide insights and knowledge gathered from discussions held between the two authors and people in their circles.

Within the African, Caribbean, and Black (ACB) experience, LGBTQ+ concerns are often left behind, or inclusion is tokenized. As more ACB LGBTQ+ people participate in community-based organizations, attend postsecondary institutions and spiritual spaces, join in politics and research, and assume leadership positions, the needs and concerns of ACB queer people are shifting from the margins to the centre along with their self-identified concerns.

When the editors received the abstracts for this book, we discovered that none of the authors had focused on ACB queer people. After assessing the gaps in the submissions, we agreed that ACB queer experiences had to be included in this book and that we were obligated to take deliberate actions to ensure this goal was met. So, we reached out to colleagues who self-identify as queer, asking whether they might be interested in submitting a chapter for the book. Although we received positive responses from everyone who replied, for a number of reasons, including managing the impacts of the pandemic, respondents were unable to commit to the submission deadline. After further discussions, the editors decided that in order to have ACB queer voices represented in this book, we would coauthor the chapter with someone with lived experience.

I, Delores, approached Wesley Crichlow and pitched the idea of partnering with him to write the chapter. Wesley rarely says no to working on projects, so I felt confident that we would have a first-voice account of the ACB queer experience in the book with his input. Wesley and I had one preliminary discussion before finally meeting to have a deeper conversation, with a series of text messages, emails, and phone calls punctuating the time in between. During our conversations, we asked ourselves a series of questions: "What do we know about how Black queer communities are being affected by COVID-19?"; "What support services are available to the community, and are they using these services?"; "How is spirituality playing a role in their lives?"; and "What kind of social support are they receiving?" The stories and discussions in this chapter are informed by the questions we asked; our observations, perceptions, and experiences; and our understanding of how the Black queer people, including elders, within our circles have been navigating the COVID-19 pandemic and showing resilience. The chapter is divided into two sections: (1) Social and Physical Care and (2) Spiritual and Mental Health. We begin by discussing how Black queer people came together to support each other as a community.

Social and Physical Care: We Are All in This Together

Within a short time after the COVID-19 pandemic was declared, Black people realized that they would be hit hard. We watched the rising death toll among African Americans and the swift reaction to Black Americans calling attention to the impact of anti-Black racism. Not long after, ACB Canadians began to also sound the alarm, by that time realizing that they were in it together, which meant they would have to care for each other during this pandemic. Black communities came together online and in person. In many cases, the historical divisions between and among Black people shifted to focus on people's needs. This is not a romantic retelling or putting ACB queer bodies up for entertainment; it is genuine care. What brought us to this place? What was the difference in the way Black people talked with each other? We observed that the conversation about race framed how people discussed the impact of COVID-19 by highlighting our racial differences from other racial groups, which created the opportunity for bonding around our Blackness regardless of other social identities.

COVID-19 created a feeling of heightened risk that brought our communities together, and we began to understand belonging differently. Questions about genderqueer, gender nonconforming, and non-binary ACB are frequently asked to gain an understanding. There is an additional piece to the acceptance in that sometimes cisgender Black people overcompensate in their actions because of feelings of guilt for not being supportive in the past. This means that for the first time in our history, Black queer people could talk about their sexual orientation and identities with families and friends, which helped reduce the trauma of hiding. In other words, the understanding of a shared trauma created unity and openness for people to talk and listen. COVID-19 depathologized Black queer people during the pandemic. Other things happened too: ACB queer people became brave and talked more openly about their struggles, and our communities responded so that they would receive support and care. Black queer people's longstanding commitments and concerns are more visibly intersectional, so their concerns became the larger ACB community's concerns as well. In some cases, non-queer and trans Black people became more open to thinking differently. Some within the ACB queer communities observed that their non-queer friends and family were openly worried about them or others dying before they had had the chance to tell them that they loved them. These are some of the incredible relationship-rebuilding efforts and displays of love that we see.

Community Activism and Self-Education

We have seen an uptake of intergenerational activities of ACB people across all age groups, challenging systems and barriers for Black queer people in an unprecedented way. The Black Lives Matter (BLM) movement, comprising mostly of Black queer youth, pushed Black queer concerns forwards and called attention to systemic and structural concerns and barriers. Black youth outside of the BLM movement also advocated for ACB elders. Black-led healthcare groups, community organizations, and practitioners—such as Access Alliance, Black Opportunity Fund (Health Care Group), Health Association of African Canadians, and Black Physicians of Canada—also mounted strong campaigns to provide vaccine access for those who wanted it, aggregated data collection among ACB people, and increased funding for research. This intergenerational activism opened spaces for conversation and education to occur.

COVID-19 also gave us the opportunity to self-educate, seek out, and participate in education about Black LGBTQ+ people. There seems to be less stigma attached to Black queer people within some parts of our communities. Within this area of newness, two things happened: First, the racial history of trans identity was less hidden, with trans people speaking openly about their genders and identities. Second, in some cases, ACB communities embraced them. In one of our social media family chat groups, many conversations about trans people generally and Black trans people specifically occurred. Some members spoke meaningfully and genuinely, trying to understand the concepts and realities of Black LGBTQ+ people, with others warmly commenting that they "look pretty." A few individuals shared educational information from social media posts, such as TikTok and Facebook. People were less interested in knowing about sexual habits, activities, and trans people's sex organs and more interested in their lives wholistically. We saw a shift towards Blackness and how it intersects with other forms of discrimination first, so less emphasis was placed on sexual and gender identities. For the first time in our history, Black people knew a lot about Black trans people, including the names of some who were sick and who died from COVID-19 and other illnesses. At the same time, Black people were offering significant social support to Black queer community members.

Social Support

Queerness is defined through a white lens that also determines Black LGBTQ+ queerness. White, queer-perceived uniformity seriously affects Black queer people because support services are designed based on the needs of white LGBTQ+ people. This leaves little room for racially and culturally appropriate services for Black queer people. If the services were inaccessible before COVID-19, they became even more so during the pandemic. From our own experiences and watching others around us, we know that Black people historically have had to care for each other because they were either barred from accessing formal services, received inferior informal care, or were denied care entirely.

Friends made time to talk with each other frequently on the telephone, and this frequent verbal connection brought people closer. Their phone conversations were deliberate. They genuinely wanted to find out how people were doing, especially those who lived alone or were estranged from their families. We saw and heard of individuals reaching out to others that they had not seen or connected with for a long time. ACB queer people also recreated severed relationships with some in their circles. We saw and heard of relationships being rebuilt where people were bonding again, reconnecting, and developing healthier relationships with the individuals in their lives. The need for both social connection and physical touch meant people were ignoring social distancing restrictions, with queer folks hugging and kissing each other and nonqueer folks despite the fear of contracting COVID-19.

Medication delivery and grocery shopping were done through informal support. Some spaces—such as apartment buildings, cooperatives, and condominiums—naturally create a stronger sense of belonging, which allowed individuals to feel more comfortable asking for help. People often disclosed their personal circumstances when asking for help. They might have said, "I'm immunocompromised, can you shop for me?" and they would get the help they needed. This indicates that a community of care is based on an acceptance of community members, including older adults.

Elder Care

Black queer people are particularly vulnerable under normal circumstances. But as we noted earlier, circumstances got worse for Black queer people under COVID-19; this was even more true for Black queer elders. However, informal community support was fully engaged and kept older queer Black adults physically safe as pposible. Older ACB queer adults rely on their community of Black people, especially their circle of friends. Black social care during COVID-19 led to older queer adults and non-queer ACB people bonding in a way that has never happened before to our knowledge. Elders were supported with resources and education that taught them to use technology to connect with community members, family, and friends. We saw an increase in elders' use of social media and videoconferencing technology to socialize, receive counselling, share information, attend spiritual gatherings, stay connected, and support others, which was particularly important, as leisure events and spaces were closed initially for lengthy periods. Community members needed to provide leisure for each other, so ACB family and friends created new kinships to facilitate social and leisure opportunities. The use of technology also allowed older migrants to reunite and communicate internationally with kinfolk from "back home," including those who had travelled to other countries with whom they had lost contact.

Community members remain concerned about older Black queer adults who reside in foster care or public institutions and wonder how to best support their friends. Wesley feels a real shift in things. For him and others, it no longer feels like "it's this big, homophobic place right now." In some circles, a keener focus on aging and a sense of care developed in which elders' unique needs are recognized. Black queer people, particularly older adults living with episodic disabilities, such as HIV/AIDS and cancer, received strong social support from Black-led organizations and Black medical practitioners (physicians, nurses, etc.), who provided access to COVID-19 vaccines, particularly for those who are immunocom-promised.

Spiritual and Mental Care

Research tells us that a lot of Black LGBTQ+ people are members of faith-based communities and have strong connections to their religious communities but are often shunned (Elliot). Many have various spiritual practices that are important in their lives. Some LGBTQ+ people have tenuous relationships with their religious communities but have found other communities to fill this gap. Black queer people found privacy, peace, and support among religious members during the pandemic. For example, online services created a sense of security and safety for all attendees, reducing the transphobic and homophobic religious violence previously experienced by some. Online, Black queer people could dress how they wanted without worrying about criticism and scrutiny. They did not have to show themselves on camera and could also attend services anonymously. Religious groups were encouraging new people to join their virtual services, saying "everyone is invited," and services focussed more on hope, gratitude, and thanks.

When Black LGBTQ+ people did attend religious spaces in person, there was also the welcoming and acceptance of gender nonconforming individuals, such as gay men wearing dresses to church, which has traditionally been frowned upon and not accepted, and as noted by Lawrence Brown, the church has been silent to the violence perpetuated towards Black LGBTQ+ communities (9). In an extraordinary turn of events, we share the story of a long-time church member who shared his story with us. He never openly identified as being gay for fear of being driven from his church, but he said the members assumed his sexual identity because of his effeminate mannerisms and the male companions he regularly brought to service. He was often isolated and not allowed to hold any post in the church. However, he got support from his fellow church brethren when he was unable to access community services. Church members were more interested in advocating with him and on his behalf to ensure he got what he needed rather than judging or excluding him. He said COVID-19 changed his life in ways that he never expected. Church members now frequently call to ask how he is doing and whether he needs anything.

Mental Health

ACB queer people show a different and better understanding of trauma now than prior to COVID-19. A lot more people now know about depression, and they know where to reach out if they need help. Individuals regularly reminded each other to check their mental health, so discussing concerns around mental health became easier during the pandemic. The ongoing mental-health-related discussions in the media, institutions, schools, and in religious and spiritual spaces have helped make this conversation easier. Given that many people in society were emotionally affected by COVID-19, Black queer people felt less stigmatized and fearful of discussing their mental health concerns. Black-led organizations and service providers, such as the Black Community Resource Centre and Black Health Alliance, encouraged ACB community members to access free virtual mental health support, which resulted in an increase in ACB people going for therapy. Black people are reluctant to seek therapy, given their experiences with anti-Black racism, including the lack of culturally and racially relevant therapeutic modalities, lack of access, and long waitlists (Crichlow et al.). In addition, they often lack time, money, and extended healthcare, which is aggravated by the shame of their perceived deficits. These conditions are exacerbated for ACB queer people and more so for our elders, as their lifestyles and personhood are stereotyped as conflicting with their Blackness.

The history of conversion therapy (Haldeman)—an aspect of some religious counselling and psychotherapy that forces young queer people to reject their sexual and gender identities—has had a lasting impact on the queer community's openness to consider therapy. Online counselling reduced the risk for many because they did not have to appear on camera during the free, virtual counselling sessions, nor did they need to disclose personal information, and formal institutional files were not kept on them. Black-led community organizations and service providers reported an increase in queer Black men accessing counselling. Black people have begun connecting the social determinants of health with Blackness and their own mental health and wellbeing. It has helped reduce Black queer people's feelings of vulnerability, isolation, victimhood, and their sense of just surviving rather than living.

COVID-19 pushed some people to either return to or begin using alcohol and drugs to cope with the grief and loss they experienced. We are aware of some individuals who had developed different ways of coping with life challenges but returned to using alcohol and/or drugs during the pandemic. At the same time, some sought out harm-reduction programs to try and stay healthy—a significant difference from past behaviour in using without support. We heard people say that in the absence of human contact, COVID-19 brought out their hidden or forgotten strengths and skillsets "because we couldn't tell people that we were gay."

Furthermore, some people among the ACB queer community are more exposed to violence, such as domestic and familial violence. Being forced through public health measures to stay in a hostile home environment was particularly difficult for those living at home with unsupportive parents or roommates or for those who are not out to others (Akpan). However, this group also found ways to connect online with others outside of their immediate environment and get support.

This chapter only retells the stories and experiences of a small number of Black LGBTQ+ people from the authors' perspectives, one of whom self-identifies as queer. We know that Black queer people went from feeling the love and warmth of friends and others in their circles and visiting and socializing with each other and having vibrant lives prior to the pandemic, to being instantly isolated at home, often in violent environments. We are not suggesting that homophobia is no longer a reality in Black communities because we also know that some members of the trans population in particular are unable to access medications and online counselling and are still excluded from ACB communities and the formal service sector. This chapter is also limited by a lack of analysis of the larger Black queer communities locally and globally; those who are not out to their parents and families, for example, and those who were isolated pre-COVID-19 and remain so. Our intent is to show what possibilities are potentially available within our communities to live, love, and support each other regardless of gender and sexual identity.

Works Cited

Akpan, Paula. "How the Pandemic Is Affecting Black LGBTQ+ Communities around the World." *Vogue*. 5 June 2021. www.vogue.in/culture-and-living/content/how-the-pandemic-is-affecting-black-lgbtq-communities-around-the-world. Accessed 8 Aug. 2023.

Brown, Lawrence T. "The Movement for Black Lives vs. the Black Church." *Kalfou: A Journal of Comparative and Relational Ethnic Studies*, vol. 4, no.1, https://doi.org/10.15367/kf.v4i1, 19 May 2017.

Crichlow, W, E. Faulkner, and K. Leach. "Lesbian, Gay, Transgender and Queer Access to Mental Health Services." *Africentric Social Work*, edited by D. V. Mullings et al., Fernwood Publishing, 2021, pp. 184-198.

Haldeman, Douglas C. "Introduction: A History of Conversion Therapy, from Accepted Practice to Condemnation." *The Case against Conversion 'Therapy': Evidence, Ethics, and Alternatives*, edited by D.C. Haldeman, American Psychological Association, 2022, pp. 3-16.

Chapter 7.

Intimate Partner Violence and Domestic Violence in the United Kingdom

Bo Ebuehi

You who were hurt and not believed
You who were not valued or protected
You who were not seen or saved
May you be protected by the divine as you heal.

Although the coronavirus has wreaked havoc on almost everyone, anywhere, there is nothing equal to the impact that COVID-19 has had on African, Caribbean, and Black (ACB) communities in recent times. COVID-19 not only created health inequities but also exposed and exacerbated long-standing inequities affecting ACB groups in the United Kingdom (UK), adding to existing social and economic inequities. Lockdown restrictions and, in particular, stay-at-home orders were put in place to impose social distancing and to combat the spread of COVID-19. They were also put in place to help reduce a person's risk of getting the virus and decrease the spread of the virus to others. These restrictions and stay-at-home orders negatively affected some people's health. As more individuals spend time at home because of these restrictions, and as a result of disruptions to support services, there has been an increase in intimate partner violence (IPV).

By themselves, the norms, social structures, and gender roles within the community greatly influence women's vulnerability to violence.

IPV is a social norm in many countries globally and is about power and control rather than social circumstances. Furthermore, anxiety and frustrations about the COVID-19 pandemic did not cause IPV. However, increased social, financial, health problems, and economic pressures coupled with isolation and being isolated in small spaces with others helped to increase anxiety about contracting COVID-19, and frustrations related to quarantine and/or lockdown, economic uncertainty caused by job loss, excessive consumption of alcohol and drugs (illicit and prescribed), and other COVID-19-related stresses have exacerbated the increase of IPV.

IPV includes all types of violence in all types of relationships between intimate partners. For some individuals, it is an inescapable life sentence that incorporates physical, sexual, economic, mental, and psychological violence on a former or current intimate partner. Individuals can be exposed to IPV directly or indirectly, whether it is the survivor who experiences the physical, sexual, or emotional violence or the individual hearing or seeing the event.

Anyone can experience IPV regardless of their gender, age, or ability. However, it is well known that ACB communities are disproportionately affected by IPV (Brixi et al.). Women experience increased risks of abuse resulting from deep-rooted systems of discrimination and barriers to accessing care and support, some of which include language differences, religion, higher rates of poverty, fear of deportation, concerns about confidentiality, and cultural stigmas. IPV is also experienced by men and members of 2SLGBT+ relationships.

Men are the overwhelming perpetrators of IPV against women, and some men experience IPV. The ManKind Initiative, a well-established nonprofit in Britain offering support to male victims, recently reported an increase in call volumes compared with the prelockdown period. In addition, the number of visitors to the ManKind Initiative website during the week of April 27, 2020 was three times higher than before the lockdown (ManKind Initiative).

Racism and discrimination have an overarching negative impact on the experiences and lives of ACB individuals and families, and this negative impact has continued throughout the pandemic. The stress associated with being discriminated against based on race and ethnicity affects mental and physical health; this, coupled with being required to remain in close proximity with an abuser, has caused a spike in IPV reports.

Across the UK, IPV reports spiked during lockdown, not least because perpetrators and survivors were spending more time at home together. Some tended to face additional pressures; women wanted the abuse to stop, but they were cautious and suspicious about what might happen when Black men are in police custody—they may end up injured or dead.

The risks associated with COVID-19 restrictions also exacerbated the housing challenges faced by a large number of communities. Unfortunately, the home is not a safe place for countless women who have found themselves locked in with their abusive partners and locked out of safety. Reports from around the world show an alarming increase in gender-based violence and intimate partner violence against women and girls (Brixi et al.).

Because there are few access to general pathways for connections, it becomes harder to reach out to get the help and support that is needed. So, it is simply a back-to-basic planning—like Black women survivors styling their hair in a manner that is less likely to be pulled and scanning the home and marking out places of shelter where there is no easy access to knives (so not running into the kitchen), reducing the likelihood of serious injury if an attack ensues.

The curtailment of social activities has also meant that ACB communities have lost the support of friends and family members, which has prevented victims and survivors from accessing important social supports from communities that were part of their support systems, thus increasing the risks for IPV. Many lost colleagues or family members to COVID-19, and nearly all are seeing the impact of the virus on their communities along with the significant social, physical, and mental health repercussions and complications.

Economic inequities for ACB communities in the UK are not new. Before the crisis, incomes were already lower for most of these groups, and amid the pandemic, less than a third of ACB employees who had been able to work received the government's furlough package. Seeking help can be difficult for many reasons, such as financial dependency, lack of access to divorce, or feelings of shame.

Migrant women face barriers to getting critical services. Their abusive partners use their immigration status to control them or prevent them from seeking help, and they may fear approaching authorities because of the risk of detention, deportation, or separation from their children. People on visas, such as spousal or fiancé visas, have no recourse to public funds under the Immigration and Asylum Act 1999, making them ineligible for most government benefits (2020).

In response to the increased levels of IPV reports across the country, a national campaign called UK SAYS NO MORE was launched to raise awareness to end IPV and sexual violence across the UK. The program provides online safe spaces for survivors to access specialist support services, all of which can be accessed through a series of untraceable web pages, allowing those in danger to access the help and support they need discreetly. These campaigns often erase ACB communities by being designed for the white experience or failing to account for compounding issues unique to ACB people.

In addition to the online spaces, other campaigns have launched: The Safe Spaces campaign works in partnership with independent pharmacies across the country to provide safe spaces in their consultation rooms for people experiencing IPV and other forms of abuse. These safe spaces increase the opportunity for victims and survivors to access specialist support, providing a space for them to phone a helpline, contact a support service, or talk to a friend or family member. As part of this scheme, survivors can seek help discreetly by giving a code word to pharmacists. If someone asks for "Ani" at one of the participating pharmacies, they will be given the chance to go to a private space to talk and to see whether they need help from police or other services, such as domestic abuse helplines. The name is an acronym for "action needed immediately." Perceived control and hope are both factors thought to be associated with resilience. ACB survivors of IPV demonstrate certain factors that predict higher levels of resilience. These factors include more spirituality, less violent relationships, and greater social support.

Faith communities have also played a vital role in engaging with communities and were a trusted source of information, leadership, and engagement for ACB communities. Their involvement is needed to better engage in future efforts to build community resilience and prepare communities for the immediate and long-term challenges of COVID-19, in particular, IPV. Faith provides an important foundation for community resilience through recovery and bereavement. The importance of faith in ACB communities should be reflected better in the support and guidance provided to survivors of IPV. Faith cannot be separated from people's lived experiences—faith is part of the solution.

As lockdown restrictions began to ease, ACB communities started to set up small support bubbles/groups and initiatives that directly addressed their needs and the best ways to support one another around life circumstances, including domestic violence and IPV. They found ways to bypass the bureaucracy and communicate directly with one another; being in direct contact provided the opportunity to eliminate the need to edit or filter their truths. Having a space where people can talk about what happened or is happening to them is critical; talking can help birth healing as well as support others who are going through similar things.

There are support organizations, such as Sistah Space, that have independent ACB advisors for ACB women experiencing IPV—the only service of its kind in London. This special place enables ACB women and girls to see themselves reflected in the service providers and the environment. It is a space where they can interact with someone who understands their hair, skin, and food without feeling stupid, inferior, and abnormal. Staff run training sessions inside the venue—for example, cultural competency training that accounts for the cultural nuances and barriers, colloquialisms, languages, and customs that make up the diverse ACB communities. Police can conduct interviews, and ACB survivors can visit or be part of the community whenever they want to just be in a protective environment—a comfortable, friendly, and sociable environment, where service providers are knowledgeable and skilled in working with and understanding ACB women holistically.

Sistah Space caters their services to the situation, dealing with housing needs, refuge, midwives, police, and even sexual health clinics as needed to protect service users. And it has become a community, a place people come back to, where they feel at home. Women that benefited from the help of these spaces when they needed help are now helping run the organization. So, it is full-circle kind of establishment; it certainly feels like a facet of ubuntu.

Although existing ACB safe spaces have experienced financial hardship during the pandemic, they have found ways to thrive through small donations; sometimes this has meant that support has come from simply meeting up with friends or family at local parks just to stay connected or get some relief, even if for very short periods. There continues to be a lack of investment in Black communities when it comes to public services. Most ACB community safe spaces have been created by ACB people who have experienced IPV, survived, and are on a journey towards healing themselves. These spaces, like Sistah Space, were set up to ensure that Black women would have a venue where they could see themselves reflected.

The sisterhood, spirituality, and energy that exists in these spaces drives them; they raise funds, raise awareness, and continue to apply for funding. It is hard work that can be draining, as support staff also need some form of therapy, too, but this does not deter them. These spaces are clear examples of what ACB victim-survivors need: support services that are racially and culturally sensitive and reflect their lived experience. Other interventions came as campaign groups, and women's nonprofit agencies called on hotel chains and the government to offer alternative accommodation to help women and children escape abuse, asking them to open rooms to those fleeing IPV. The response from hotels, including some of the country's largest chains, has been overwhelmingly positive. However, the hoteliers say that the UK government must follow the lead of France and Italy and now offer financial support to underwrite the costs of opening their rooms and providing meals to occupants.

The helpline for perpetrators of IPV and domestic abuse who are seeking help to change their behaviour received more calls as the COVID-19 lockdown continued. The Respect phone line offers advice to individuals who have been violent towards their partners or are fearful that lockdown conditions will lead to them losing control of their behaviour. The confidential phone line received a significant increase in calls during the first UK lockdown compared with the two months before the lockdown began. Their website also received an increase in hits in the same period.

Some smaller nonprofit organizations were able to offer virtual conferences over Zoom that provided a platform for victim-survivors, service providers, and stakeholders to discuss the challenges experienced by the ACB and minority communities in accessing and receiving support for domestic violence across the country.

Although IPV is experienced predominantly by women, a small percentage of men, nonbinary, and trans people also have violent partners. I close with two questions: What needs to be done to seriously address IPV to eradicate it, and what needs to be done in the interim to promote zero tolerance of IPV towards women?

Works Cited

Brixi, H., Fu, H., and Uribe, J. P. "Global Crisis of Violence against Women and Girls: Tackling It with New, Better Data Use." *World Bank Blogs*, 5 Jan. 2022, https://blogs.worldbank.org/opendata/global-crisis-violence-against-women-and-girls-tackling-it-new-better-data-use. Accessed 8 Aug. 2023.

Pezzali, A. "UK Failing Domestic Abuse Victims in Pandemic." *Human Rights Watch*, 8 June 2020, https://www.hrw.org/news/2020/06/08/uk-failing-domestic-abuse-victims-pandemic. Accessed 8 Aug. 2023.

ManKind Initiative. "Media and Policy Briefing: Male Victims of Domestic Abuse and Covid-19 Briefing (3): 27th April to 3rd May 2020." https://www.mankind.org.uk/wp-content/uploads/2020/05/3-03-05-2020-ManKind-Initiative-Covid-19-Briefing-Male-Victims-of-Domestic-Abuse.pdf. Accessed 8 Aug. 2023.

Chapter 8.

Ottawa-Led Coalition Helps Rescue 41 Black International Students from Ukraine

Bruce Deachman
(Reprinted with the permission of Post Media)

The route from Kherson, Ukraine, to freedom, in neighbouring EU countries Poland or Slovakia, is extremely long and uncertain. Yet many are determined to escape the Russian-occupied city on the Dnieper River in the south, not far from Odessa, some setting off on the more than one-thousand-kilometre journey on foot.

But with the help of the Ottawa-led Global Black Coalition, forty-one Black international students have successfully made their way to safety, with more expected to follow in their footsteps in the coming days.

"These students were waking up and going to bed to the sounds of bombs," says Gwen Madiba, founder of Ottawa's Equal Chance Foundation, one of the groups involved in the coalition. "They were living in fear, and they wanted to escape. They can now sleep in peace."

The Global Black Coalition is made up of numerous international organizations that have come together to assist the estimated fifteen hundred Black international students and families in Ukraine. According to Hector Addison, executive director of the African Canadian Association of Ottawa, many Black people and others from marginalized groups have been prevented from leaving the war-torn country as the result of racism and discrimination.

"When the crisis started, and the trains were moving, we had people preventing Black people from getting on board," he said in an earlier interview. "There were people kicking people, pushing them back."

The Kherson students, according to Madiba, reached out to the coalition. But because of the danger involved in fleeing Ukraine, they were counselled not to leave.

"We're not recommending that people try to leave," she says. "We talked to them about the danger of escaping and would never encourage them to escape without a safety corridor. But we'll help any that have made the decision to do so. We've been talking with students, some of them for weeks, who've told us that they love what the coalition has done, and they trust us, but that we have to respect the fact that they need to leave. They say, 'The fear of dying is heavy. Either we die here, die trying, or survive trying, and we want to survive trying.'"

"And these students were determined to walk," she adds. "The way people are determined to escape this war is taking strength to another level. They took their courage into their own hands, and we have to respect that."

The help the coalition is providing includes financial assistance, key in arranging passage via taxi or minivan. "We've contacted taxis in Kherson and around the city," Madiba says. "After many gave us hope, most failed and either called back to decline, fearing for their lives, while others took an advance of funds and then turned off their phones or blocked us."

The cost to pay the drivers who helped, she adds, is steep—between twenty-five hundred and four thousand US dollars for each taxi ride for five students.

Of the forty-one students and families the coalition has so far helped escape, about half are French speaking. They have been relocated to Paris, where they have secured free accommodation through Airbnb, which has made thousands of homes across Europe available, at no cost, to Ukraine refugees for up to thirty days.

"This is life saving," Madiba says, speaking from the Red Cross offices in Paris. "And it's wonderful just to see the smiles and relief on their faces, knowing they're in a city that is safe."

The other twenty or so refugees in the group are currently in

Medyka, Poland, where Madiba was headed Wednesday to help with their resettlement. She says she hopes some of the students can come to Ottawa, with University of Ottawa Prof. Boulou Ebanda de B'béri, the school's special advisor on antiracism and inclusive excellence, and Corrie Scott, associate director of University of Ottawa's Institute of Feminist and Gender Studies, working to enrol them there.

"Although fleeing the same war, Black students don't enjoy the same benefits as white Ukrainians," Scott says. "Pushed off trains and to the back of the line at border crossings, Black students are being told that their lives don't matter. This is unacceptable."

Madiba hopes some of the students will arrive in Ottawa within the next two weeks.

"We can't let them down. They are now part of us. They are now our family."

Meanwhile, she adds, there are more students to help leave Ukraine. "There are lots that we didn't even know were there, but word of mouth moves fast. We cannot leave these people empty handed, and we can't force them to stay. We don't encourage them to leave, but they're leaving anyways, so we have to do our best to protect them."

Visit the Instagram accounts @globalblackcoalition or @equalchance for more information or to donate.

Chapter 9.

Supporting Care Leavers' Resilience through Innovative Community-Based Practice in Jamaica

Khadijah Williams and Sydney Henry

Introduction

Schools in Jamaica were suspended from March 13, 2020, to June 8, 2020, due to the COVID-19 pandemic, which significantly affected students. The stay-at-home orders issued by the state were subsequently extended following the increase in COVID-19 cases. At the time of Village Academy's closure, the study site, most of the students attending were in transition to independent living from being in state care—that is, they were seventeen years and older and were in the process of reuniting with their families of origin. One approach used by the state to facilitate this reunification process was to enrol the care leavers in training programs, such as the one in this study, a residential training school, to equip them with the necessary skills for employment or entrepreneurship.

The pandemic served to highlight the complex issues concerning young people and their experiences with the care and education systems, some of which existed before COVID-19. The school had a firsthand account of the dynamic expressions of these experiences of young people, their exercise of agency (Oswell) in a pandemic, and how they navigated the decisions made by them, with them, and for them. At the start of the pandemic, the global reality was that over 70 per cent of students who could not be contacted to be engaged, lived in rural areas and over three-quarters came from the poorest 40 per cent of households (UNICEF, *COVID-19*). This is also the reality for some rural-dwelling children and young people (CYP) in Jamaica and particularly boys in transition from state care.

In 2020, there were 5890 children in state care in Jamaica (CAPRI). The state ensures that the best interest of the child is foremost and the best alternative to a family unable to care for the child. The child protection system in Jamaica has been improving its approach through foster care and adoption as alternatives to institutionalization (CAPRI) and adopting new transition-support strategies. However, as Jamaica has a low resource economy with inadequate human resources and infrastructure, the country struggles to be more effective and efficient in childcare and protection (CAPRI). These challenges, however, are mitigated through innovative approaches and partnerships, such as with Village Academy, which provides transition support.

This chapter illuminates the lived experiences of some of the most vulnerable CYP in Jamaica during the pandemic and demonstrates how effective public-private partnerships (PPP) and community support can help enable their resilience. The individual resilience of CYP leaving care is underscored but with an understanding that these young people require additional systems of support to promote their demonstration of resilience (Ungar), thus increasing protective factors for them. The authors, therefore, take an ecological view of resilience, which is more effective in promoting sustainable futures for CYP.

This chapter explores the following questions. How were young males transitioning from state care navigating the COVID-19 pandemic? What mechanisms are required to support male care leavers in their transition to independent living, particularly during a crisis such as a pandemic?

Literature Review

Caribbean scholarship related to children transitioning to independence from state care is scant, and development in this area is needed. This need is particularly acute, since residential childcare remains a last resort measure but the most used in practice to protect children, suggesting that the experiences of this group need to be carefully examined. As such, reference will be made to literature from countries where African, Caribbean, and Black children experience state care, and in some instances white, non-Caribbean authors are referenced.

A racialized dimension to care has been documented in child welfare systems internationally, which has gained the attention of many academics in the diaspora. African Canadian CYP were reported to be overrepresented in the Ontario child welfare system with culturally inappropriate services and supports, poorer outcomes for Black CYP, systemic racism, and structural inequities (Ontario Association of Children's Aid Societies). In the UK, Claudia Bernard and Anna Gupta have examined the experiences of Black African families in the child protection system, and the importance of culturally appropriate services among professionals. Similarly, Paul Bywaters et al. have focussed on sociocultural and ethnic factors that contribute to inequities leading to CYP as recipients of child protection services in the UK. Applying theoretical frameworks of critical race theory and critical race feminism, Jennifer Clarke has provided insights into the experiences of children within the child welfare system and how they are further criminalized due to institutionalized racism, sexism, and classism.

Applying an understanding of children's agency, critical social work and relational care, Khadijah Williams has demonstrated the relational aspects of children's participation in care with the caregivers and the institutional processes in Trinidad and Tobago and how these care experiences were more transformational than transactional and affected care leavers' successful transitioning to independence. This ground-breaking work out of the Caribbean provides deeper insights into the complexities of child protection and residential childcare experiences for Caribbean CYP.

Despite efforts to promote the agency of children in the Caribbean through the advancement of child rights, this remains an ideal in societies that preserve traditional views of children and suffer the effects of structural and systemic barriers to children's demonstration of their agency (Williams). The ability of children to make their own decisions is even grimmer for those on the lower-socio-economic strata. We argue that the group of young people highlighted in this study are at a greater disadvantage, and for us to assume that they have fair life chances would be presumptuous. The view of transformative childhood (Henry-Lee) does not adequately recognize the diverse structural and systemic inputs that affect a child's outcomes and agency. Contrary to this perspective, we analyse the interconnections between the personal and structural elements in which CYP engage and demonstrate their resilience. This approach further interrogates what is deemed to be the necessary engineering of inputs that support the agency of the child towards achievable meaningful and sustainable transformation—the role of community, PPP, the caregiver/teachers, social care professionals, and CYP policy.

Jamaica's children are significantly affected by the violence that plagues the country (Henry-Lee; Crawford-Brown); 79% of Jamaican children witness community violence and/or violence in their homes (UNICEF). In addition, children of lower socioeconomic status also live in environments where police harassment and brutality are commonplace and normalized (UNICEF). Moreover, children in care are more likely to come into conflict with law enforcement than children living in family environments (Xavier; Taylor). The criminalization of children in care (Littlechild and Sender) coupled with an environment that does not support aftercare transition presents a good recipe for the further criminalization of a young person. CYP leaving care are also at greater risk of negative outcomes, which include poor housing and accommodation, homelessness, substance abuse, and offending behaviours (Ryan)—all factors that predispose persons to coming into conflict with the law.

In 2018, the Child Protection and Family Services Agency (CPFSA) stated that there was a mental health crisis in Jamaica among children fourteen to seventeen years old (Mundle). Children in care and leaving care experienced mental health challenges that were not adequately treated. In 2020, "there were only four psychologists to serve children in state care, which suggests that access to psychological support was almost non-existent" (CAPRI 25). Studies have shown the direct relationship between mental health and care leavers due to the stressors related to transition (Ryan). Thus, there is a need for care leavers to be involved in community-based mental health programs that will help them to transition successfully into mainstream society. The urgency outlined in a recent poll by UNICEF highlights this plight, which notes that the COVID-19 pandemic has had a significant impact on the mental health of young people in Latin America and the Caribbean (UNICEF, "About.").

Methodology and Research Ethics

The present study uses ethnography and case studies. Data collection methods included participant observation, documentary analysis, unstructured individual interviews, and focus group interviews. The ethnographic portion of our study provided us a deep understanding of the participants' lived realities, norms, and values (Silverman) in the context of the pandemic. Participants were interviewed before the pandemic, in September 2019, as part of an enrolment exercise, and then again in March 2020, June 2020, September 2021, and March 2021. Thematic analysis (Boyatzis; Braun and Clarke) facilitated the identification of common themes, codes, and patterns in the data.

Five cases were examined in detail; all were male and had been wards of the state for five to ten years. They were classified as "children in need of care and protection" or "children in conflict with the law." They were between the ages of seventeen and nineteen years and provided their consent to participate in this study. Two focus group interviews were completed as well as five in-depth ones. For minors, caregivers or a parent/guardian provided consent. In addition, all measures were put in place to safeguard the young people as stated in Village Academy's safeguarding policy, which guides the practice, research, monitoring, evaluation, and learning agenda. The Economic and Social Research Council (ESRC), UK (SRA) Ethical Guidelines provided useful guidelines. As an agency funded by a UK institution, Village Academy was required to engage in ethical research, which is consistent with UK standards, in addition to other local guidelines involving researching human subjects.

Theoretical Application and Data Analysis

Critical social work, as developed by Jan Fook, provides a useful framework for understanding the issues presented in this research. It facilitates the analysis and understanding of context, such as the lived experiences of subjects within social structures and their capacity to be reflective, construct their reality, and influence social change (Allan et al.; Fook). This approach helps us to recognize, confront, and work in the best interest of children in difficult situations (Fook). In this regard, the work of Devon Carbado et al. was useful for providing an inter-sectional analysis. The theory of intersectionality explains how culture, class, race, and gender intersect and compound existing injustices for vulnerable groups, such as those in this study. Seen as an amalgamation of injustices with devastating outcomes rather than individual challenges, responses to oppression must also involve intersectional solutions or innovations. As Carbado et al. explain, "Intersectionality's movement in the international arena draws attention to how contextual differences generate alternative engagements with the theory" (308). This theory will help to illuminate how the Village Academy navigates class, cultural, and gender structures to develop holistic, innovative approaches that will support CYP in demonstrating their agency and resilience.

The social ecology of resilience theory (Ungar) acknowledges the interdependence between individual and environmental factors, wherein facilitative environments provide the potential for children to do well (4). The context in which CYP exists therefore takes precedence in determining their resilience as they require external agency to help put them on the path of resilience. The ecological conditions affecting CYP therefore need to be the focus when facing adversity and not the child as previously advanced (Garmezy). This perspective complements the approach taken by Village Academy as an enabler of CYP resistance. Village Academy brought relevant resources together to facilitate sustainable and meaningful transformation as evidenced in the cases presented in this chapter.

The Agency Context: Village Academy

Village Academy is a community-based educational institution, which provides academic and vocational training and support services to youth in rural settings. It is a residential school, which integrates psychosocial development and agriculture to create a social agriculture concept for youth development. One of the school's fundamental principles and requirements is action research, which supports its monitoring, learning, and evaluation (MEL) framework. Integrating research and evidence-informed practice is therefore critical to the sustainability of the program. As such, this study was appropriately aligned to the objectives of the institution. Village Academy was an option for care leavers of the child protection system and is considered innovative. The program evolved over time to include a component of training specifically designed for care leavers in transition to independence based on the increasing demands to serve this population. Five cases, using pseudonyms, are presented below.

Don

A seventeen-year-old male, Don returned to his mother who was unable to accommodate him, which left him to fend for himself. While staying in a friend's home in a community that was regularly under police surveillance, Don was detained under the existing security orders during a joint military and police exercise. This was his second encounter since the school closure order. He was consequently released, and he contacted Village Academy seeking refuge to avoid being arrested during another military exercise in his community. After successfully completing the Village Academy program, he was hired to work on the school farm.

Marlon

Marlon is a seventeen-year-old male, who was hospitalized in March 2020 after experiencing a severe mental breakdown, and he stayed there for over three months. He lived independently under the limited supervision of a relative, but the stress of independent living amplified during the pandemic lock down. He was reported to have underlying mental health concerns, but this was never diagnosed while in state care. When he recovered, he drew upon his resources to treat his mental health challenges and identified the support systems he needed. Through Village Academy, he was connected to social services, which assisted him in receiving accommodation and long-term treatment.

Jessy

Jessy is a seventeen-year-old male, who returned to the overcrowded home of his family where he was not welcomed, as they could not afford to physically accommodate him. The lack of resources included an inability to feed him and support his online educational needs, as his many other siblings had competing needs. He was able to mitigate the challenges in his relationships at home through the life skills taught to him at school and the ongoing support he continued to receive as part of the school's intervention.

Zac

Zac is an eighteen-year-old male, who was unable to integrate into his community as an adult due to discrimination and prejudice. Among his peers and his family, he was rejected because of his sexual identity. His circumstances were untenable as a result of threats against his person. He returned to school a few weeks after he left for home with a request for accommodation at one of the school's dormitories. He benefited from the accommodation and the reinforcement of his confidence to represent himself in a less than welcoming society.

Fenton

Fenton is a nineteen-year-old male, who lived with his older brothers and had to provide for himself. His mother expressed concerns that she was unable to accept him at home because of the overcrowding, and being with his brothers was unsuitable as he was at risk of joining his brothers' gang. He however demonstrated the capacity to make decisions beyond his mother's expectations and to transcend the stereotypes and decisions of his siblings by returning to school to resume his studies and gaining employment.

Findings and Discussion

There are common themes in all five cases that represent the intersecting issues within juvenile justice, mental health, and family reunification. The elements needed to support CYP transition to independent living and their resilience were apparent. These are discussed under the central themes of "navigating pre-existing and emergent inequities and injustices during the COVID-19 pandemic" and "the efficacy of child and youth focussed systems in support of CYP resilience and agency." They are discussed below.

Navigating Pre-existing and Emergent Inequities and Injustices during the COVID-19 Pandemic

From the interviews and focus groups with the young people, they were unable to fully relate to the urgency and seriousness of the pandemic initially. For them, they had grown accustomed to situations of restraint and monitoring. Their response was not reflective of the sensitivity or level of empathy that was expected in a pandemic. This was because all they knew was how to survive, regardless of the circumstance. For some, community lock downs were a normalized experience in which their rights were withheld, as was generally experienced in the Zone of Special Operations[1] (McKenzie). For Jessy, upon returning to his family, he experienced inequity among his siblings in a space of limited resources to support his education, personal care needs, and wellbeing. These experiences provide a window of opportunity to examine issues of family reunification and how young people are able to reclaim their place in their biological families.

The community of origin remains a challenge for these young people in that the social stigma attached to it did not change. Its hostility and poor social support did not provide a healthy environment for youth development. When the only place called home is not appropriate for a care leaver, chances for success are diminished, and the likelihood of youth offending is increased. The stigma of the community, the discrimination facing marginalized youth, and the impartial response of the justice system make for an unhealthy developmental space, as seen with Don. The experiences highlighted also raise concerns about the state of readiness for care leavers for the world of work and the requirements for the opportunities that exist. Transitioning from a place where their basic needs were met to one in which care leavers needed to be prepared to meet their own needs responsibly proved to be a frustrating experience for young people who were not adequately prepared.

In terms of their demonstration of resilience, the young people represented their interests and secured short-term employment (Fenton) as an alternative to engaging in illegal activities; they also drew upon the available resources and employability skills taught to them (Marlon, Fenton, Don, Zac, and Jessy) as well as navigated technologies to their benefit (Jessy). They all sought assistance when needed. While there may be some anxiety among older people about what the future holds, the young people demonstrated the ability to live in the moment, appreciate what was happening, and make the best of it. Of importance is that structured support during the pandemic could have reduced their risks and vulnerabilities and increased their chances of engaging in more fulfilling activities to a greater extent. Additionally, the fact that they are also resilient by nature does not mean that their needs should not be prioritized.

The Efficacy of Child and Youth Focussed Systems in Support of CYP Resilience and Agency

School was a relief or safe place for the young people. Consistent with the findings of UNESCO ("Guidance"), we found that there was heightened anxiety and frustration as a result of being away from school. In order to participate in online classes, youth were at risk to a greater extent because of the lack of support systems to access mandatory internet services to complete school assignments. However, they were able to come up with innovative ways of participating in online classes while navigating their environments. For example, they found open access networks in their communities and negotiated flexible training times with teachers.

A juvenile justice system is also critical to safeguarding children who come into conflict with the law (UNICEF, *Achieving*). Those leaving care may be more prone to be in conflict with the law and possibly join gangs (Gayle; Taylor). Criminalizing care leavers, as seen in this study, cannot promote the positive changes that are needed. The criminalization of care leavers such as Don—who reunite with other traumatized and displaced care leavers who they identify with as peers in unstructured settings—poses a challenge to national security and the justice system. Antigang legislation may further support their incarceration, as they sometimes naively transition into a vicious cycle that awaits them. As such, promoting their participation and strengths in their aftercare planning will help to decriminalize children in and out of care and promote more meaningful citizenship.

The ongoing problems of stigma, marginalization, and discrimination against LGBTQ+ peoples in Jamaica (Human Rights First, 2015) are also evident in this study. Young people who are LGBTQ+ face emotional and physical abuse regarding gender identity. Others may be homeless and must survive on the streets due to rejection by family and community members. In this study, we saw where Zac's parent refused to have him return home because of his identity and his parents' opposing beliefs and values. One parent was adamant on a follow up call that "He nah come back yah cause ah how he wa live. There is no place for him here." For over a year, Zac sought shelter at friends' homes, and there are indications that he may have engaged in sex work to survive. The experience of Zac is common (Human Rights First), but he had a supportive system to rely on, and he used it. The empathy demonstrated by Zac's school peers was remarkable, as they demonstrated support and encouragement, such that he was able to complete his course along with all other students involved in this study. Zac also utilized available resources the school provided when he needed to make decisions about his wellbeing. Zac also indicated that he felt supported by the school staff and his peers, who did not judge him but made him feel as if he was a part of a family. This finding is consistent with earlier studies that highlight the importance of youth programs in promoting positive peer relations, a family atmosphere, and supportive adults (Nelson et al.).

The fact that Village Academy enabled resilience among CYP is apparent in this study. Village Academy re-engineered partnerships, such as with the Child Protection Department, training sites, and international partners who became more flexible in their accountability measures. The agency worked to ensure that the emergent public health protocols were met so that young people could have a place to live. The Academy was able to provide residential training one year after the closure of schools and employed three of the trainees on the farms where they were eligible for employment, which provided some level of security, sustenance, and comfort for them. Our partners also assisted with providing tablets for trainees to complete online training, and where in-person learning tours were a requirement for training, some of our partners created virtual tours, shared information online, and served as guests on our online channels. Parents and caregivers were also instrumental in providing opportunities for practical training at home on their farms and overseeing projects, which was useful in providing and maintaining healthy relationships.

As an active participant in Village Academy, the young person became more equipped to demonstrate his agency and resilience even when he returned to his home during the lockdowns. The curriculum was amended to include activities in the trainees' immediate communities and also ensured that trainees received ongoing remote psychosocial support through telecounselling and weekly follow-up calls. Local partnerships supported their introduction to and use of new technologies, which included online learning. A platform that encouraged and supported independent learning and personal responsibility was a core pivot in their training and consequently in their ability to respond to their current circumstances. Thus, CYP resilience is not an individual experience but one facilitated by support (Ungar). In this regard, and similar to Clarke, et al.'s suggestions, a community-based model with integrated services is beneficial for youth.

Policy and Practice Recommendations to Support the Resilience of CYP in Transition to Independent Living

The following recommendations highlight the individual, systemic, and structural elements that are required to support the resilience of CYP leaving care so that the positive experiences such as those highlighted in this study can be achieved.

Juvenile Justice, Child, and Youth Care

A national standard that puts care leavers on a positive path must be established should they come into contact with law enforcement agencies. To encourage resilience among CYP leaving care, designated transition facilitators are required for young people to assist them with reintegration into society. These facilitators should bring fresh perspectives and renewed energy to confront new challenges and should be fully integrated into the new child protection and juvenile justice approaches.

Mental Health

Early detection of mental illnesses is vital to promoting the resilience of CYP. Treating young people's mental health problems is required, as they will only worsen in adulthood. Many young people leave care with undiagnosed mental health issues (CAPRI), which worsen over time, as our study indicated with Marlon when he was faced with societal pressures. Investments to support interventions promoting positive mental health are therefore needed, such as walk-in stations at the community level where support is readily accessible.

Children transitioning from care to independent living require special support for healthy family reunification. Since these children have had adverse experiences (Burke Foundation), specialized services should be made available to facilitate successful transitioning. Families and community spaces must be ready and equipped to receive these young people. Interventions with these designated families need to be integrated fully into the childcare process. Providing family support in preparation for receiving these children is essential to a model of reintegration. Where family reunification is not in the best interest of the child, this should be identified early, and measures should be put in place to facilitate a supportive network beyond care. Components of skills training, life skills and civics training should be a priority for this group, where there are adults who embrace care ethics (Noddings, 2012). The structural problems of the state need to be informed by a culturally relevant interpretation of the needs of these CYP who are citizens, and as such this interpretation is translated into practical systems of support beyond the generalized approach.

Supporting positive small group home experiences, such as those being developed in Trinidad and Tobago (Williams), can create solutions in which family environments do not exist. Aiming to make the group homes as close as possible to family environments should be the goal while recognising the individuality of the care leavers. Support beyond the institutional arrangements should allow for adequate time for the care leaver to build supporting partnerships, demonstrate their resilience, identify passions, develop skill sets, and have access to all other relevant constructs of a community to support a satisfactory quality of life.

Public-Private Partnerships

The state clearly has some challenges in meeting the needs of the CYP in state care (CAPRI). As an entity, it requires the support and collaboration of other partners to meet its commitment to care for children unable to benefit from living in a family environment. The community stakeholders, which include the private sector, can improve the quality of life of CYP through their investment in helping boys leave care. Policies to support male care leavers could inform hiring and mentorship programs, employee assistance programs, scholarships, and internships to name a few. Professionals in social work, policy, child and youth care, and education can lead the required multidisciplinary and multisectoral approaches, such as those being explored in other countries, which we can learn from (UNICEF, *The*

Role). An interdisciplinary approach is the best reflection of what a well-functioning family would provide in response to meeting the complex needs of care leavers.

The Village Academy model should also become part of a broader policy framework so that more care leavers and young people at risk can benefit from such interventions. Village Academy, as a transition facility to support care leavers through skills training and psychosocial support, provides a unique model for analysis in which integrated services are applied using a multidisciplinary approach to youth development and independent living.

Conclusion

The pandemic has highlighted some important lessons for CYP transitioning from state care. It is important to consider the agency of CYP as an integrated construct of their inherent competencies as well as the external support systems that facilitate the transition process. The crisis of the pandemic has revealed the agency of CYP in their ability to respond to its demands as they have responded positively to an environment fraught with frustration, anxiety, and increased risks. This capacity was an outcome of the intervention at Village Academy.

COVID-19 has provided an opportunity for rethinking and reinforcing approaches to interventions around safeguarding CYP and preparing them for independent living. Partnerships such as the ones described here were re-engineered to meet the needs of CYP and to support the demonstration of their agency. This construct ought not to revert after the pandemic.

Endnotes

1. Zone of Special Operations (ZOSO) was a military exercise which utilized curfews in response to violence and criminal behaviours in high risk communities in Jamaica.

Works Cited

Allan, June, Linda Briskman, and Bob Pease. *Critical Social Work*. Allen & Unwin, 2009.

Barrow, Christine. *Caribbean Early Childhoods: Socialisation, Motherhood, Poverty and Rights*. Sir Arthur Lewis Institute of Social and Economic Studies, 2011.

Bernard, Claudia, and Anna Gupta. "Black African Children and the Child Protection System." *The British Journal of Social Work*, vol. 38, no. 3, 2008, pp. 476-92.

Boyatzis, Richard. E. *Transforming Qualitative Information: Thematic Analysis and Code Development*. Sage, 1998.

Braun, Virginia, and Victoria Clarke. "Using Thematic Analysis in Psychology." *Qualitative Research in Psychology*, vol. 3, no. 2, 2006, pp. 77-101.

Burke Foundation. "Adverse Childhood Experiences. Opportunities to Prevent, Protect Against, and Heal from the Effects of ACEs in New Jersey." *Burke Foundation*, www.https://aces-report.burke foundation.org/. Accessed on 24 Oct. 2021.

Bywaters, Paul, et al. "Out of Sight, Out of Mind: Ethnic Inequalities in Child Protection and Out-of-Home Care Intervention Rates." *The British Journal of Social Work*, vol. 47, no. 7, Oct. 2017, pp. 1884-1902.

CAPRI. *Fix the Village: Governance and Accountability for Children in State Care in Jamaica*. Caribbean Policy Research Institute, 2021.

Carbado, Devon, et al. "Intersectionality: Mapping the Movements of a Theory." *DuBois Review*, vol. 10, no. 2, 2013, pp. 303-12.

Chevannes, Denise. "Focus on Adolescent Pregnancy Prevention." *Jamaica Information System*, 29 Nov. 2020, https://jis.gov.jm/focus-on-adolescent-pregnancy-prevention-dr-chevannes/. Accessed 10 Aug. 2023.

Clarke, Jennifer, et al. "Imagining a Community-Led, Multi-Service Delivery Model for Ontario Child Welfare: A Framework for Collaboration Among African Canadian Community Partners." *Journal of Law and Social Policy*, vol. 28, 2018, pp. 42-66.

Crawford-Brown, Claudette. *Children in the Line of Fire: The Impact of Violence and Trauma on Families in Jamaica and Trinidad and Tobago*. Arawak Publications. 2010.

Creswell, John. *Educational Research: Planning, Conducting, and Evaluating Quantitative and Qualitative Research*. Pearson, 2012.

Fook, Jan. *Social Work: Critical Theory and Practice*. Sage Publications. 2002.

Fook, Jan. *Social Work: A Critical Approach to Practice*. Sage Publications. 2012.

Gayle, Herbert. "Light on Violence: Here's Why Boys Join Gangs." *Jamaica Gleaner*, 2017, https://jamaica-gleaner.com/article/news/20170127/light-violence-heres-why-boys-join-gangs. Accessed 10 Aug. 2023.

Garmezy, Norman. *Risk and Protective Factors in the Development of Psychopathology*. Cambridge University Press, 1992.

Henry-Lee, Aldrie. *Endangered and Transformative Childhood in Caribbean Small Island Developing States*. Palgrave Macmillan, 2020.

Human Rights First. "'The World As It Should Be.' Advancing the Human Rights of LGBT People in Jamaica." *Human Rights First*, 2015, https://www.humanrightsfirst.org/sites/default/files/HRF-Jamaica-Report-final.pdf. Accessed 3 Oct. 2021.

Littlechild, Brian, and Sender, Helen. *The Introduction of Restorative Justice Approaches in Young People's Residential Units: A Critical Evaluation*. University of Hertfordshire/NSPCC, 2010.

McKenzie, Imaro. *Community Violence in Jamaica and Child Rights*. 14th Annual Caribbean Child Research Conference, UNICEF, Jamaica, 2019.

Mundle, Tanesha. "Mental Health Crisis among Jamaican Children." *Jamaica Observer*, 2018, https://www.jamaicaobserver.com/news/mental-health-crisis-among-jamaican-children_137268 Accessed 10 Aug. 2023.

Nelson, Annabelle, et al. "Storytelling Narratives: Social Bonding as Key for Youth at Risk." *Child & Youth Care Forum*, vol. 37, no. 3, 2008, pp. 127-37.

Noddings, Nel. "The Language of Care Ethics." *Knowledge Quest*, vol. 40, no. 4, 2012, pp. 52-56.

Oswell, David. *The Agency of Children: From Family to Global Human Rights*. Cambridge University Press, 2013.

Ryan, Mary. *Promoting the Health of Young People Leaving Care*. National Children's Bureau, 2008.

Silverman, David. *Interpreting Qualitative Data.* Sage Publications, 2006.

Social Research Association. *Ethical Guidelines.* Social Research Association, 2021.

Taylor, Claire. *Young People in Care and Criminal Behaviour.* London: Jessica Kingsley Publishers, 2006.

Ontario Association of Children's Aid Societies. *One Vision One Voice: Changing the Ontario Child Welfare System to Better Serve African Canadians. Practice Framework Part 1: Research Report.* Ontario Association of Children's Aid Societies, 2016.

Ungar, Michael. "The Social Ecology of Resilience: Addressing Contextual and Cultural Ambiguity of a Nascent Construct." *American Journal of Orthopsychiatry*, vol. 81, no. 1, 2011, pp 1-17.

UNESCO. *Guidance on Open Educational Practices during School Closures.* UNESCO, 2020, https://iite.unesco.org/wp-content/uploads/2020/05/Guidance-on-Open-Educational-Practices-during-School-Closures-English-Version-V1_0.pdf. Accessed 10 Aug. 2023.

UNICEF. *Situation Analysis of Jamaican Children.* UNICEF, 2018.

UNICEF. *COVID-19: Are Children Able to Continue Learning during School Closures? A Global Analysis of the Potential Reach of Remote Learning Policies Using Data from 100 Countries.* UNICEF, 2020.

UNICEF. "About Mental Health during COVID-19." UNICEF, 2020, https://www.unicef.org/lac/en/impact-covid-19-mental-health-adolescents-and-youth. Accessed 10 Aug. 2023.

UNICEF. *The Role of Small-Scale Residential Care for Children in the Transition from Institutional to Community-Based Care and in the Continuum of Care in the Europe and Central Asia Region.* UNICEF, 2020.

UNICEF. *Achieving Justice for Children: A Review of Innovative Data Initiatives around the World.* UNICEF, 2021.

Williams, Khadijah. "Child Protection, Paternalism and Participation: Re-framing Children's Participation in Care: A Case Study from Trinidad and Tobago." *Caribbean Journal of Social Work,* vol 14, 2021, pp. 58-80.

Xavier, Julie. "Exploring the Links between Victimization and Delinquency among Caribbean Youth: Using an Ecological Perspective to Review the Literature. Soul of Society: A Focus on the Lives of Children & Youth." *Sociological Studies of Children and Youth*, vol. 18, 2014, pp. 219-51.

Chapter 10.

More than Just Food: Exploring the Intersection of COVID-19, Food Insecurity, and Black Communities in Canada

Preeyaah Clarke

A t the age of fourteen, I became acutely aware of the issue of food insecurity, particularly among Black and racialized communities. This sparked a personal interest in nutrition and food, which led me to pursue it academically. Upon completing my master's degree in health science with a specialization in nutrition in 2020, I found myself entering a world gripped by the COVID-19 pandemic. Equipped with scientific knowledge and skills in nutrition and food, I was determined to make a positive impact during this global crisis. The convergence of the pandemic and my studies on food insecurity, particularly within racialized communities, compelled me to closely observe the situation affecting Black communities in Canada. The devastating effects of the pandemic only exacerbated existing challenges faced by Black individuals and families. These experiences profoundly influenced my practice as a registered dietitian.

In this chapter, I delve into the intersection of the COVID-19 pandemic and global food insecurity, with a specific focus on the impact on Black communities in Canada. I also explore the efforts of food banks in the Greater Toronto Area (GTA) to tackle food insecurity while emphasizing the need for comprehensive public policies and income solutions to address this pressing public health issue. However, it is important to note that while food banks temporarily fill gaps; they are not a long-term strategy for combating food insecurity.

The second part of the chapter examines the transformative power of food in the context of family and community during the pandemic. I share personal stories of how my own family came together, utilizing food as a source of joy, healing, and cultural preservation. Amid the challenges, I discovered the importance of sourcing culturally appropriate food, adapting to online platforms for connection, and finding resilience through the act of cooking and sharing meals. Additionally, I highlight a promising strategy developed to address food justice within Black communities in Brampton, Ontario—the establishment of a Black-owned, youth-led farm. This initiative aims to increase accessibility and affordability of local, culturally appropriate fruits and vegetables while also providing education, employment, and holistic health and wellness services for Black youth. Through personal involvement in this project, I have witnessed the potential for positive change and the empowerment that stems from community-driven solutions.

The chapter concludes with reflections on the lessons learned during the pandemic. It emphasizes the need for dietitians and other healthcare professionals to engage with Indigenous, Black, and racialized communities to address the disproportionate impacts of racism and systemic inequities in the food system. I also explore the importance of race-conscious perspectives and structural interventions, challenging prevailing beauty standards, and body image issues perpetuated by society. Finally, the chapter culminates with a poignant poem titled "Food is Love; Food is Justice," penned by Jennifer Clarke, which encapsulates our collective love for food and the imperative nature of food justice.

By delving into the experiences of Black individuals and families during the COVID-19 pandemic, this chapter aims to shed light on the resilience displayed in the face of food insecurity. It underscores the urgent need for systemic change and equitable solutions that foster nourishment, health, and empowerment within Black communities.

COVID-19 Pandemic and Food Insecurity

Global Food Insecurity

With the World Health Organization officially declaring the pandemic on March 11, 2020, cities and states worldwide implemented strict measures, such as stay-at-home mandates and business closures, to mitigate the virus's transmission. Unfortunately, this led to a surge in illness, job losses, and reduced working hours, exacerbating the already existing global food insecurity problem. To address this pressing issue, both short-term economic emergency relief and long-term global food strategies were crucial.

The Food and Agricultural Organization of the United Nations' report, *The State of Food Security and Nutrition in the World*, highlights the alarming reality that the world is not on track to achieve zero hunger by 2030. The COVID-19 pandemic's health and socioeconomic impacts have worsened the situation, particularly for the most vulnerable populations. In 2020 the United Nations reported that approximately 2.37 billion people, or one in three individuals worldwide, lacked access to adequate food, signifying an increase of about 320 million people. Notably, African, Caribbean, and Black (ACB) communities, including those in Africa, Latin America, and the Caribbean, have borne a significant brunt of this hunger crisis, further compounded by systemic anti-Black racism.

Food Insecurity in Canada

The Public Health Agency of Canada (PHAC) has highlighted the impact of COVD-19 on racialized communities, including Black Canadians (PHAC, "Food Insecurity"). PHAC data show that race matters when examining the stark inequities across Canada, which disproportionately affects the health and wellbeing of Black and racialized Canadians. Unfortunately, because we do not collect disaggregated race-based data, it is more difficult to address the specific needs of diverse communities. In Canada, the number of people who struggle to put adequate food on the table is increasing because of the layoffs and the economic downturn caused by the pandemic (CFCC). Canadians who were absent from work due to COVID-19 were almost three times more likely to be food insecure than those who worked (Statistics Canada). Not surprisingly, food insecurity negatively imapcts on physical well-being, increasing susceptibility to chronic conditions, such as heart disease, hypertension, and diabetes. People who are food insecure have more difficulty accessing nutritious food and, as a result, consume a reduced quantity of fruits and vegetables, resulting in decreased vitamin intake. Food insecurity also puts significant strain on our healthcare system because of the chronic diseases that result from people who lack access to healthy and nutritious food.

Canada's one million Black population between the ages fifteen and sixty-nine has been hit hard by the economic effects of the COVID-19 pandemic and continues to be significantly impacted by financial and employment challenges. The reality is that approximately 30 per cent of ACB households' experience food insecurity, which has been deepened by the structural inequities of the pandemic (PROOF). Statistics Canada found that the COVID-19 pandemic has disproportionately affected Black workers across the country both in terms of higher unemployment and lower wages (Statistics Canada; Langton). For instance, the unemployment rate for Black Canadians was 13.1 per cent compared to 7.7 per cent for whites, and in the twenty-five to fifty-four age group, the unemployment rate was 9.4 per cent for Black Canadians versus 6.1 per cent for white Canadians. The jobless rate for Black Canadians rose by 5.3 per cent between January 2020 and January 2021, compared to 3.7 per cent for whites (Gordon). Black Canadians also earned significantly lower wages than white workers at $26.70 versus $30.62, respectively. The jobless rate of 30.6 per cent for young Black Canadians aged between fifteen and twenty-four is almost double that of white youth at 15.6 per cent. Black youth in Canada aged between fifteen and twenty-four also experienced a significantly higher rate of unemployment than other youth—96 per cent difference (Statistics Canada; Congressional Research Service). As a result, about one-third of Black Canadians (33.2 per cent) live in households that were challenged to meet basic financial needs over the past four weeks of January 2021 compared to 16.6 per cent of white Canadians. Addressing food insecurity among Canada's ACB populations will require dismantling anti-Black racism and other inequities in the labour market, and other systems (e.g., health and education), including the food system.

Food Insecurity in Ontario

For many Black Canadians, living in Ontario, the likelihood of becoming food insecure is 3.5 times more likely than their white counterparts (PROOF, Tarasuk and Mitchell). In addition, Black children were 34 per cent more likely to be food insecure, compared to 10 per cent of white children. This disparity can be associated with an increased risk of chronic diseases and poor health outcomes, poor educational outcomes, low self-esteem, and other detrimental effects to one's physical and mental health (Tarasuk & Mitchell). Furthermore, food insecurity is deeply felt among the people in the Region of Peel. Almost one out of ten households experienced food security problems in 2013–2014 (Peel Region).

Black-Owned Food Banks and Food Insecurity

Many people in Brampton and the GTA have started Black-owned food banks to help ACB people who are food insecure. Recent research shows a trend that Black-owned food banks and food security driven programs in Brampton see stability in their future, with few anticipated changes; they are motivated by their desire to support and uplift their communities. Similar to mainstream food banks, Black-owned ones are supplied by nonprofit organizations (such as other food banks and food security-focused organizations), for-profit grocery stores—which provide community donations and advertise their services through church programs—word of mouth, and recommendations from supporting community organizations. Although Black-owned food banks fill an immediate need for access to food, especially for culturally appropriate food, as a strategy, they do not address the structural challenges of food insecurity, which are rooted in anti-Black racism. Access to land to grow food, especially culturally appropriate food, is a more sustainable strategy. One promising strategy is the recent development of a Black-owned youth farm in Brampton. This strategy, discussed below, may help to give ACB people some control over access to food.

Food, Family, and Community Justice

In this section, we talk about our "new normal" during the pandemic, specifically how we used food to create joy and healing, sourcing culturally appropriate food and staying connected with families through technology. Although COVID-19 changed how we connected physically with each other, it forced us to get more creative with socially distanced engagements, such as connecting with family and engaging with the community. We discuss the challenges, barriers, and creativity that emerged in the process as well as how we created joy and healing through cooking and baking, while building resiliency as a family. It closes with brief stories about my experiences in helping to develop a Black youth-led farm.

Creating Joy and Healing through Food

Similar to numerous other households, my family has faced severe challenges during the pandemic, including job loss and the loss of family members. Whereas some families were privileged to shop in bulk and stacked their pantries or engaged in panic buying during the early weeks of the pandemic, my family, among others, had to be more cautious and intentional about purchases, especially as unemployment among Black communities increased. As discussed earlier, Black people, in particular Black women, have faced disproportionate negative impacts of unemployment from the pandemic, which has remained high (13.4 to 18.6 per cent). This has been a challenge and an opportunity for us as Black families to get creative with our limited resources and to utilize the time to support each other in grief and job loss and to heal from racial violence and trauma.

Being of Jamaican cultural background, food is central to how we show care, love for one another, and celebrate life. My family, which is a kaleidoscope of different bodies—Black, mixed race, able bodied and disabled, cisgender, heterosexual, queer, Rastafarian, Christian, Muslim, and other complex and intersecting identities—all have their own relationships with food. The pandemic gave us time to share food stories from our cultures, to develop new recipes and exchange recipes from generations of our ancestors, and to do live cooking and baking together even though we live in different parts of the world and in different time zones. Planning meals together, swapping recipes, and having virtual meals together as a family helped us learn more about each other, our food preferences, and our bodies and how to take better care of our physical, mental, social, and spiritual health and wellbeing using food.

I spent a lot of my time during the pandemic developing recipes and creating menu plans for my clients to help them care for their bodies in a healthy way. I provided nutrition education classes in fun and interactive ways with hands-on workshop activities to lighten the heaviness of the pandemic and teach cooking skills at the same time. Participants were informed how to make better choices, read food labels, and understand the importance of eating local, sustainable food that supports optimal health. The prolonged isolation revealed the importance of being in community with family, friends, and neighbours. Everyday acts of kindness and being charitable by giving food to food banks for those in need replaced eating out with friends and family. Learning self-compassion and finding joy in the everyday helped us cope with the enormous loss, grief, and isolation. The immense acts of kindness among community members and neighbours as well as the connections with families near and far were foundational to creating joy, hope, and healing.

The opportunity to connect virtually with family, locally and internationally, as well as neighbours and community members, allowed us to develop a deep sense of community spirit that helped to fill the longing for socialization and connection. Through cooking and baking together, we learned that survival as human beings, especially during times of crises, does depend on connection and interdependence. Although we live in an individualistic society, the pandemic taught us to rely more on each other for support and care. As people of African descent, we have always centred the collective over the individual, and helping family members and friends to heal and cope through cooking and baking contributed positively to all our lives. We learned from the stories of our elder grandparents, aunts, and uncles about how they adapted and adjusted to crises such as natural disasters over the years. We drew upon their strength and resilience and found joy in connecting through food and stories.

Creativity and Innovation in Sourcing Culturally Appropriate Food

Due to safety concerns and social distancing protocols, many people avoided large crowds and began to shop online. According to recent data, almost four in ten (37 per cent) Canadians were shopping more online, with 22 per cent of Canadians specifically noting that they were buying more groceries online due to COVID-19 (Statistics Canada). Some local Black-owned business owners enjoyed increased revenues during the pandemic, but many lost their businesses as customers lost their incomes, and it became difficult to operate and maintain their businesses (Statistics Canada). When the federal government imposed travel restrictions, access to culturally appropriate food was reduced. The importation of food from the Caribbean was halted or limited, and sourcing our ethnic food required creativity and innovation in terms of identifying which stores had what food and sharing the information with family and friends. The pandemic also created challenges for businesses with increased transportation and shipping related costs, which led to simultaneous increase in retail prices for Carribean produce (Black Youth Led Farm Project). Moreover, there were delays in shipments and decreases in the quantity of produce delivered, resulting in a shortage of products from the island (Black Youth Led Farm Project). We had to learn to survive without our regular menu of yam, cassava, and sweet potatoes from the islands. To complicate matters, we observed that the prices had increased significantly, which affected our purchasing habits.

With pandemic restrictions and no Black-owned grocery stores in my community, my family and I spent more time in the international aisles of the regular grocery stores trying to source culturally appropriate and affordable foods, such as Jamaican ackee, yams, mangoes, and other produce from the Caribbean. Since mainstream stores have less options for Jamaican food, we had limited access to food from our culture.

Some individuals and Black-owned businesses got creative during the pandemic and turned to mobile food services. In the GTA, there was an increase in the number of Black-owned ethnocultural mobile food delivery services, as demands for ethnocultural food and produce grew. One study found that COVID-19 had a moderate but disruptive impact on Black communities' grocery experiences, impacting the frequency of grocery shopping (80 per cent), spending on groceries (64.7 per cent), and where households buy groceries (62.7 per cent). This disruption represents an opportunity to offer consumers an alternative, affordable, safe, and convenient option, like mobile food services (BYFP). The racial injustices that were occurring during the pandemic also led some people to intentionally support Black-owned businesses, including mobile food services. Individuals and businesses were delivering freshly cooked meals, groceries, and fresh produce boxes during the COVID-19 pandemic (BYFP). However, affordability was a factor for many community members who expressed concern about increasing food prices and delivery costs (BYFP). Nonetheless, the confluence of the pandemic and racial injustice seemed to have resulted in more socially conscious community members wanting to purchase food and other supplies from Black-owned businesses to uplift and strengthen our communities.

Developing a Black Youth-Led Farm Project

As a Black female registered dietitian, I am aware of the inequities in the food system—from consumers to producers—and the ways that Black people have experienced systemic anti-Black racism in their communities around food. Historically, Black people have been enslaved to build white wealth, dispossessed from their homeland, and marginalized through disinvestments in their communities—with little opportunity to access land and grow, distribute, and consume fresh, organically grown, culturally appropriate food to promote good health. As the pandemic surged, the structural and systemic barriers around food insecurity and food justice became more prominent, and I wanted to help address food inequity for Black communities. Below, I briefly share stories of my experience and feelings around my participation in helping to develop a Black-owned, youth-led farm in Brampton, Ontario.

I was on many farms as a child to pick apples and strawberries. When we visit my grandparents in Jamaica, I also get to spend time on their farm eating fresh produce from the garden. However, the greatest lessons came from my involvement in helping to develop a Black youth-led farm. From speaking to consumers about their food purchases and access to organic produce as well as asking restaurateurs and entrepreneurs about their partnerships with local farmers and organic growers, I learned that developing a Black youth-led farm involves more than just food. I learned how to work with city officials to secure access to farmland and to partner with school boards to deliver nutrition education curriculum to Black youth in schools. Although I know a lot about nutrition and health, I know little about crop production, soil health, or the pricing of food. Through the work on this farm project, I learned to connect the dots between food systems, health, and agriculture.

The Black-owned, youth-led farm in Brampton is a collaboration between the Asase Institute (AI) and En'tyce Mentorship and Community Services (EM&CS), with a strong youth steering committee, which consists of twelve Black youth of various backgrounds. Other youth were also hired as research consultants, videographers, and program workers to lead the development of programming for Black families to grow their own food and support their local community food banks. One of the key goals is to break down barriers and racist land use to support the Black community in accessing fresh organic produce that is locally grown. The farm will also engage youth as volunteers and offer opportunities for learning about growing their own foods and increasing food literacy and partnering with local food banks.

As a dietitian, I am often thinking about the important role of food in the lives of people and how to use food to preserve and improve health and wellbeing. Being a part of this project has been inspiring in many ways, primarily because it acknowledges the inequities and systemic racism that the Black community has experienced historically and presently in relation to land and access to food. I am still learning about these concerns, but protecting the land and providing the opportunity for the Black communities in Brampton to have access to locally grown organic food is important, as is removing the barriers to agri-food industry jobs for Black youth. Dismantling anti-Black racism in the agri-food industry and food production is needed to shift the balance of power and address health disparities around access to healthy food.

Since being involved in this farm project, I have come to appreciate how connecting to the land can be therapeutic. Not only did I learn about food production in a very practical way, but I also learned to attend to sustainability issues. Even though the pandemic made it hard to be sociable, obtain employment and plan our futures, we learned to survive and thrive, individually and collectively as Black youth.

Concluding Reflections and Lessons Learned

The road to recovery from this pandemic must include dietitians and other health professionals working in Indigenous, Black, and racialized communities. Being a dietitian, people often want to talk with me about weight loss, restoring their relationship with food, or creating a healthy diet. As the pandemic prolonged and face-to-face interaction with clients halted, I learned that I needed to utilize social media and other virtual platforms to continue to engage with people and offer food literacy classes, food justice education, and cooking classes. Through these online interactions, I learned that many people were living alone and feeling lonely and were isolated from friends and family, and some turned to food for comfort. It became important for me to teach about the importance of healthy eating, cooking skills, recipe development, and other nutrition-related knowledge, such as reading and interpreting food labels as well as food safety procedures. These virtual discussions and classes resulted in nutrition related knowledge being disseminated to people of different racial and cultural backgrounds and increasing their understanding of healthy eating, especially around eating fruits and vegetables to improve their physical health.

I also recognized that people do not often talk to me about racism in our food system. However, as a Black dietitian, I am aware of the dis-proportionate impact of racism on racialized communities, specifically Black communities. Race needs to matter more to dietitians, especially given the grave inequities the pandemic has highlighted for Indigenous, Black, and racialized communities (Robertson et al.). Working on the Black youth-led farm project in Brampton during the pandemic showed me that a race lens is needed to understand the challenges of food insecurity in Canada (e.g., experiences of anti-Back racism, lower income for Black employees, etc.) and how these inequities can impact the health and wellbeing of Canadians. Not only individual but structural interventions are needed.

Another lesson that I learned is that even during times of separation and isolation, such as the challenging periods brought about by a pandemic, the power of food remains a unifying force. Food has the unique ability to connect people across boundaries and cultures, fostering a sense of togetherness and empathy. As we share and savor dishes from various corners of the world, we not only celebrate diversity but also reduce racism within our food system. This shared appreciation for culinary traditions and flavors helps break down barriers, bringing people closer and reinforcing the importance of coming together, even in the face of adversity. It reminds us that in times of crisis, as in times of joy, food is a universal language that transcends physical distance and strengthens the bonds of our shared humanity. Taking time to reflect on and interrogate these negative messages have become an important part of my everyday practice and are essential to my social justice food practice. The lessons learned during this pandemic provide the impetus for further race analysis on food justice and the role that Black dietitians can play to help address this problem. The chapter concludes with a poem by the second author, which summarizes our love of food and food justice as well as the importance of food to our bodies, minds, and social lives.

Food Is Liberation Practice

Jennifer Clarke

Food is love, food is justice
Food is rights and access practice
Food nourishes bodies, brains, and minds
Filling hungry bellies and bowels
Ignoring calories, values, and vowels

Food injustice is complex, more than body mass index
Food enters bloodstream and mainstream
Pushing through bureaucracy and white supremacy
Blending cultures
Crushing stereotypes
Squeezing local into global

Food builds bonds of love and friendship
Food tells tales of slavery ship
Food holds memories good and bad
Food uplifts spirits when we're sad

Food is love, food is justice
Food is community care in practice
Food eases pain of grief and loss
Food gives escape to worried thoughts

Food is love, food is justice
Food is humanity and resilience practice
Food is celebration and restoration
Food is healing in all colours
Food is legacy
Food is liberation.

Works Cited

Congressional Research Service. "Unemployment Rate during the COVID-19 Pandemic: In Brief." *CRS*, 2021, https://crsreports. congress.gov/product/pdf/R/R46554/7. Accessed 10 Aug. 2023.

Community Food Centres Canada. "Beyond Hunger: The Hidden Impacts of Food Insecurity in Canada." *CFC Canada*, 2021, https:// cfccanada.ca/getmedia/57f5f963-af88-4a86-bda9-b98c21910b28/ FINAL-BH-PDF-EN.aspx?_ga=2.196139236.999427921. 160146 3920-807604576.1601463920. Accessed 10 Aug. 2023.

Food and Agriculture Organization. "Urban Food Systems and COVID-19." *FAO*, 2020, www.fao.org/publications/card/en/c/ CB0407EN. Accessed 10 Aug. 2023.

Food and Agricultural Organization of the United Nations. "The State of Food Security and Nutrition in the World," *FAO*, 2020, https:// www.fao.org/publications/sofi/2020. Accessed 10 Aug. 2023.

Gordon, J. "Black, Minority Women in Canada Left behind in COVID-19 Job Recovery." *CTV*, 2020, https://www.ctvnews.ca/ business/black-minority-women-in-canada-left-behind-in-covid-19-job-recovery-1.5232390. Accessed 10 Aug. 2023.

Langton, J. "Black Canadians Suffer Higher Unemployment and Lower Wages." *Advisor*, 24 Feb. 2021, https://www.advisor.ca/ news/economic/black-canadians-suffer-higher-unemployment-and-lower-wages/. Accessed 10 Aug. 2023.

Peel Region. "Household Food Insecurity." *Peel Region,* https://www. peelregion.ca/strategicplan/20-year-outcomes/household-food-insecurity.asp. Accessed 10 Aug. 2023.

PROOF Food Insecurity Policy Research. "Household Food Insecurity in Canada." *PROOF*, 2023, https://proof.utoronto.ca/food-insecurity/. Accessed 10 Aug. 2023.

Public Health Agency of Canada (PHAC). "Food Insecurity in Canada." *PHAC*, 2021, https://www.cpha.ca/food-insecurity-canada. Accessed 10 Aug. 2023.

Public Health Agency of Canada. "From Risk to Resilience: An Equity Approach to COVID-19." *Canada*, 2021, https://www.canada.ca/ en/public-health/corporate/mandate/about-agency.html. Accessed 10 Aug. 2023.

Robertson, A., et al. "Statement from Black Health Leaders on COVID-19's Impact on Black Communities in Ontario." *Alliance*, 2 Apr. 2020, https://www.allianceon.org/news/Statement-Black-Health-Leaders-COVID-19s-impact-Black-Communities-Ontario. Accessed 10 Aug. 2023.

Slaughter, G. "Study Will Test Black Canadians for Antibodies to Explore Racial Disparity in COVID-19 Cases." *CTV*, 15 Sept. 2020, https://www.ctvnews.ca/health/coronavirus/study-will-test-black-canadians-for-antibodies-to-explore-racial-disparity-in-covid-19-cases-1.5106681. Accessed 10 Aug. 2023.

Statistics Canada. "Impact of COVID-19 on Small Businesses in Canada, Second Quarter of 2021." *Statistics Canada*, 3 June 2021, https://www150.statcan.gc.ca/n1/pub/45-28-0001/2021001/article/00022-eng.htm. Accessed 10 Aug. 2023.

Tarasuk, V., and A. Mitchell. "PROOF's Research Shows That Food Insecurity Is a Policy Decision That Requires Income-Based Interventions to Solve." University of Toronto, 2020, https://proof.utoronto.ca/. Accessed 10 Aug. 2023.

Chapter 11.

Placemaking in a Pandemic: Beating the Odds, Buying Properties, and Starting Over

Anita Ewan

I remember when we moved into our first townhouse in downtown Toronto. It was a four-bedroom, three-storey home; it was public housing. But my mother decorated it with elegance. There was a white Italian couch set with plastic over it in the living room and a marble coffee table with matching side tables. In the dining room was a large, dark, wooden dining-room table, big enough to seat our seven-person family. My family consisted of my stepdad, my mom, my elder sister, my younger sister, my two younger brothers, and me. There was enough room for everyone. It was a fresh start for us.

My mom kept the place spotless despite having five young children. Whenever our home became messy, I knew my mom was either stressed or overworked. I think this is why I keep my home spotless now. It gives me the feeling that everything in life is in order. It gives me peace.

As we grew older, our spotless home became less so. My mom taught us to clean up after ourselves, and we would, but a few things happened that made it impossible to keep it clean like when we first moved in—like how my mom would. My mom went into a deep depression. Anyone who's suffered from serious depression knows how it can sap your motivation, how it steals your energy. Our public house was also in disrepair; it was infested with bedbugs and cockroaches, which were nearly impossible to get rid of. There was no help with either of these things from our housing provider. I'm certain that my mom must have felt as though she were drowning in a literal mess, being weighed down to the bottom by her circumstances. Drowning, though, is silent. And my environment gave me anxiety. I moved out of my home at age seventeen, right before my daughter was born.

Twenty-two years later, I found myself in a similar situation as I did all those years before, living in a house too small to sufficiently accommodate my growing family. My children were suffering, and so was I. We needed a change, and we needed it yesterday. But living in publicly funded house is challenging. It's not as simple as packing up and moving. There's a process, you know. There are people I needed to ask, and others who got to decide. There's a matter of qualifying. There's a matter of waiting. It's scary not being in control, even on the best of days. For the sake of my and my children's health, I began thinking strategically. I had to take control.

My children and I moved into the townhome my mother lived in after she separated from my stepdad. There was enough room because most of my siblings had moved out, and my younger brother lived downtown with my stepdad. Moving into my mom's townhome was lifesaving—a new start just like it was in 1997, when we moved into our first townhome downtown. My children had room to grow and play. I had room to care for my newborn baby I brought home a week after moving into my mom's townhome. I successfully defended my PhD dissertation in this home with enough space in my bedroom for all my children and my mom to come in and congratulate me. This could not have happened in the home I'd just left. I was so grateful for this space. I was once again at peace.

I knew I would eventually have to find a new home. My mom's place wasn't forever, and if I couldn't secure something permanent for my family and me, I'd be sent back to the two-bedroom townhouse. This was out of the question, so my only option was to seek housing through the private market. But no one would rent to us. I had solid credit and a decent income. But no one would rent to us. For the eleven years I lived on my own, I never paid my rent a day late. But no one would rent to us. I provided a letter of support with every rental application and viewed several homes. But no one would rent to us. I showed I could afford it; I provided all the supporting documentation required. But no one wanted to rent their homes to us. What was it, I wondered, about me and my family that made us so undesirable? I have my suspicions, but rental discrimination is surreptitious and nearly impossible to prove.

Although I was now living in my mom's spacious and clean townhome, I was no longer at peace. It was stressful knowing that I may have to return to the hell hole I'd escaped.

And then the COVID-19 pandemic hit. Next, we were on lock down. Combine the pandemic with the instability of my situation, and I was experiencing a new level of fear and anxiety. Everything was uncertain. Everything was fluid. Thank God for my mother's home. But what if they sent us back? What if we were stuck in that home downtown?

I was job searching in hopes of securing work that would allow us to rent outside of Toronto. And then an opportunity arose all the way out in Edmonton. Despite being in the middle of a pandemic, my fear of having to return downtown was great enough to motivate me to pick up my small children—with another one on the way—and fly to an entirely new province. Moving in the middle of a pandemic was difficult, with the tight restrictions on mobility and rules around social distancing. Plus, I also needed to stay strong and reassuring, at least on the outside, for my kids. I was alone and nervous, but this is what I had to do for the sake of my children and for me.

Everything fell into place once we got to Alberta. Within two months, I had delivered my new baby, secured a well-paying job, and started house hunting. This was something I could never have imagined doing in Toronto. The Toronto housing market had barred us from being able to afford to buy a suitable family home, and the discrimination we experienced in the city precluded us from renting there.

In September 2021, my dream became a reality. I bought my own five-bedroom, three-bath house in Alberta. The minute I signed the papers, I felt a wave of relief wash over me. I felt the peace return to my heart, mind, spirit, and bones. As chaotic as the world was outside with the pandemic, I was able to protect my children with a home to call our own. I no longer had to worry about being forced along with my children into a harmful, too-small space. I no longer had to worry about being forcefully displaced and relocated. I found my home, and I found my peace. I'm in control. And no one can take that away from me now.

Chapter 12.

Employment, Self-Employment, and Entrepreneurship in Nigeria

Olasumbo Adelakun and Oladele Aishida

Nigeria: The Paradox

On many occasions, Nigeria has teetered on the brink of collapse, such as the country's transition to democratic rule, successive elections, security challenges, the Ebola epidemic, insurgency, and more recently the COVID-19 pandemic. In each of these situations and other crises, experts predicted that the country would implode as a consequence; however, these experts were proven wrong because against all odds, Nigeria has always managed to survive, adapt, and rebound.

Nigerian people are known for their resilience, can-do attitudes, and success. As the saying goes, "Give a Nigerian a little space and basic tools, and they will make things work!" The average Nigerian believes that unity of purpose is their greatest strength, and they possess a love for life that makes them fight for it. Nigerians do not wait for the government to provide amenities for them; they simply take matters into their own hands. They put wells in areas where there is no running water, buy generators where the electricity supply is unstable, and build private schools where government-funded public ones are inadequate.

Some will argue that this is not resilience but an unwillingness to change the status quo or a reluctance to challenge authority and hold leaders accountable in order to change situations. The bottom line is that Nigerians always find a way.

Common phrases—such as "e go better" (it will get better), "where there is life, there is hope," or "it is well"—sum up the thought process of the average Nigerian with regards to issues that plague the country and challenges they face individually.

Then there is religion. Nigerians are deeply religious, and this enables individuals to step forwards in faith when faced with difficult circumstances—again with the conviction that they will overcome the challenges. When they want something badly enough, they are known to be unstoppable despite the country's unpredictability and shifts from one extreme to another.

For decades, Nigeria has faced numerous challenges in both its economic and health sectors as a result of a dearth of effective policy implementation, infrastructural decay, lack of political will, and little development in health care to meet the standards required of national health systems in the twenty-first century.

The Federal Ministry of Health acknowledged the importance of effective infectious disease outbreak discoveries in the country today and admitted that Nigeria is still in a difficult position, as outbreaks, prevention, response, and control cannot be managed properly. Little has been done to stem the recurrent tides of such outbreaks and the devastating effects they have on both human lives and economic activity (Muhammad et al. 6). It is in this context that the COVID-19 pandemic struck.

The Wuhan Health Authority in China issued an alert of this new coronavirus on December 30, 2019. The disease then spread across the globe, and on March 11, 2020, the World Health Organization declared the disease a global pandemic. Whereas the disease devastated parts of Asia, Europe, and the Americas, Africa was almost untouched by it until the first case was reported and recorded in Egypt. At this point, it was inevitable that the disease would eventually reach Nigeria, a country with the largest economy on the continent and a population of over two hundred million. The first confirmed case, an Italian national was reported on the 27th of February 2020 (Amzat et al., 2020)

Since countries like the US, Italy, and Spain suffered a great number of fatalities, it was speculated that the continent of Africa would experience the worst devastation of all. The logic of this prediction was based on the fact that most African countries have for decades been viewed as underdeveloped with inadequate healthcare facilities. As of April 30, 2021, the American Centers for Disease Control and Prevention reported that approximately 101 million persons in the US had been fully vaccinated against COVID-19, compared with 1.6 million Nigerians. Thankfully, despite the deplorable vaccine inequality gap globally and low vaccination rates across Africa, the catastrophe expected to occur on the continent has not happened (Lawal 118).

According to the Africa Centres for Disease Control and Prevention (ACDC), in August 2020, there were about a million confirmed cases and twenty-two thousand deaths across the continent. By September 2021, as many African countries reported experiencing a third wave of infections, ACDC reported 8.1 million cumulative cases, 202,613 deaths, and 7.2 million recoveries on the continent. For now, Nigeria, like many other countries, has not flattened the curve; testing is inconsistent, and confirmed cases are on the rise. Yet, ironically, the fatality numbers are much lower than those of more advanced countries with better health systems in place. This situation is not unusual in Nigeria, and the expectation of uncontrollable chaos in the country has not materialized almost eighteen months into this pandemic. Therein lies the Nigerian paradox.

Impact of COVID-19 on the Microeconomy

Nigeria is comprised of thirty-six states and has the largest population in Africa. The World Population Review predicts that Nigeria's rapid growth will see its population hit 264 million by 2030 (World Population Review). Before the pandemic, the rapid population growth in the country caused by increased birth rates and porous borders, combined with a collapse in global oil prices, placed Nigeria, the largest oil-producing country in Africa, in a recession. Although the country's economy had been steadily improving before COVID-19 struck, this lethal combination increased the number of poor Nigerians by about two million, and the high levels of poverty and inequality were estimated to affect six people every minute. Beyond the loss of life, the COVID-19 pandemic was projected to push about five million

Nigerians into poverty in 2020 alone, with the poorest and most vulnerable groups disproportionately affected (Adebayo).

The ninety million Nigerians who live in extreme poverty live on less than US$1.90/day, with unemployment and underemployment rates at 23 and 20 per cent, respectively, creating a significantly vulnerable population.

The United Nations defines "poverty" as follows:

> A denial of choices and opportunities, a violation of human dignity. It means a lack of basic capacity to participate effectively in society. It means not having enough to feed and clothe a family, not having a school or clinic to go to; not having the land on which to grow one's food or a job to earn one's living, not having access to credit. It means insecurity, powerlessness and exclusion of individuals, households and communities. It means susceptibility to violence, and it often implies living in marginal or fragile environments, without access to clean water or sanitation. (United Nations)

Poverty, thus, limits people's choices and increases their risks of exposure to violence, natural disasters, and disease outbreaks, as seen with COVID-19 (World Bank). In Nigeria, women frequently fall into this category, and the poor are often relegated to the rural areas of the country. The patriarchal nature of the society also subjects them to discrimination, resulting in limited access to education and lack of political power.

Nigeria, the biggest economy in Africa was once ranked the world's sixth-largest oil producer. However, it has experienced its fair share of economic challenges. The country has relied heavily on oil exports and short-term financial flows for decades. Oil represented more than 80 per cent of its exports, 30 per cent of its banking-sector credit, and 50 per cent of overall government revenue. With the recent collapse in oil prices, coupled with the COVID-19 pandemic, however, the country's economy will likely be plunged into another recession and one worse than the country experienced in the 1980s. Government revenues also fell by over 3 per cent of the gross domestic product, the equivalent of USD $15 billion, at a time when funds were urgently needed to stimulate the economy, address the health impacts of COVID-19, and protect the livelihoods of its citizens (Adelaja).

According to a 2020 World Bank report titled *Nigeria In Times of COVID-19: Laying Foundations for a Strong Recovery*, if the spread of COVID-19 has not been contained by the third quarter, Nigeria's economy would likely contract further, by about 3.2 percent, in contrast to the 2 per cent economic growth predicted prior to COVID-19, resulting in a higher level of poverty and inequality than already exists (Joseph-Raji et al.).

Entrepreneurship and Employment: Nigeria in the COVID-19 Era

In Nigeria, an estimated 56 million people rely on micro-business or trading for their employment and daily subsistence in this developing nation. The social interactions that ensue as a result of this serve as resilience mechanisms for millions of citizens. Therefore, during this pandemic, lockdown policies, though crucial for disease containment, competed with the economic and social aspects of survival and resilience of the country's most vulnerable. The informal business sector consists mainly of women; therefore, all disruptions in the flow of activities in this sector affected a large proportion of women who work and trade within these markets daily.

At the beginning of the pandemic, these markets were the first places to be shut down by the government, and movement was abruptly restricted. This singular act crippled the income streams and livelihood of traders, and the resulting economic downturn has had substantial implications for gender equality, as these disruptions to their daily livelihood significantly affected their ability to meet their most basic needs. The inability to travel to work and conduct business, not to mention the skyrocketing food prices, had vendors and traders struggling to feed their families.

The effects of COVID-19 on gender equality were investigated by Titan Alon et al. They argue that social distancing measures affected employment rates, which put many women at a disadvantage on the socioeconomic ladder, especially since sectors requiring the strictest social distancing measures employed more women. Working mothers were also faced with childcare challenges as a result of school and daycare closures, forcing many to re-evaluate their work commitments.

In the formal sector, women are more likely to be hired in the service industry for administrative work as receptionists and cashiers, service attendants in hospitality, airline workers, and health and social workers—roles that leave them susceptible to unemployment or temporary job losses during economic downturns. In Nigerian families, women are also mostly responsible for childcare; therefore, school closures caused by the COVID-19 pandemic mean that many women with school-aged children had to stay home to look after their children while men resumed work, further exacerbating the challenges of gender inequality and women's income loss. Since the pandemic, however, businesses have re-evaluated their policies by putting flexible work schedules in place, and fathers have begun taking a more active role in the care of their children (Akpan). Restrictions on movement also affected the income-generating capacity of families, thus reducing their consumption expenditure and their consumption of nonessential commodities in general. For them, this meant spending primarily on essential goods and services only.

Resilience of the People: Strength amid the Storm

Nigeria, like many African countries, is a collectivistic society in which strong, long-term relationships are fostered, and communal lives where people take responsibility for other members of their community is the norm. Therefore, when the first cases of COVID-19 were confirmed, and the federal government imposed a five-week lockdown requiring all except essential services to close, there was a lot of resistance from citizens and a demand that the government's response measures be adapted to the realities on the ground.

Understandably, the government's priority is to protect the lives and health of their citizens; however, outbreaks unfold differently in different communities based on social conditions, and the lessons learned from previous outbreaks and crises around the world have proven that one size does not fit all. The approach, strategies, and solutions implemented in developed nations would not necessarily be successful in Nigeria (de Waal and Richards). The Ebola epidemic of 2014 was tackled successfully without the need for lockdowns.

Research has shown that markets and social networks, such as family, friends, and neighbours, are critical sources of resilience in protracted crises, particularly in a nation like Nigeria where formal governance is largely weak or absent altogether. Studies also show that self-efficacy, conviction, and confidence in the future can predict an individual's or a household's ability to escape and remain out of poverty during a crisis (Krishnan).

Therefore, it was not surprising that as the pandemic progressed, resilience and seeking a means of livelihood birthed unofficial networks with person-to-person interactions, especially within vulnerable communities, rendering government lockdown policies for disease containment ineffective.

In Nigeria, where these social networks of family and community are important and shaped around strong societal norms, many business owners were able to rely on these support systems to facilitate collaborations and positive contributions to ensure the survival of their businesses. Families resorted to sharing material resources with each other, with neighbours, and with other community members to cope with food shortages in their homes.

Many outside the formal sector—such as taxi drivers, artisans, food vendors, hairdressers, and street traders—were not only affected by the effects of the pandemic but also faced the challenges of interlocking oppressions of tribe, class, gender, and susceptibility to job losses.

Despite the economic woes created by the pandemic, many citizens, through sheer resourcefulness and creativity, found themselves forced to adapt to these setbacks to survive through the failed promises of financial assistance from the government. Out of this adversity, a new, temporarily sustainable economy emerged that includes small-scale farmers, grocery store owners, artisans, and service providers with a primary collective goal of making it to the next meal.

In local produce markets within some low-income settlements, traders returned to trading by barter, where they exchanged goods and services instead of money. This practice was well established between African countries, Asia, and Europe in the 1500s, primarily because traders were unable to understand one another's languages. It had also slowly disappeared since the advent of legal tender.

Roadside kiosk owners and mini-markets repackaged food items— such as sugar, rice, and grains—into small portions so that low-income families could afford to buy groceries and the retailers themselves could move their products.

Historically, small- to medium-scale enterprises (SMEs) are principally motivated by basic survival needs and incentives, and this strategy has helped entrepreneurs succeed in business. In addition, the concept of the "side hustle" is popular in Nigeria in relation to SMEs within the context of the overall economic situation. This system is based on additional sources of income for individuals and has been the saving grace for many since the pandemic struck.

In the formal sector, for example, disruptions in the domestic food supply chain forced some SMEs in the food industry to pivot to community-based platforms to connect consumers with farmers. Whereas some businesses started actively expanding their product portfolios, others used emergency funds or raised money through private bonds. Small businesses furloughed staff or ran skeletal operations, just enough to ensure nonfurloughed staff were paid salaries, although these came with significant pay cuts.

In the produce industry, through creativity and innovation, some business owners developed new products and implemented new technologies, such as substituting processed spice businesses for fresh fruit and vegetables delivery, based on market research, demand, and a focus on only locally available products. Technology has been used to enable business owners to reach their customers and provide delivery services to keep these customers happy.

Needless to say, with the challenges caused by curfews and lockdowns, running a business in Nigeria is both stressful and difficult. Supply chain, sales, and production have been negatively impacted, causing many businesses to fail and close their doors permanently. Local fish farmers, for example, faced scarcity of both fish and feed, and when feed eventually became available, the costs had soared by over 30 per cent and feed could only be purchased when the government allowed movement. Because of this scarcity, fish farmers were forced to ration the feeding, ultimately slowing the growth of fish, which reduced sales and resulted in revenue losses.

Although a strong and proactive initial approach to preventing COVID-19 community spread enabled Nigeria to handle the health aspects of the pandemic better than many African countries, the damaging aftereffects are still taking a toll on the country and its vulnerable groups. Now the disease is largely concentrated in Nigeria's biggest cities, with the largest concentration of confirmed cases in Lagos state, representing over 40 per cent of the country's confirmed cases.

Resilience, a Prerequisite for Survival

Even though the pandemic affected Nigerians across the entire economic spectrum, the impact has been felt more by the urban poor because of their dependence on the informal economy. The combination of poverty, reliance on the informal economy, and high cost of living has made urban poor communities extremely vulnerable to the economic effects of the COVID-19 pandemic. Within this informal sector, access to financial help continues to be limited or completely nonexistent.

The strength and resilience of some citizens was captured in the *Corona Diaries* of Temilade Adelaja. She narrates the story of a mother of seven who because of the lockdown went from working as a university cleaner for thirteen years to taking on two jobs when she lost her cleaning position; she was unable to make ends meet and had no access to benefits. Her family went from three meals to one meal per day. She, like others in her community, claimed not to have seen evidence of widespread and severe COVID-19-related illnesses or fatalities around them. According to her, people were out and about, using public transportation, and not getting sick. She claimed markets and buses were congested, so it was difficult to comprehend why there was so much suffering around her, but she knew she had to keep going to feed her family.

Similarly, a photographer who had lost his job because of the lockdown said that lack of money and other resources made his family decide that a different member of his household would be chosen daily to go without food. He said neighbours had been surviving by showing love to each other and by sharing the little they have because they could not watch one another starve (Adelaja).

In January 2021, the federal government set up a COVID-19 cash transfer project with the aim of alleviating the cash flow problems of the urban poor. However, out of the 24.3 million poor and vulnerable individuals (about 5.7 million households) that were registered to be beneficiaries of this social assistance and emergency cash transfers, only 921,445 households received the transfers between March and April 2020, and this tapered off as the crisis wore on (News Agency of Nigeria). Others have had to rely on handouts from privately funded nongovernmental organizations and churches or take on small bank loans to purchase food, goods, and services.

Preconditioned for Survival: What Does the Future Hold for the Majority of Nigerians and Nigerian SMEs?

Amid the uncertainty, the future actually looks promising for Nigerians—a resourceful, resilient and determined people regardless of social standing or socioeconomic status. For the most part, Nigerians believe no matter how tough things are, there is always light at the end of the tunnel.

It is predicted that by 2050, Nigeria will be the third most populous country in the world, providing many business opportunities that are not available today (Okafor). Despite the challenges people have faced, culture has continued to play a significant role in strengthening resilience and the bond of unity within the different communities. The ability of the people to channel their energy towards activities to help keep their mental health in check has been a saving grace for many.

With social distancing orders still in place, families who have the space endeavour to gather together to talk, take the pressure off, and get through day-to-day challenges. Known for their vibrant, popular culture, Nigerians also continue to gather together to celebrate important occasions. Event planning businesses and their vendors have stayed in business by offering in-home services to affluent clients who have the space in their homes to accommodate guests without breaking government social distancing or capacity rules and restrictions. Artisans with no access to vaccines have resorted to consuming local herbal remedies to prevent COVID-19 so that they can continue working daily to earn a living.

Already, the country is listed as part of the Next Eleven group of promising economies, and it also belongs to the MINT (Mexico, Indonesia, Nigeria, and Turkey) bloc of emerging economies by virtue of its young demography and economic viability. Therefore, the likelihood of attracting foreign investment and new business opportunities is high once borders are fully opened, easier cross-country travel is permitted, and the country has been able to respond to the economic effects of the pandemic.

Final Thoughts

According to Kendra Cherry, resilient people are aware of their own emotional reactions and the behaviour of those around them. By remaining aware, they can maintain control of a situation and think of new ways to tackle problems. In many cases, resilient people emerge stronger after such difficulties. The COVID-19 pandemic is disproportionately affecting Africans, yet many developed countries continue to exercise a me-first approach to vaccine access by acquiring more than 50 per cent of the world's total supply.

It has also been reported that developed countries are destroying unused, expired vaccines, leaving developing countries with no supplies and the task of trying to figure out a way forward. As things stand, many developing countries will not receive their vaccines before 2024. Many Nigerians have never really been in the vaccination and are therefore not fazed by these statistics. They continue to push on in their usual manner. They are innovative and are ready to face any challenges ahead as they emerge.

Their optimistic spirit and resilience are evident even in names sometimes given to children, such as Godspeed, Mercy, Blessing, Testimony, and Goodluck. Survival in this COVID-19 era is based on an unfaltering belief that no matter the hardship, no condition is permanent.

This resilience undoubtedly accounts for the ability of Nigerians to continue to thrive despite all the challenges they continue to face.

Works Cited

ACDC. "Coronavirus Disease 2019 (COVID-19): Latest Updates on the COVID-19 Crisis from Africa CDC." Africa Centres for Disease Control and Prevention (ACDC). Accessed 1 July 2021, africacdc. org/covid-19/.

Adebayo, Bukola. "Nigeria Overtakes India in Extreme Poverty Ranking." *CNN*, 26 June 2018, www.cnn.com/2018/06/26/africa/ nigeria-overtakes-india-extreme-poverty-intl. Accessed 12 Aug. 2023.

Adelaja, Temilade. "'Between Hunger and the Virus': The Impact of the Covid-19 Pandemic on People Living in Poverty in Lagos,

Nigeria." *Human Rights Watch*, 28 July 2021, www.hrw.org/report/2021/07/28/between-hunger-and-virus/impact-covid-19-pandemic-people-living-poverty-lagos. Accessed 12 Aug. 2023.

Alon, Titan, et al. *The Impact of COVID-19 on Gender Equality.* National Bureau of Economic Research, Working Paper 26947, Apr. 2020, doi:10.3386/w26947.

Cherry, Kendra. "What Is Resilience: Characteristics of Resilient People." *Very Well Mind*, www.verywellmind.com/characteristics-of-resilience-2795062. Accessed 12 Aug. 2023.

de Waal, Alex, and Paul Richards. *Coronavirus: Why Lockdowns May Not Be the Answer in Africa.* BBC News, 15 Apr. 2020, www.bbc.com/news/world-africa-52268320.

Fischer, M. "COVID-19 Vaccine Breakthrough Infections Reported to CDC." *CDC*, 26 May 2021, https://www.cdc.gov/mmwr/volumes/70/wr/mm7021e3.htm. Accessed 12 Aug. 2023.

Joseph-Raji, G. et al. "Nigeria in Times of COVID-19: Laying Foundations for a Strong Recovery." *Nigeria Development Update, World Bank Group*, June 2020, documents1.worldbank.org/curated/en/695491593024516552/pdf/Nigeria-in-Times-of-COVID-19-Laying-Foundations-for-a-Strong-Recovery.pdf. Accessed 12 Aug. 2023.

Krishnan, V. "Role of Markets in Strengthening Social Resilience Capacities in Northeast Nigeria." *Mercy Group*, www.mercycorps.org/sites/default/files/2021-05/NENigeria_RapidLearning Brief _4-26-21.pdf. Accessed 12 Aug. 2023.

Lawal, Yakubu. "Africa's Low COVID-19 Mortality Rate: A Paradox?" *International Journal of Infectious Diseases*, vol. 102, Jan. 2021, pp. 118-122.

Muhammad, Faisal, et al. "Major Public Health Problems in Nigeria: A Review." *South-East Asia Journal of Public Health*, vol. 7, no. 1, 31 Dec. 2017, pp. 6-11.

News Agency of Nigeria. "1m Nigerians to Benefit from COVID-19 Cash Transfer, Osinbajo Says." *The Guardian Nigeria News - Nigeria and World News*, 20 Jan. 2021, https://guardian.ng/news/1m-nigerians-to-benefit-from-covid-19-cash-transfer-osinbajo-says/. Accessed 12 Aug. 2023.

Okafor, C. "Nigeria to Become the 3rd Most Populous Country by 2050. What Does This Mean?" *Business Insider Africa*, 1 Oct. 2022, https://africa.businessinsider.com/local/lifestyle/nigeria-to-become-the-3rd-most-populous-country-by-2050-what-does-this-mean/svlm3xz. Accessed 12 Aug. 2023.

United Nations. "Statement of Commitment for Action to Eradicate Poverty Adopted by Administrative Committee on Coordination." *United Nations*, 20 May 1998, www.un.org/press/en/1998/19980520.eco5759.html. Accessed 12 Aug. 2023.

World Population Review. "Nigeria Population 2022." *World Population by Country*, https://worldpopulationreview.com/countries/nigeria-population. Accessed 12 Aug. 2023.

Chapter 13.

Overcoming Overencumbered: A Toronto University Student's Experience

Eboni-Rai Mullings

Pandemic, lockdown, quarantine. Three words that we have always known but whose significance will be altered forever for anyone who was alive to remember the COVID-19 pandemic. For me, a younger millennial who had never really heard those words used outside the context of fiction or school drills, the pandemic was eye opening. It gave me the opportunity to learn about how the world works, and in so doing, I learned more about myself. But let's start at the beginning.

To say that it was a March like any other would not be exactly true for me. In the weeks before the first lockdown, I'd been trying to settle into my life again after moving in with my sister, and my retail job had dispersed all the employees from my store to other locations so that our store could get a much-needed renovation. The only part of my life that had not changed at all was school. Over 2019, my enrolment at Toronto Metropolitan University (formerly Ryerson) in Toronto had become the most important thing to me. While the rest of my life was stressful, chaotic, and unstable, my education was my lifeboat. I dove into my studies because my inner need for control demanded something to hold onto—something that could keep me afloat while it felt like everything else was sinking. And I succeeded. I was able to maintain my place on the dean's list with each semester. So, with some major stressors dealt with, I returned to my life as it should be. And 2020 was supposed to be easy. Then, day by day, the word "corona" began to seep into everyone's vocabulary. People started working from home, shops were closing, and my school sent the official email that we were moving to online classes while I was sitting in my philosophy class on March 23, 2020.

Truthfully, I thought we were all going to die. As a sci-fi and fantasy fan, I immediately accepted corona as an apocalyptic-like event from which the world could not possibly recover. If you've ever seen *The Walking Dead*, that is what I imagined would happen. Cars abandoned on the road, ghost towns, total loss of institutional power, colonies of strangers coming together for survival, 5 per cent chance of zombies manifesting in our society. So, when my retail company did mass layoffs, and I no longer had to endure the shoulder-to-shoulder commutes to campus, I was relieved. With no need to leave the house for work or school, pre-existing behaviours of having groceries delivered every week, and no compulsion to exercise, my opportunities for exposure were low. *I might survive the end of the world as we know it,* I thought. Although there were many lives tragically lost to the COVID-19 virus, it became clear to me that this would not be the catastrophic event that television had prepared me for. To protect ourselves and each other though, we in Ontario stayed in lockdown until August, but that protection had consequences of its own. It may not have been an apocalyptic-like event, but everything changed in those five months.

Our culture here in Toronto alone essentially disintegrated. Having to stay inside during the colder months might not have been such a loss, but the summer months are when I find the city to be at its greatest. The annual outdoor events that we all look forward to were cancelled to prevent overcrowding and reduce chances of COVID-19 transmission, but it meant that all the beautiful ways we get to celebrate the communities in the city every year, together, were gone. The Pride Parade, which is one of the biggest LGBTQ+ festivals in the world, was cancelled. Toronto Caribbean Carnival, better known as Caribana, which draws in visitors from all over the world and celebrates one of the biggest communities in the city, my community, was cancelled. Salsa on St. Clair, VELD Music Festival, Taste of the Danforth, Canadian National Exhibition, Toronto International Film Festival, and so many more event organizations all cancelled their in-person activities. Parks and beaches were emptier, even trains and buses that were normally packed to capacity were empty. All our ordinary human interactions were gone, and the ties that connected us as a community and as a city were severed, leaving all of us to face any hardships in our lives alone and without the benefit of interaction or external distractions.

For me, school, which was my lifeline, instantly became more difficult. With students adjusting to learning online and professors adjusting to online teaching technology, we all struggled. I tried to forget about the two courses I had done years ago through distance education that went horribly for me. When I was enrolled in those courses, I found it difficult to hold myself accountable for getting all the work and readings done on time. Having a professor remind the class that an assignment is due in a few weeks or having class discussions and quizzes every week that encourage the class to stay on track with readings are things I depend on for success. I worried that the pandemic would leave students on an island alone. Without that structure that made me successful, part of me worried that I would fall behind. But I had survived 2019, and I told myself I would make it through Zoom University, too. In my mind, there was no other choice. I simply refused to not do well, sending my inner need for control into overdrive once again.

My organizational skills were forced to evolve; there was now an obscene amount of colour coordination, pages of handwritten notes from research articles, and course content taped to my wall; outlines meticulously written and rewritten were also fixed to my wall or desk. I created daily schedules for myself on my whiteboard—reasonable ones that accounted for productivity, rest, and free time—and finished the first semester of online learning with great marks and true knowledge applicable beyond the classroom. Eventually, I was forced to accept that even if the city started to open up again, it would likely be a long time before we returned to campus. But after having proven to myself that I could continue to meet my own goals and expectations in my education without being in a physical classroom or having other students to learn from in the way I was used to—and with the recognition that life would maintain some sense of normalcy amid the upset of the pandemic—I enrolled in online summer classes.

Each virtual semester was a little sad, though. I missed the banalities of the physical classroom and the campus experience: getting to class early to make sure I got the same seat every week; stopping by the little cafe for a tea, banana muffin, and a quick conversation with the woman at the register; looking for familiar faces in class and forming study groups; collectively laughing when the professor made a joke or looking collectively confused when tackling a new concept; enjoying spontaneous class discussions; having the opportunity to learn from my peers in a way that is more fluid and stress-free; and locating my favourite study spots in the Student Learning Centre. But by the beginning of the spring-summer semester in 2020, it seemed that I would continue to have little to do and nowhere to go, so throwing myself into school was an obvious choice. How else would one spend an infinite number of days indoors, right? Not only was I glad for something to do, but I was also happy to be working towards something and grateful that I had the opportunity to put my undivided attention into my education. No work to balance and no social life to consider, my schedule was as clear as I always wished it could be. *There's no stopping me now,* I thought. But 2020 had more surprises for us.

Despite my easy schedule, my mind was becoming heavy. On May 25th, in Minneapolis, George Floyd was murdered by police officer Derek Chauvin during an arrest. Chauvin, a white man, knelt on the neck of Floyd, a Black man, for over nine minutes while ignoring Floyd's pleas that he could not breathe. This murder was recorded on a cellphone by a witness who later released the video online, where it quickly went viral. George Floyd's death was an international catalyst for addressing issues of institutional anti-Black racism and racism, police brutality, and white privilege, ultimately relighting a fire under the Black Lives Matter (BLM) movement that had lost momentum in 2016. BLM 2020 was widespread and heavily discussed, and it produced one of the largest protests the United States had ever seen. As a young Black woman, I found it encouraging to see issues I had grown up learning become mainstream. I found it remarkable to see people, particularly white people, all around the world rallying behind us, supporting the fight against systemic anti-Black racism and other struggles, and in some cases, physically shielding us from police. I believe that COVID-19 provided us the opportunity for this movement to take hold as it did. With most of us staying home with little to do, and many of us using TikTok, Instagram, and Facebook more than we did before, we were better able to share information and spend the time to understand people's perspectives. Many people learned about what racism can look like, how internalized racism develops, and the effect of colonialism on societal norms and expectations. But, of course, no movement is ever entirely well-received. Out of Black Lives Matter came All Lives Matter and Blue Lives Matter. And with every Black life lost at the hands of police, of which there were many, conversations and debates about blame and accountability on social media ensued. To see every day that another life was unfairly taken from this world and to see that there are thousands of people who do not understand or agree that there are issues of race involved in the loss of that life was exhausting. And to make matters worse, the United States presidential election was nearing.

Although I am a proud Canadian, I do feel that the American political climate often seeps into our country. Their issues become ours; their beliefs become ours. With He-Who-Must-Not-Be-Named building his presidency on a platform of sexism, racism, and general distastefulness, those qualities became socially acceptable in the US and then in Canada as well. It felt as though the moral centre of the world were at stake. And with the election following closely on the heels of the resurging BLM movement, there was no rest for an exhausted mind or disappointed heart. Social media, one of humanity's favourite tools of distraction, continued to be saturated with social issues and political agendas. I was torn between needing to know what was going on and needing to unplug completely to spare myself the constant head and heartache, but the need to know always won. At the height of it all, I was spending time almost every morning and evening online and on social media to stay updated. I wanted hope, order, and balance in my life; I needed the information, to see the conversations, and to understand as much as I could to not be blindsided by politics and popular beliefs again.

Truth be told, the weight of the political climate in 2020 was most of the mental and emotional load for me during this pandemic. Many of us were struggling with being isolated at home and not being able to connect with loved ones in person, particularly people who live alone, but I was quite fortunate in this case. I have had the great privilege of living with my older sister, with whom I get along famously. It was fairly suffocating to be stuck in a condo without being able to go out to eat (something I did often as a student who frequented downtown Toronto) or study at the library on campus for a change of scenery (which I enjoyed doing on a regular basis), but at least I was not alone. My sister and I had each other, and we had our cat. Our life at home changed very little. Sure, I was spending much more time at home, and we washed our hands more, but those changes were insignificant compared with the changes in the outside world. Luckily for me, or unluckily depending on the perspective, my university courses primed me for understanding social issues differently than I ever had before. It became a burden I did not expect. Ignorance truly is bliss. Sometimes, I wish I had not learned how deeply engrained anti-Black racism, xenophobia, and antifeminist ideals were in our society, but I did. With the added weight of those issues and the aforementioned need to know, I realized I had to find ways to keep my head above water.

Some of my coping strategies involved maintaining my organized school schedule. Keeping that part of my life as stress free as possible was one of the easiest ways for me to stay sane. But routine is just one part of the process. I also had to find ways to feed my soul without leaving my home. School is a big part of my life, but it is not all that I am. The introvert in me knew that I needed to recharge and focus on acts of joy and self-love. By not putting all my energy into my student identity and honouring the other parts of myself, I was able to stay more grounded. The part of me that is creative and hands on enjoyed using free time for crafting and revamping parts of my bedroom—transforming an old piece of furniture into something that better fits my personal style, redesigning the aesthetic and layout for my space, or carefully crafting pieces with my closet full of hoarded materials and crafting tools. These are small things but important for me as a distraction from the stresses of a rapidly changing society and to help me not lose sight of myself.

I also made efforts to explore my spirituality. Although I still have much to learn and improve upon, I found some meditation guides and helpful literature, invested in many candles because candlelight always brings me peace, and even began learning to make my own candles. I valued time by myself in my own space, but being social was an important part of managing the weight of the outside world. A break to bother the cat or chat with my sister was a frequent necessity, but we all had to learn to be social in other ways as well. Human beings are social creatures, and being stripped of that element on a large scale was difficult. Many of us adapted by having Zoom parties, but I used popular social media apps. Keeping in contact with my closest friends regularly was easiest for me on Snapchat. This app allows the user to easily take and send pictures, videos, texts, or voice memos to friends in a chat that disappears after being opened. They allow for a more personal connection than simply sending a text message but do not demand the immediacy that a phone call requires. So, even though lockdowns prevented us from seeing each other, we weren't without the benefits of those interactions. And being able to share things with friends and family across apps keeps us close when we're all so physically far from each other. My family keeps in touch via group chats, but to be honest, I have never really been able to keep up with them all.

Experiencing the social stressors on social media during this pandemic also made me less inclined to want to spend the extra time on my phone to stay caught up in those conversations. That said, I have a small circle of friends and family that I connect with regularly. We do our best to support each other from a distance in the ways we know how and share our hope or frustrations of this difficult time. With them, I realized that I didn't need an army of loved ones to make it through the year; I only needed a few great ones.

The pandemic helped me understand in a different way the value of rest and finding joy in the little things. Even now, I make sure that I give myself time to recharge every day. Whether my studies are keeping me busy, or my work schedule is packed, or there are a million things to take care of at home, I always make sure to have time to just stop and rest. In this world that is changing so quickly in more ways than we can count, with new stresses being brought to our attention regularly, the best we can do is make sure that we feel good inside our own hearts, minds, and souls before we try to tackle the doom and gloom of society. I believe it is important to understand what goes on in the world to understand one's place in it, and I have always said that it is hard for me to know where I am going if I don't know where I am. If I don't understand the changes in the world, how can I plan for tomorrow, or next year, or the next decade? I need balance and to know what the next steps will be, but with all the changes, I have had to work hard to not stall. So, despite needing to understand the world, I have learned that perseverance and resilience for me lie in letting go.

The essence needs to know but my soul does not. I find comfort in preparation, but I find peace in acceptance. I will never be able to know how and when the world will change, and, yes, many of those changes will undoubtedly affect me. But it does not mean that I have to carry the weight of those changes. There is a video game I like in which your player moves slowly when they are carrying too many items. "You are over-encumbered and cannot run" it says, and only after dropping some of the items in your inventory can you run again. It is the same in life. We can only control so much, and we only have so much space in our minds and hearts to hold onto things. Sometimes we have to stop and let some go. It is okay to create a level of distance between yourself and external things, especially the ones we cannot control and most especially when they have a negative impact. We only have the power to control what we do right now. For me, accepting that is how I thrive, and to maintain that positivity, I will choose to fill as many of my life's moments with relationships that fulfill me, activities that replenish me, and things that bring me joy. That's all any of us can do.

Chapter 14.

Sistah Circle: Black Women's Stories of Pregnancy, Birth, and Support During COVID-19

Jennifer Clarke, Tamar Hewitt, Tina Hewitt,
Preeyaah Clarke, and Stacy Diedrick

Introduction

B lack women deserve safe and healthy pregnancies and births if they choose to become mothers—even during the COVID-19 pandemic. We challenge the construction of Black women as "bad mothers," "welfare queens," and "single mothers" who are undeserving of motherhood (Ewan, Mullings, and Clarke) and turn the gaze on the white supremacist, anti-Black, violent, and hetero-patriarchal healthcare system that has ignored pregnant Black women in Canada. In this system, Black women lack access to high-quality reproductive and maternal health services from trusted medical providers. Due to anti-Black racism, misogynoir and other systemic barriers, Black women's bodies are regulated, surveilled, disciplined, and punished by health professionals, even as they seek prenatal care, negotiate complicated delivery, and access postnatal care.

In this chapter, five first- and second-generation Black women share their narratives of how they created a virtual and in-person community called Sistah Circle (SC) as a transformative space for support and healing to assist a young Black mother (Tamar, second author) during pregnancy and the birth of her child during COVID-19. The chapter is framed through an Africentric and anti-Black racism lens and organized around two main themes: the pregnancy and premature birth of a Black child during COVID-19; and the powerful spiritual, physical, and emotional support that the mother received from a group of Black sistahs who have had their own lived experiences of pregnancy and child loss, which inspired and informed the type of support they offered this mother. Our narratives provide insights into the complexities and nuances of being Black and pregnant in Canada, and more specifically, our experiences, perspectives, challenges, and creative strategies for navigating prenatal and maternal care during COVID-19. Our brief stories of pregnancy and birth loss will serve as a backdrop to inform the type of support we curated for Tamar during a crisis. The chapter builds on other research on Black maternal mortality, racialized birth trauma and supporting birth persons during the pandemic (Davis-Floyd et al.; McKinnon). We do not shy away from the emotional pain and challenges experienced, even while we support this young mother through her pregnancy and birthing process. We acknowledge that not all people giving birth to Black children identify as women or mothers. However, we identify as women and mothers and have written this chapter from that perspective.

Pregnancy during the COVID-19 Pandemic

In March 2020, as the world grappled with the COVID-19 pandemic and lockdown regulations and policies became effective, we found ourselves isolated from one another and daily life as we knew it had changed. Tamar and Stacy, like many Canadians, were concerned about being furloughed from their jobs and educating their children at home via online classes. Preeyaah completed her graduate studies during the pandemic and did not have a graduation. Becoming pregnant was not part of the plan for the SC, especially during a global pandemic. However, at the beginning of fall 2020, Tamar revealed she was pregnant. Not only was she pregnant, but it was a high-risk pregnancy, like her two previous pregnancies. "I immediately knew that this pregnancy was going to be the toughest of all my pregnancies," she stated. The medical experts were clear that the coronavirus was particularly dangerous for people with compromised immune systems and pregnant individuals, especially Black and racialized women (Ellington et al.). Before the pandemic, research consistently showed racialized inequities and disparities in maternal outcomes for Black pregnant women (Oparah; Arega et al.; Oparah and Bonaparte; Oparah, Salahuddin et al.; Petersen et al.; Tangel et al.).

Due to COVID-19 restrictions, Tamar's early appointments with her doctor were virtual or via the telephone. Once in-person appointments began for ultrasounds, COVID-19 restrictions banned any support person from attending, so Tamar went alone without support from her partner or family member. At one of these appointments, Tamar got the news that no pregnant woman would want to hear: "My OB told me that my placenta was not functioning properly. That I had Inter uterine growth restriction (IUGR) meant I would likely have to deliver my baby before I got to thirty weeks gestation." Tamar was already experiencing fear and anxiety due to the pandemic and loss of employment, and this news worsened her stress and worry. Having experienced a previous child loss, she was well aware of the risks and uncertainties surrounding the survival of her unborn child as well as the various medical complications that could arise from giving birth at that gestational stage. Extensive research has shown the detrimental effects of stress and anxiety on both mother and the unborn child. There is a scarcity of studies exploring anxiety, depression, and stress, specifically among mothers facing high-risk pregnancies, particularly Black women (Fannte-Coleman and Jackson-Best; Quenby).

In January 2021, Tamar was put on bed rest and had to be followed closely by the special pregnancy unit of the hospital. This marked a turning point for our SC, as we knew she had to learn to navigate the ever-changing landscape of COVID-19 policies and regulations on her own. We knew that each biweekly appointment carried the possibility that Tamar could be admitted to the hospital. In an earlier appointment, her doctor told her to "have an overnight bag ready for the occasion." Reflecting on her experience, Tamar shared that these appointments had always left her on edge: "They are anxiety-inducing." She further explained her concern this way: "I knew that once admitted, a caesarian section would follow in a few days, and I did not want to have another c-section because of the issues with recovery, and the fact that it was major abdominal surgery." Tamar had good reasons to be concerned about having a c-section, given the inequities in health care for Black women due to anti-Black racism (Adhopia; McKinnon, et al.).

Research in both the US and UK shows a distressing statistic: Black women are four times more likely to experience maternal mortality than their white counterparts (Centre for Disease Control and Prevention [CDC]; Knight et al.). In the UK, for instance, there were thirty-four Black deaths among every one hundred thousand Black women during childbirth (Knight et al.). Furthermore, Black women undergo c-Sections at a higher rate than other ethnic groups. This disparity mirrors the US, where research shows that Black women receive more c-sections than women of other races (Knight et al.). In Canada, c-section rates have risen from 21.4 per cent in 2000 to 28.8 per cent in 2019 (Statistics Canada). Although current data on induction rates could not be found, in earlier decades, induction rates rose from 12.9 per cent in 1991 to 21.8 per cent in 2005. Although Canada does not systematically collect race-based data on the health and wellbeing of Black mothers, Black women have experienced generations of systemic anti-Black racism in the health system during pregnancy and childbirth, leading to a dismissal of their prenatal symptoms and needs. To understand how the pandemic may have worsened these inequities for Black mothers and their babies, data must be made accessible to the public (Adhopia). Although Canada does not have the data and the level of demographic tracking by race, as it pertains to Black women's death or risk of death and miscarriages of Black babies, we know from research in the UK that Black women face a 40 per cent higher risk of miscarriage than their white counterparts (Knight; Quenby et al.). We also know that approximately 12.7 per cent of Black women and 8 per cent of white women deliver prematurely (Adhopia).

On February 9, 2021, during Tamar's visit to her doctor, she received the dreaded news that she needed to head to the hospital, as there were signs that she would deliver the baby in the next few days. The situation had become critical, and she needed to be monitored closely in the hospital. Tamar reached out to her sister, Tina, and requested her help to care for her six-year-old daughter, who was navigating online school and helping prepare for the baby's arrival.

When Tamar arrived at the hospital, there were strict COVID-19 protocols in place, which she had to adhere to before being admitted. After the screening, she was sent to the antenatal unit to be admitted and monitored. Tamar's husband could not join her in the hospital room. This left her feeling frightened and isolated, facing the challenges of a high-risk pregnancy within a healthcare system embroiled in anti-Black racism. The pandemic and newly implemented hospital policies to curb the virus spread meant that women like Tamar would not have the support they needed. The absence of her partner, sister Tina or Sistah Circle, who could provide valuable support and ask relevant questions during these challenging times, compounded the situation. Tamar vividly recalled the lonely and isolating experience this way: "I even had to go downstairs to the hospital entrance to meet my husband the following day when he brought me some basic supplies." The weight of the risks and uncertainties she faced added to her distress. The lack of attention given to Black maternal health and anti-Black racism in Canada further fuelled Tamar's concern that she might receive sub-standard care.

The morning following Tamar's admission to the hospital, she had a major scare when the nurse responsible for monitoring the baby could not detect a heartbeat. When the nurse paged for help, Tamar knew the situation was serious. Tamara recalled moments later, "A team of medical professionals, including the OB/GYN, nurses, and ultrasound technicians, rushed into the room." In Ontario, approximately 78.8 per cent of babies are born under the care of an OB/GYN (Born Ontario, 2016). Tamar vividly remembers her immense relief when a bedside scan successfully found her baby's heartbeat, confirming the baby was active. Throughout this ordeal, she was overwhelmed by the team of unfamiliar specialists, leading to a panic attack. She described her anxiety as "being through the roof" because of the prospect of "undergoing another c-section and the uncertainty of the baby's wellbeing." In Canada, research is scarce on pregnant Black women's mental health, specifically stress and anxiety issues during pregnancy and childbirth. Research conducted in the U.S. shows that Black women face significant mental health challenges pre-and postdelivery (Howell et al.; McKinnon et al.).

Later that night, Tamar was moved to the labour and delivery area for monitoring in case of any further complications with the baby, which could require immediate transfer to the operating room (OR). Tamar recalled feeling "extremely scared throughout the monitoring process." Initially, everything was going well during the monitoring session. However, by early Friday morning, Tamar's daily ultrasound showed that things had deteriorated. She was promptly moved to labour and delivery and placed on the list for a c-Section later that day. "The swiftly shifting and fragmented care scared me, and I felt vulnerable and helpless," Tamar recalled. Research conducted in the US shows that Black women receive more c-sections and inductions and experience more premature births than other women (McKinnon, et al.). However, no studies were found addressing Black women's experiences in Canada. Tamara found momentary relief and joy upon learning that her husband could join her in the hospital, as she was about to give birth. COVID-19 policies and regulations only allow a partner or support person to be present with a woman about to give birth after community protests (Davis Floyd et al.).

The Premature Birth During COVID-19 Pandemic

Baby D was born at 7:25 p.m. that night at twenty-seven weeks and weighed only 1 lb. 6 oz. "I was only able to see him for a brief moment after he was born because they had to take him to be assessed by paediatrics in the Neonatal Intensive Care Unit [NICU]," Tamar recalled. The baby would stay in the NICU for the first three months because he was premature and needed extensive medical attention. Being separated from her newborn was emotionally difficult for Tamar, although she knew that he needed to be nurtured and cared for by the medical team. In our SC, she shared that one of her major fears was the quality of care her Black baby would receive in her absence: "I prayed every day that the doctors and nurses would not inflict racism on my son but address the needs of a little Black baby, weighing less than two pounds with care."

Canada had an estimated 380,000 births in 2018, with nearly one-third occurring in Ontario (Statistics Canada). There is limited research exploring the childbirth experience of Black women in Canada, and available data do not show the number of babies born to Black mothers. A 2015 study by McGill University found that 8.9 per cent of babies born to Black women in Canada were preterm, compared to 5.9 per cent of white babies (McKinnon). As Black women who have experienced pregnancy, birth, and loss of children, we are acutely aware of the troubling gaps and disparities despite the dearth of data to understand the extent of the problem in Canada. We are intimately aware of the lack of attention to Black women's pain in prenatal and birthing and navigating and advocating for culturally appropriate care during complications and postnatal periods.

Tamar was discharged from the hospital only two days after giving birth to her premature baby. Research shows that African American women have been experiencing expedited hospital discharges during the pandemic, often receiving little information on how to care for themselves, their wounds, or how to breastfeed their babies (Adhopia). Once at home, Tamar could not see her baby until she had recovered and could travel to the hospital about a week later. During Tamar's healing, her husband would go to the hospital to be with their baby. When Tamar regained her strength, she began to visit her baby in the NICU, but COVID-19 protocols prevented the parents from sharing the joy of being with their new baby together, as only one parent could be in the room at a time. Reflecting on the situation, Tamar shared, "We had to alternate every other day so that we could both take part in his care—feeding him, changing his diaper, taking his temperature, and engaging in skin-to-skin contact."

For the first three months of their baby's life, Tamar and her family had to take extra precautions in their daily activities to stay safe from the coronavirus or risk losing the opportunity to visit with their baby in the NICU. To minimize interactions with the public, they paid for private transportation, such as taxis, instead of using public transit. They also resorted to online grocery shopping with home delivery, even though it incurred added costs. Their focus during this period revolved around going to the hospital and returning home. While these self-imposed pandemic restrictions ensured their ability to visit their baby safely, they placed a significant financial strain on the family, particularly as Tamar was furloughed, and they had to rely on one income to sustain themselves. The Sistah Circle (SC) offered their support.

Sistah Circle (SC): A Support System Borne Out of Love, Pain, and Resilience

The SC evolved from the first author's vision of advancing racial trauma care to support pregnant Black women during COVID-19. The SC began as a WhatsApp group and transformed into a powerful virtual community to support Tamar during this challenging time and her increased pregnancy risk. It became a safe space for five Black women to meet and offer support to each other around COVID-19, organize practical support for Tamar during her pregnancy and birth of her baby, and help her navigate and resist against anti-Black racism in the health system. The SC wanted Tamar to be empowered so that she could advocate for herself during doctor's appointments, as COVID-19 protocols prevented her from having a support person on these visits. From our experiences of pregnancy, child loss, and childbirth, we know that Black women have multiple vulnerabilities, and anti-Black racism is the main culprit. We have all lived through the effects of maternal death and child loss on our families.

Although we live in different cities in Ontario and are of different ages, we are a family and share a common experience with pregnancy and child loss at the intersection of race, gender, and class. What makes our narratives unique is the development of a SC amid a global pandemic and racial injustice reckoning. Forming the SC and talking about our experiences as Black women who have lost precious Black lives because of disparities in Black maternal healthcare gave us the fuel needed to identify and resist systemic anti-Black racism in the health system and more specifically around medical trauma and obstetric justice. The SC became an authentic space for community, support, empowerment, and healing. We maintained regular contact via phone calls, texts, and video calls and provided individual and collective support. Most importantly, we supported Tamar throughout a high-risk pregnancy and premature birth while simultaneously experiencing fear, anxiety, and uncertainty of the pandemic.

The SC carried out specific actions to support Tamar during her pregnancy and the birth of her baby. These actions were based on our lived experience as Black women and mothers and included offering emotional and social support, providing correct COVID-19 information, providing nutrition information, practising spirituality and prayer, and sharing material and practical resources, such as baby items from our children. Woven into our actions are themes of love, support, sistahood and community that are grounded in resistance and resilience. Specifically, our narratives will detail the emotional, social, spiritual, and material resources offered. For example, we offered humour, laughter, and prayer to uplift her spirits while ensuring she had correct COVID-19 information to ease her worries and fears. There was help with parenting responsibilities, such as supporting her daughter with online schooling as well as allowing her time to prioritize her wellbeing and that of her newborn. Additionally, the SC offered nutrition information to support a healthy pregnancy and fulfilled basic material needs through maternity care packages for herself and newborn items for the baby, as a traditional baby shower could not be held due to COVID-19 restrictions and stay-at-home orders.

Support Fuelled by the Pain of Child Loss and Anti-Black Racism

As Black women, we were acutely aware that when we entered the maternal health system, we were vulnerable to anti-Black racism and other health inequities. Living in a racist society, we understood that neither our education nor economic status could shield us from racial inequity in healthcare. However, we did not expect the blatant acts of anti-Black racism we experienced from healthcare professionals at various levels of the system. These experiences, coupled with the already challenging complications of our pregnancies, compounded oppression and heightened our stress levels. Consequently, we grappled with high blood pressure (preeclampsia), gestational diabetes, and anxiety. We were constantly worried about our survival, the wellbeing of our babies, and whether our needs and concerns would be addressed or dismissed. Given this background, concern about racial disparity in maternal health was persistent and ever-present in the SC.

Jennifer shared her story of child loss and how her need for pain medication was ignored during labour as if she could not feel pain or did not deserve ease. She described this as "a very traumatic experience." Those experiences fuelled her to provide Tamar with information to advocate for herself but also to understand how self-advocacy can be perceived as a "problem patient" by some medical professionals. Stacy shared how her pregnancy complications and the fear of being labelled problematic forced her to remain quiet because she "feared getting bad care." Tamar and Tina have had babies die at birth (stillbirth) or shortly after birth. Their pain of child loss has also fuelled their passion for creating a strong support system as well as for self-advocacy and resisting anti-Black racism. At times, these sisters' pain of loss was palpable, even as the joy of a new birth was imminent.

As Tina contended, "When systemic anti-Black racism and misogynoir [Bailey] converge, we are bound to receive less care. Tamar prayed for her wellbeing and her baby's survival throughout the birthing process. The SC fervently discussed implicit bias and anti-Black racism in maternal care towards Black people giving birth and how to navigate mistrust so that young Black mothers will be more likely to seek treatment.

Love and Support from Family and Friends Near and Far

The COVID-19 pandemic and related travel restrictions and physical distancing policies prevented Tamar's parents from being with her during pregnancy and the birth of their grandchild. "Had it not been for the pandemic, my parents and sister would be part of the birthing experience with me," Tamar explained. Separated by geographical distance, Tamar described how the love and support she received from her parents, sister, extended family, friends, and SC helped her to cope with stress and anxiety. She shared that receiving love and support from the collective—parents, aunties, friends from back home, husband's family, sister and cousins near and far—provided a sense of wellbeing, including the emotional and social support she needed to cope with a high-risk pregnancy. These connections helped her navigate the challenges and protocols of COVID-19 to receive prenatal care and the routines of everyday life following the birth of her baby. Tamar described the love and support she received this way: "All of our families rallied around us; even those who were not in Canada were here in spirit, on phone calls, video chats, emails, direct messages." She shared how her mother would call daily from the Caribbean to tell her which church and community members were praying for her or who had asked about the pregnancy and birth of the baby: "The extended community of support gave me a sense of spiritual and religious grounding and the strength to cope with the stress and anxiety I was experiencing."

Love, Laughter, and Information

Tamar also received love and support from family, friends, and the SC through kindness, prayer, empathy, and information as she expressed concern and worry about her high-risk pregnancy. She recalled how "the SC listened to me and allowed me to vent and express my emotions without judgment." She added, "My cousins here in Canada would call regularly to check in on me, pray with me and offer encouragement to support me." She laughed as she recalled how one cousin would tell her positive stories of other people's pregnancy challenges and how they overcame, "giving me jokes to make me forget the fear, stress and anxiety I was feeling." Others would inquire about doctors' appointments. They would encourage her to ask lots of questions and even provide questions to ask the doctors and would share the latest research to help her better understand the particular challenges she was having with her pregnancy. Family, friends, and SC would stay on the phone with her at night when she was worried and could not sleep. Others ensured that Tamar received correct COVID-19 information on protecting herself when travelling to and from the hospital without continuously watching the news, which made her more anxious. Another SC offered nutrition information and discussed the importance of healthy eating as well as the importance of prenatal vitamins to support the health of both mother and baby.

Practical Material Resources and Support

The SC also supported Tamar with necessary material resources, such as baby items (e.g., clothing, bedding, and car seats), to help her prepare for the baby's arrival. These items included newborn clothes, diapers, onesies, baby shoes, a crib, crib sheets, blankets, towels, a playpen and bouncer, a stroller, and, most importantly, a car seat to take the baby home. Tamar recalled, "One SC provided the majority of baby supplies, which was a blessing during the pandemic because the stores were closed." She continued: "The SC's gifting of clothes and other material items from their children was significant, as it meant that I only needed to purchase a few things, which helped to ease the financial burden on us during the pandemic." Tamar understood that without this type of collective practical and material support from the SC, family, and friends, the confluence of a high-risk pregnancy and having a premature baby during a pandemic could have been potentially tragic for her family.

It is important to note that while the SC lovingly supported Tamar, some struggled with grief and pain from losing their babies. Although Tamar appreciated the collective love and support from the SC, family, and friends in Canada and abroad, one of the most crucial supports was her sister, Tina. Their narratives show how pain connects and transforms them individually and collectively.

Caregiving, Memories, and Grief

Tamar and her sister, Tina, grew up in a close-knit family of four, are close in age, and are always "sounding boards for each other," as Tamar put it. She described Tina, her younger sister, as a "lifeline" and "the one person I knew that I could count on to move into my house and help me to parent my daughter and assist with online school so that I could follow doctor's orders for bed rest." She continued: "She was my rock throughout the entire process. She moved in with us to help with the housework, cooking, laundry, and being my nurse aid as I recovered from a c-section." Tina recalled the day she "packed a bag and moved in" to offer emotional and practical support to Tamar and her family. She added, "I wanted to be a presence and support in my niece's life, who was doing online schooling and to help her adjust to being a big sister and to the shift in the dynamic of her family." Their closeness was clear in Tina's statement, "There was never a question in my mind if I would step up and support my sister when she was surprised with a positive pregnancy test." Tina continued: "I remember the night vividly: ribbing her and her husband about this huge out-of-left-field surprise. It was funny because my sister and brother-in-law planned to have another child, but not during a global pandemic, which added a slight undertone of hilarity." The sisters recalled how the momentary surprise and excitement swiftly shifted to figuring out how to manage and manoeuvre the safest possible ways for Tamar to have a successful pregnancy and birth during a pandemic.

While Tina ensured that Tamar, her newborn baby, and her young daughter received the care they needed, she had to live physically apart from her husband, which she described as "a sacrifice to help my sister," whom she believed would do the same for her. Tina shared that there were times when she was caring for Tamar and her family, she was triggered and became emotional as she was still grieving the loss of her baby: "Having recently lost my own baby, my first pregnancy as a stillbirth, there was definitely a pit of dread that opened up as my sister advanced in hers." She continued, "There is no stopping the mind from walking along the darker edges of our existence. However, there is also light, a spark of hope to let us know there is a way to open to relief." Tina is an avid reader and shared this: "My sacrifice was rewarded with books. Plus, I had time to breathe, reflect, assess, and tune in to approaching changes."

Faith, Spirituality, and Hope

Faith, hope, and spirituality were central to how we connected to support Tamar and one another during the uncertain time. Even as a highly spiritual circle, the fear of Tamar contracting COVID-19 at the hospital, in transit to and from the hospital, or during delivery was never far from our minds. As one SC said: "COVID-19 has tested our faith, yet our hope for a positive outcome and our belief that God would intervene kept our spirits alive—faith over fear." Tina lamented: "My faith took a massive hit after my loss, but I leaned into prayer and positive thinking during my sister's pregnancy, and I am so glad that I did." We laughed, cried, prayed, and shared our stories of child loss, inequities we experienced in the health system, our fears of future pregnancy risks, the trauma of pregnancy loss to our bodies, and how we were coming along in our grief. As Jennifer pointed out: "Grief never leaves, but it changes as we heal and grow." Stacy concurred: "As long as we are honest with ourselves about what we are feeling—feeling and grieving go together." The SC became a space to discuss our experiences with pregnancy loss, miscarriages and stillbirth and our hope for a future that centres Black maternal healthcare. As Preeyaah reflected: "If not for the SC discussions, my faith and hope for a positive outcome would have been shattered." She continued: "The sistahs that stayed connected to their church community online and offered prayers and messages of hope helped me find spiritual and religious grounding." The SC looked to the Black community and culture for spiritual sources of strength and sustenance. When COVID-19 limited our financial resources, we drew on our collective cultural traditions and wisdom for guidance and strength. This spiritual connection sets the foundation for sharing, acknowledging, and healing.

Reflection as Healing and Resilience

The SC became a space for us to share our varied pregnancy journeys, child loss, and childbirth. We shared stories and strategies for over-coming personal crises, physical and emotional pain, bereavement, loss, stress, and trauma, and how we moved forward with our lives. Jennifer reflected on how she overcame "racial trauma in multiple systems" and the myth that Black women do not feel pain and should not express emotions. At the same time, Stacey shared how she survived "medical trauma and shame." Tina lamented the difficulties revealed after her pregnancy loss: "Being designated high-risk, being made aware of inherent placental problems that would impact any future pregnancies really did a number on my dream of becoming a mother." For Tina, healing meant accepting how carefully she must manage pregnancy going forwards and finding meaning after loss (Bailey, Hannays-King et al.). She continued: "COVID-19 forced us all to slow down and gave me time to reflect on why I wanted to become a mother and if biologically was the way to go." She added, "I am still walking a path that has diverged from what I thought once in a committed partnership, and I am fine with that." Tina continued: "I will not lie. I still have days when I waver, but that is my choice because it is my body, my mental and emotional wellbeing that will irrevocably change depending on the outcome of my final decision." Furthermore, she added, "Right now, I am enjoying being there for my sister and niece and happy for the expansion of our family."

The SC afforded us a space to connect, make sense of our distress, and reflect on our feelings of pain, trauma, and what we have been through as Black women on our journey to becoming mothers. Reflecting on our experiences with pregnancy and child loss allowed us to be present for our sistahs and draw strength from one another. Meeting with other women with similar life experiences has shown us that having a dedicated support system is critical to our physical, social, emotional, and spiritual wellbeing. For us, resilience also includes validation, celebration, and resistance.

Resistance as Healing and Resilience

Writing about the preterm birth of a Black child during the COVID-19 pandemic and the worldwide Black Lives Matter movement for racial justice weighed heavily on us as we recall our own experiences with anti-Black racism in seeking maternal care. Jennifer recalled how a hospital denied her requests for pain medication several times while in labour and told her the pain was not significant enough to require medication. She received pain medication only after her partner complained on the fourth attempt. Years later, at the same hospital, as she cried at the loss of her baby, a racialized male doctor chided her: "Why are you crying? You will have lots more babies; you people always do." The pandemic has underscored existing inequities in the education, employment, and justice systems, and Black maternal health is no exception.

Black women's resilience to exist in a society that caters to the ease and satisfaction of white people is difficult. "When you are pregnant, there are more barriers stacked against you," said Tina. She recalled that while giving birth to her dead baby, there were perceptions that she "was tough and could tolerate the pain." She sighed deeply as she remembered: "There was no support offered to me around grief and bereavement after that horrific ordeal." She later challenged the healthcare system for grief support. Tamar said, "There were definitely biases along the way through my two pregnancies and birth." She continued, "I just learned to 'tough it out,' walk in my truth and power and thrive." Preeyaah regularly shared news and research on how Black medical professionals are resisting anti-Black racism in the health system, specifically around COVID-19 and how it was hitting Black communities especially hard in both Canada and the US: "Even to this day, safeguards and medical care opportunities are still either poorly geared towards or inaccessible to us as Black people." As research shows, our collective resistance to systemic anti-Black racism and other challenges of COVID-19 promoted our healing and resilience while strengthening our bonds of care and support (Bailey, Akhtar, et al.).

Black women have endured the brunt of health inequities since modern medicine began, and COVID-19 has compounded and complicated these systemic failures. Our bodies have been sites of experiments, our pain has never been taken seriously, and our mental health has never been prioritized. Our awareness of the neglect to collect disaggregated race-based data, despite the disproportionate maternal and infant mortality, and our own experiences of systemic anti-Black racism inspired us to form a SC and take back our power. The SC became a critical source of support for Tamar—a Black pregnant mother who needed correct information to navigate an already racist healthcare system that was further impacted by the pandemic. Tamar had to advocate for herself as no one, not even her partner, could go with her to doctor's appointments. The SC became a space of resistance to anti-Black racism and an opportunity to connect Black women with anti-racist strategies, stories of wisdom, resources, and healing practices. Although Tamar did not experience blatant acts of racism this time, she feared leaving her preterm baby at the hospital to be cared for by an all-white medical team. "I could not sleep sometimes. I had nightmares thinking what could happen to my baby in my absence," she recalled.

Conclusion

The SC was an inclusive, culturally relevant space for supporting a pregnant Black woman. We used a wraparound care strategy—a type of safety net that could be adapted to support pregnant women beyond the pandemic. The SC highlights the need for and importance of a dedicated support system to help Black women cope with and survive high-risk pregnancies and the birth of their babies. It shows the collective power of individual women's stories to help others understand the structural dimension of our oppression as Black women and better strategize how to navigate anti-Black racism in our lives at the intersection of race, gender, and class. Through this crisis, we have had the privilege of reclaiming our personal power and connecting in a deeper, more meaningful way, thus strengthening our sistahood.

Implementing the SC was our attempt to show that Black sistahood heals. By supporting a Black sistah, we increased her chance of having a healthy and safe pregnancy and childbirth. Although the SC played a small part in Tamar's pregnancy and childbirth journey, her successful pregnancy and childbirth rested with her medical team, supportive partner, extended family and friends, and her sister Tina, who was paramount, and all served as important protective factors during her pregnancy and childbirth.

While the full impact of the COVID-19 pandemic on Black maternal and infant health is yet to be fully understood, Tamar's story, along with the experiences shared with the SC, illuminates the profound significance of being a part of a community that comprises Black mothers. This community offers a space to share stories of grief and loss of our babies, to express struggles encountered as Black women seeking care, and to confront the challenges of navigating high-risk pregnancies in a racist healthcare system. Having experienced lives marginalized within intersecting systems of care, we assert that systemic changes are imperative to address the pervasive racial inequities that are deeply rooted in the healthcare system. This change must begin with actively listening to the voices of Black pregnant women and genuinely valuing our bodies, lives, and the lives of our precious babies.

Works Cited

Adhopia, V. "Why Doctors Want Canada to Collect Better Data on Black Maternal Health". *CBC*, 23 June 2021, https://www.cbc.ca/news/health/canada-black-maternal-health-1.6075277. Accessed 13 Aug. 2023.

Bailey, A., M. Akhtar, et al. "Intersecting Individual, Social and Cultural Factors in Black Mothers' Resilience Building Following Loss to Gun Violence in Canada." *Women's Mental Health: Resistance and Resilience in Community and Society,* edited by N. Khanlou and B. F. Pilkington, 2015, Springer, pp. 311-25.

Bailey, A., C. Hannays-King, et al. "Black Mothers' Cognitive Process of Finding Meaning and Building Resilience after Loss of a Child to Gun Violence." *British Journal of Social Work,* 43, 2013, pp. 336-354.

Bailey, M. *Misogynoir Transformed: Black Women's Digital Resistance.* NYU Press, 2020.

Born Ontario. "Better Outcomes Registry and Network." *Born Ontario,* 2016, https://www.bornontario.ca/en/index.aspx. Accessed 13 Aug. 2023.

Davis-Floyd, R., G. Kim, and D. A. Schwartz. "Pregnancy, Birth and the COVID-19 Pandemic in the United States." *Medical Anthropology* Vol. 39, no. 5, 2020, pp. 413-27.

Ellington, S., et al. "Characteristics of Women of Reproductive Age with Laboratory Confirmed SARS-CoV-2 Infection by Pregnancy Status—United States, January 22–June 7, 2020." *MMWR Morbidity and Mortality Weekly Report,* vol. 69, no. 25, 2020, pp. 769-75.

Fante-Coleman, T., and F. Jackson-Best. "Barriers and Facilitators to Accessing Mental Health Care in Canada for Black Youth: A Scoping Review." *Adolescent Research Review,* vol. 5, 2020, pp. 115-36.

Howell, E.A., et al. "Racial and Ethnic Differences in Factors Associated with Early Postpartum Depressive Symptoms." *Obstetrics & Gynecology,* 105, 2005, pp. 1442-50.

Knight, M., et al. *Saving lives, Improving Mothers' Care-Lessons Learned to Inform Maternity Care from the UK and Ireland Confidential Enquiries into Maternal Death and Morbidity 2016–18.* National Perinatal Epidemiology Unit, University of Oxford 2020.

McKinnon, B., et al. "Comparison of Black-White Disparities in

Preterm Birth between Canada and the United States." *CMAJ*, vol. 188, 2016, p. 1.

Oparah, J. C., H. Arega, et al. *Battling over Birth: Black Women and the Maternal Health Care Crisis*. Praeclarus Press, 2018.

Oparah, J. C., and A. D. Bonaparte. *Birthing Justice: Black Women, Pregnancy, and Childbirth*. Routledge, 2015.

Oparah, J. C., F. Salahuddin, et al. "By Us Not for Us: Black Women Researching Pregnancy and Childbirth." Research Justice: Methodologies for Social Change." *Academia*, 2015, https://www.academia.edu/40662223/By_Us_Not_For_Us_Black_Women_Researching_ Pregnancy_and_Childbirth. Accessed 13 Aug. 2023.

Petersen, E. E., et al. "Racial/Ethnic Disparities in Pregnancy-Related Deaths—United States, 2007–2016." *MMWR Morbidity and Mortality Weekly Report, 68*, vol. 35, 2019, pp. 762-65.

Quenby, S., et al. "Miscarriage Matters: The Epidemiological, Physical, Psychological, and Economic Costs of Early Pregnancy Loss." *Lancet*, vol. 397, no. 10285, 2021, pp. 1658-67.

Tangel, V., et al. Racial and Ethnic Disparities in Maternal Outcomes and the Disadvantage of Peripartum Black Women: A Multistate Analysis, 2007-2014." *American Journal of Perinatology*, vol. 36, no. 8, 2019, pp. 835-48.

Chapter 15.

COVID-19 Impacts, Resistance, and Strategies: An Intersectional, Global Review

Roberta K. Timothy, Falan Bennett, and Denessia
Blake-Hepburn

Introduction

This chapter discusses the results of a scoping review conducted between June and August 2020 on the experiences and impact of COVID-19 on African/Black communities within the Canadian and global context during the first year of the pandemic. The goal of the review was to support interventions and research in this area at a time when the impact of COVID-19 on global African/Black communities was not considered.

First, the context of structural violence in the lives of transnational African/Black communities is outlined, using Canada as an example. Second, the method and sources used are presented. Third, the findings of the review are explained concerning the following topics: African/Black health and race; intersecting identities; policing, surveillance, and criminalization; economic marginalization; the coronavirus context of employment; anti-Black racism as a global and colonial standard; housing apartheid; government responses to the COVID-19 pandemic; and African/Black interventions and resistance.

Global History of Anti-Black Racism and COVID-19

For over four hundred years, structural, violent practices—maintained and sanctioned by ideologies and actions that harm African/Black peoples—have sustained anti-Black racism by mainly white settlers of European descent under the guise of economic and racial superiority. This history started with the enslavement of Indigenous Africans. The transatlantic slave trade trafficked and displaced up to twelve million Africans from the sixteenth to nineteenth century, creating a triangular trade route that led to the continued economic prosperity of today's Western countries and the economic underdevelopment and capitalist apartheid of Africa and the African diaspora (Lewis). During the Middle Passage, enslaved Africans were brutally transported across the Atlantic Ocean to the New World (Americas); of the 11.2 million enslaved Africans that survived the journey, 450,000 were transported to the United States and the remaining to Latin America and the Caribbean (Gates 2). The dehumanization and mistreatment of African/Black people continued upon arrival to the New World as they endured inhumane physical and social conditions that continued after independence (Noonan et al.). The current realities of anti-Black racism globally are intrinsically connected to historical roots of anti-Black hate, white supremacy, and economic apartheid, and anti-Black racism is directly connected to the global plight of African/Black people and COVID-19.

Africa's population is projected to increase from 1.3 billion to 4.3 billion between 2020 and 2100 (Cilluffo and Ruiz). There are about 250 million Africans living in the diaspora (United Nations, "International Decade"). In Latin America, there are approximately 113 million, with Brazil representing the largest African population outside of Africa. There are over 46 million in North America, 13.6 million in the Caribbean, and 3.5 million in Europe (African American Registry; Kajunju; Lituchy). In 2016, 1.2 million people in Canada identified as Black, comprising 3.5 per cent of the total population (Maheux and Do).

Canadian Context

Structural violence in Canada started before its creation. In the span of five hundred years, white settler governments have legally, physically, and culturally nearly eliminated Indigenous peoples (Palmater). The high unemployment rates, extreme poverty, inadequate housing, and poor social and health services of many reserves reflect the legacy of colonization of Indigenous communities (McCue). Although the government has created the Truth and Reconciliation Commission, and government officials have apologized, some have denied Canada's colonial history (Palmater), yet its effects are painfully evident: the environmental racism taking place in Wet'suwet'en territory in British Columbia concerning the national gas pipeline project (Baker); the missing and murdered Indigenous women (Native Women's Association of Canada); as well as the unmarked graves being found on the grounds of old residential schools (CBC News, "Unmarked").

Turtle Island is a site of white supremacy, where anti-Black racism is intrinsically linked to anti-Indigenous racism. This history and the current realities are critical in understanding the impact of the current pandemic on African/Black communities, as the legacies of slavery and colonization are apparent in the anti-Black racism seen in the current health crisis. As a social determinant of health, racism has had many social and health consequences for Black people, and it continues to manifest through the perpetuation of racist policies and practices (King and Redwood).

The Scoping Review

A scoping review was conducted from June to August 2020 focusing on the impact of COVID-19 on African/Black communities transnationally. Timothy's resistance education methodology was used to conduct the scoping review from a critical, intersectional, transnational, and African feminist perspective ("Resistance Education"). Intersectionality is a concept that helps in understanding how intersectional systems—such as class, race, sexual orientation, gender identity, age, and gender— connect to produce social inequality and entails a critical praxis to create social change (Collins 1; Timothy "What Is Intersectionality"). The term "transnational Africa" refers to the ways in which Africa's new and old diasporas interact to challenge and shape identities that transcend nation-states (Okome and Vaughan 10). The research questions guiding the review included the following: What was COVID-19's impact on African/Black communities? How did anti-Black structural violence affect African/Black communities' COVID-19 outcomes? How did African/Black communities resist?

The search process yielded a collection of more than 150 academic and grey literature articles as well as four YouTube videos and two academic and community-based webinars. All data and information sources were published between February and July 2020. The academic articles consisted of original studies and opinion pieces. Comparatively, the grey literature sources included newspaper articles, governmental briefs, blog posts, nongovernmental organization reports, magazine pieces, public health agency medical synopses, and epidemiological and sociological summaries. The information gathered was divided into themes that illuminated African/Black Canadian and global COVID-19 experiences.

Themes

African/Black Health and Race

The review provided evidence of a discrepancy in public health policy regarding race as a social construct and as a genetically based construct (Gannon). Understandings of race as a biological category in public health are problematic, as historical and current discourses pathologize African/Black peoples as intrinsically ill (Darity 470; Williams and Mohammed 1). Anti-African/Black stereotypes vilify Black communities as disease vectors, impacting the way Black people are medically perceived and treated in relation to COVID-19 and chronic diseases (Green; Jones). Although COVID-19 is an infectious disease, the probability of infection, severity of symptoms, and prognosis have been found to be directly related to pre-existing chronic conditions, such as diabetes and hypertension (CDC). This link is especially troubling for those who are misconceived as being genetically more likely to develop chronic comorbidities because they are Black (Siddiqi et al., "Illustrating"; Lujan and DiCarlo 414).

The COVID-19 pandemic has added a new stratum to the debate

concerning the root causes of racial health disparities. British and American governments acknowledged that a large proportion of their COVID-19 patients and deaths were African. In England, Black males and females were 4.2 and 4.3 times more likely to die from COVID-19, respectively, than their white counterparts (Office for National Statistics 2). Black Londoners were overrepresented in COVID-19 deaths, accounting for 13 per cent of the population but 16 per cent of COVID-19 mortalities (Mackintosh). Similarly, in Texas, African Americans were 3.7 times more likely to succumb to COVID-19, with 73.7 African Americans dying for every 32.4 white Americans (APM Research Lab Staff). Multiple researchers misattributed the morbidity and mortality disparities observed in England and the United States (US) to the high prevalence of chronic disease in Black communities (Aldridge et al.). This constituted a misleading argument that blamed African/Black people for their own health demise (Global News; Strings and Bacon).

In Canada, a deep history of colonialism, anti-Indigeneity, anti-Black racism, and denial has impeded the basic task of collecting racial data (Czyzewski, 2; Siddiqi et al., "A Lack of Data"; Timothy, "Coronavirus"). Discourse from officials from Canadian institutions indicated that race (as a proxy for racism) had little to no association with health and that the collection of race-based data would spur discrimination (Lapierre). Both misconceptions align the Canadian brand of racism with the reluctance to acknowledge Canada's colonial and racist realities (Tuck and Yang; Miller). Whereas the US and England described the state of their Black residents, Canada was unable to do so using direct methodologies (Mulligan et al.; Timothy, "Coronavirus"). Overall, there is a lack of race-based data in Canada, which makes it difficult to clearly identify the impacts of the COVID-19 virus on Black communities in Canada, who are reported to be the most affected (Iyayi). Data collected from the federal government included basic demographic data on infection rates among women, long-term care centres, and congregate settings (Wherry).

Provincial and municipal public health authorities from Ontario, Toronto, Quebec, and Montreal expressed commitment to collecting race-based data to document how COVID-19 affected racialized communities (Bowden and Cain). Although the Public Health Agency of Canada discussed collecting these data, no firm commitments were made.

Intersecting Identities

The concept of intersectionality is critical to understanding the complexities of Black life and COVID-19. Intersectionality refers to the fact that continental and diasporic Africans hold multiple, marginalized identities simultaneously and throughout the life course, exposing them to a variety of opportunities, disadvantages, and obstacles (Crenshaw; Davis).

African/Black communities resist institutional and systemic anti-Black racism and struggle against additional colonial, intersecting systems that impede their ability to live healthy and free (López and Gadsden; Davis). Intersectionality allows us to analyze how systems that generate oppressed realities based on patriarchy, ableism, classism, misogynoir, homophobia, xenophobia, religious persecution, and transphobia interact with and compound anti-Black racism (Crenshaw; López & Gadsden, 2; Timothy, "What Is Intersectionality"). These systems have the potential to worsen mental and physical health outcomes (Timothy, "Racism Impacts Your Health"; "Reparations"). For this reason, we sought to examine and discuss the ways in which those with intersecting disenfranchised identities experienced the COVID-19 pandemic.

Black women experienced compounded economic impacts during the pandemic, as they are the ones who generally earn less income and are more likely to be in insecure jobs and live close to poverty (United Nations, "The Impact of COVID-19"). In many countries, the first round of layoffs took place in the service sector, including hospitality, retail, and tourism, sectors in which women are overrepresented. Countries with developing economies where 70 per cent of women's employment was in the informal economy experienced a worse situation because of the limited access to social and employment protection (United Nations, "The Impact of COVID-19"). In Ghana, kayayei—women and girl head porters who carry goods on their head for a fee—experienced precarious working conditions, as they lacked social and financial safety nets after COVID-19 lockdowns (Bauck). In Kenya, 67 per cent of women reported spending more time doing chores and experiencing a complete loss of income or employment compared with men (Austrian and Abuya). Brazil has the highest rate (8 per cent) of domestic workers among women in the developing world (McCoy and Sheridan), with Afro-Brazilian representing 63 per cent of them (Sellmann). A United Kingdom (UK) report found that for all ethnic groups, Black women were much more likely to work in a key occupation, particularly in healthcare roles. South Asian and African/ Black women were reported to be 25 and 130 per cent more likely than white British women to work in these roles, respectively (Platt and Warwick). In Canada, racialized women earn 32 per cent less in the workplace (The Homeless Hub).

Working in essential jobs decreased the ability to follow social distancing guidelines, thereby increasing risk of COVID-19 infection. For instance, Kayayei women were left without incomes when the Kantamanto Market in Accra—the largest second-hand market in West Africa—closed (Bauck). They were also unable to follow social distancing and hygiene guidelines because of a lack of proper housing and sanitation systems, such as lack of washing and toilet infra- structures (Bauck). In the UK, Black women were reported to be more than 4.3 times likely to die a COVID-19-related death compared with white women (ONS). Employment neglect and the devaluing and subsequent death of Black women were evident during the COVID-19 pandemic period. In Canada, many Black women are concentrated in homecare, nursing, and caregiver roles for families, which placed them at a higher risk of infection (Jones). While women comprise slightly more than 50 per cent of the Canadian population, they account for 54 per cent of confirmed COVID-19 patients (Flanagan). In Montreal, more than half of the number of COVID-19 cases reported during the period were women (Perreaux).

There is a lack of Canadian data regarding the effects of COVID-19 on Black queer folks. LGBTQIA2S+ individuals have been found to be less likely to seek emergency or critical care and more likely to rate their own health as poor, to have underlying comorbidities, and to receive inadequate and discriminatory care, which increase their risk of contracting and experiencing a severe case of COVID-19 (Osman; Wyton). Additionally, physical distancing guidelines were forecast to be especially disadvantageous for queer individuals because they were already more likely to live in poverty and to be unemployed (Osman; Wyton). For those who are Black and LGBTQIA2S+, this was a likely compounded reality (Furman et al.).

The National Law Center on Homelessness and Poverty forecast that "homeless individuals infected by COVID-19 will be twice as likely to be hospitalized, two to four times as likely to require critical care, and two to three times more likely to die than the general population" (1). COVID-19 cases were confirmed in eleven of Toronto's shelters and respites (Shadpour). Despite the increased risk of infection in these settings, the city did not enforce federal and public health guidance, which required two metres of separation within the shelter system (Orkin 2-3). Lack of implementation of proper standards heightened risk of infection for Indigenous and Black people and people living with disabilities, who disproportionately make up the homeless population (Orkin 3).

The Canadian Emergency Response Benefit (CERB) provided income supplements to workers who had been laid off or were earning less than one thousand dollars for fourteen or more days as a result of COVID-19 (PooranLaw). Significant confusion was reported by those on social assistance regarding deductions from Ontario Disability Support Program and Ontario Works payments (PooranLaw). The federal government advised the provincial governments and territories to ensure vulnerable Canadians were accounted for and "not to claw back on CERB from those on social assistance" (PooranLaw). While there were discussions around benefits for members in Canadian society who were affected by the pandemic, these discussions often did not address the effects on Black people.

Policing, Surveillance, and Criminalization

The COVID-19 pandemic presented a similar pattern to the criminalization of HIV nondisclosure in the use of policing and the criminal justice system as mechanisms of COVID-19 containment (Bain et al.; Timothy, "Racism Impacts your Health"). When COVID-19 rates began to increase in Ontario in April, the Toronto police chief stated that police would enforce a zero-tolerance policy for physical distancing disobedience (Rocca). Black communities expressed fear and frustration with the hypersurveillance and ensuing consequences for Black communities (Maynard; Rocca; Bain et al.; Martis), as African/Black individuals in Toronto were already more likely to be street-checked, assaulted by police officers, and die in altercations involving the police (Maynard; CBC News, "Black People in Halifax"; Ontario Human Rights Commission). Various municipalities in Ontario (including Toronto, Peel, Sudbury-Manitoulin, and Nipissing District) mandated the use of masks in public, indoor venues (Vyas). Although this policy was meant to protect individuals from COVID-19, members of Black and Indigenous communities expressed fear over the ways in which masks would increase the likelihood of being profiled, harassed, or street-checked by police (Thomson-DeVeaux and Butchireddygari; Timothy, "Coronavirus"). This situation was ironic, as Black and Indigenous people were most likely to contract and suffer the worst outcomes of COVID-19 (Office for National Statistics); however, it was also Black and Indigenous people who were most likely to suffer the worst outcomes of police brutality (Maynard; Ontario Human Rights Commission; Freeze).

Economic Marginalization

The pandemic negatively impacted countries with large concentrations of Black people. The African continent accounts for 17 per cent of the world's population, yet it only holds 3 per cent of the global gross domestic product because of colonialism and neoliberal policies (Coleman). This inequality was projected to widen amid the COVID-19 crisis. For instance, Ghana reported financial and social difficulties caused by lockdown protocols (Adusei). In Nigeria, 48 per cent of the population lived in extreme poverty, and the economy was expected to decline from 2.1 per cent (Okigbo). Somalia faced a dire situation as a result of decreases in remittances, as the wages of Somalians from the diaspora also decreased (Jama and Abdullahi). In the Caribbean, the impact of COVID-19 was expected to be mostly financial because their economies are highly indebted and lack access to concessionary financing as a result of lower income levels (Meighoo). Evidence showed that the pandemic would worsen pre-existing economic inequalities.

Employment and COVID-19

In the early stages of the Canadian COVID-19 response, the federal government indicated that workers who kept society functioning and preserved life would keep working on the frontline during the COVID-19 response (Public Safety Canada). The list of essential frontline workers included those employed in health care, transportation, retail (e.g., grocery), hospitality (e.g., restaurants), and food and medication manufacturing and processing industries (Public Safety Canada). These employees were deemed essential not only because they preserved health but also because they allowed society to function through their precarious work (Lowrey). Work and race intersected, as Black individuals were often positioned in the most precarious forms of frontline work, which confined them to low-wage jobs affording little physical, social, or economic protection against COVID-19 (Cooper; Kelly; Timothy, "Coronavirus"). The nature of their work in a colonial landscape caused the marginalization, sickening, and death of Black workers because of COVID-19 and its related proxies (Cooper).

Black Brazilian maids were especially susceptible to contracting COVID-19 as they commuted to work using crowded transportation systems, resided in favelas and lived in poverty, unable to access high-quality healthcare and relied on Brazil's underfunded public health system, which was operating at capacity (McCoy and Sheridan). Afro-Brazilian domestic workers were functioning as intercommunity vectors in the unintentional spread of COVID-19 to working-poor neighbourhoods (Sellmann; McCoy and Sheridan). The earliest cases of COVID-19 in Brazil were imported by the international travels of the rich to foreign destinations (Slattery and Viga Gaier). This resulted in the death of numerous Brazilian domestic workers, including Cleonice Goncalves, who contracted the virus from her rich employee who had become infected vacationing in Italy (Slattery and Viga Gaier).

In London, offensive customers and toxic working conditions were speculated to have contributed to the COVID-19 deaths of two transportation workers in England (Weaver and Dodd). Belly Mujinga, an African Briton, died on April 5, 2020, fourteen days after reportedly being spat and coughed on by a COVID-19 positive commuter (Weaver and Dodd). Similar to personal support worker Leonard Rodriquez, Belly feared for her health, as she had been working in public without suitable personal protective equipment (PPE) (Weaver and Dodd). These cases demonstrate the ways in which Black lives and employees are disparaged and how COVID-19 was weaponized to sentence African individuals to health debilitation and death.

Anti-Black Racism as a Global and Colonial Standard

Asian people experienced anti-Asian racism as a direct result of the COVID-19 pandemic (Human Rights Watch, "Covid-19"; Lee, B.; Lee, J.). African/Black and other racialized leaders stood in solidarity against anti-Asian racism (Timothy, "Coronavirus"). Ironically, Asian people also continued to engage in anti-Black racism. According to Human Rights Watch, in China, authorities in the southern city of

Guangzhou (home to China's largest African community) began a campaign to forcibly test the African community for COVID-19; it also involved forcing them to self-isolate and/or quarantine in designated hotels. Many Africans were subjected to unfair treatment, as they were evicted from their homes and refused service from many stores, hotels, and restaurants. This mistreatment sparked outrage among several African countries, such as Uganda, Nigeria, and Ghana. Each country summoned its respective Chinese ambassador to tell them to stop mistreating Africans in China (Human Rights Watch, "China").

Housing Apartheid

COVID-19 racial disparities were attributed to living conditions. Racialized groups were more likely to live in overpopulated areas, to experience residential segregation, to live in multigenerational households, and to live further from grocery stores and medical facilities (CDC). These groups were also more likely to work in essential jobs—increasing their risk of infection if they continued to work without paid sick leave—and were more likely to have no access to health insurance (CDC).

A report analyzing non-long-term-care COVID-19 trends in Ontario neighbourhoods showed that areas with the most ethnically diverse populations reported the highest levels of COVID-19 (Public Health Ontario). These findings mirrored similar findings for diverse neighbourhoods in Montreal and New York (Bowden and Cain). In Brazil, Black Brazilians reported the highest levels; for the UK, it was Black, Asian, and other racialized groups. For Black people in South Africa, it was Nigerians who had the highest rates of COVID-19. In Australia, it was the Indigenous population (Aldridge et al.; Cousins; Friedman). Black people also reported limited access to health care, low testing rates and often low-quality health infrastructure in the US, Canada, Nigeria, South Africa, and Somalia (Jama and Abdullahi; Laurencin and McClinton; Sandoiu; UNDP Africa, "In Nigeria"; Yang et al.).

Government Responses to the COVID-19 Pandemic

Ghana implemented lockdown, tracing, testing, and treatment protocols (Adusei) and became the first country to employ Zipline drones to test for COVID-19 and to transport medical supplies from urban centres to rural areas, cutting testing times considerably (Baker).

The East African leaders of Kenya, Uganda, South Sudan, and Rwanda collaborated to combat the pandemic and agreed on multiple joint, regional interventions to COVID-19, including uninterrupted cross-border movements of goods throughout the region, border screening, testing, and tracing as well as measures to support local agriculture (Xinhua). Rwanda also used Zipline drones to deliver medical supplies (Edwards); testing for COVID-19 in this country, however, was limited because of its only having one lab (Edwards). Rwanda also reportedly intended to employ robots to assess patient temperatures, to inform security of individuals not wearing masks, and to deliver food, resources, and supplies to patients (UNDP Africa, "UNDP and Government of Rwanda Deploy").

In the Caribbean, responses to COVID-19 reportedly involved lockdown protocols (Meighoo); movement restrictions ranging from one (St. Vincent) to thirteen (Jamaica); and food security policies focussed on self-production, seed distribution, and other inputs to small farmers and vulnerable families for growing food in their own homes (Food and Agriculture Organization of the United Nations). Some countries made public land available for the cultivation of these products for public consumption and provided food to quarantined communities (Food and Agriculture Organization of the United Nations). The Jamaican government established travel bans, working-at-home restrictions, social distancing policies, and two sets of financial stimulus policies (Mera). Trinidad and Tobago's response involved developing evidence-based decision making and guidelines, financial supplements, remote work and pandemic leave policies, provisions of social support and communication services, as well as establishing a parallel health system to test and treat COVID-19 patients (Hunte et al.). Canada's COVID-19 benefits (CERB, Canada Emergency Student Benefit, and employment insurance) and subsidies were presumed to be effective (Government of Canada; Flanagan). Nova Scotia provided social supports, especially to the North Preston community (Moore).

African Interventions and Resistance

Numerous documented initiatives indicate that even though COVID-19 upended the lives of African/Black communities, their transnational resistance persists. Crowdfunding through apps was an example of African/Black resistance during COVID-19. Funds were reportedly raised for initiatives and personal needs, PPE, housing aid for trans individuals, and campaigns against police and authoritative brutality (Liu; Saybo). For Black people, the existence of several simultaneous anti-Black crises required the use of public fundraisers to garner international support from whoever was willing and able to donate (Ryssdal and Fam; Lampen). For example, the COVID-19 Black Emergency Support Fund–Toronto reported raising $136,724 to be allocated in stipends to Black families (Black Lives Matter Toronto). Anecdotal information from social media indicated that many donors were working-class individuals who were matching the donations of one another.

Multiple webinars, community check-ins, Twitter discussions, and Zoom meetings took place with the goal of providing safe spaces for African/Black individuals to share their thoughts and experiences (The Voice of Community). Other documented forms of communal healing included counselling, Black cooking initiatives, and community fitness workshops (Women's Health in Women's Hands Community Health Centre).

In Brazil, a coalition between multiple Brazilian favelas (G10 Favelas) implemented a successful COVID-19 intervention for and by residents of poor and working-class favelas that included hiring their own medical team consisting of three ambulances (with an ICU), two doctors, two nurses, drivers, and first aid workers to care for community residents (Friedman; De Oliveria Andrade). Brazilian favelas predominantly comprise African communities living with a lack of access to clean running water, reliable electricity, PPE, and soap. This situation complicated and impeded adherence to necessary hand hygiene and social distancing guidelines (Friedman; De Oliveira Andrade), which, combined with other social factors, increased the risk of contracting and dying from COVID-19. The G10 Favelas coalition created a network of 400 volunteers; each volunteer was responsible for distributing food, providing supplies, monitoring fifty families for social distance adherence, and for contacting the medical team when someone presented with COVID-19 symptoms (De Oliveira Andrade).

Conclusion

Findings from the review indicated that whereas some African/Black nations initially reported successes in the fight against COVID-19 (e.g., Trinidad and Tobago), other African/Black communities struggled to survive within inherently anti-Black societies. Responses to COVID-19 occurred in communities with realities of extreme adversity. The effect and toll of COVID-19 on African/Black communities can be attributed to the mental, physiological, and materialistically tangible tolls of living under colonial, anti-Black, capitalist, and white supremacist oppression.

Findings of the review also demonstrated the major role that neoliberal policies have played in producing and reproducing economic and health inequalities between African/Black people and other groups, which have been further exacerbated by the COVID-19 pandemic. These policies have compounded the economic and social impacts observed among Black continental and diasporic women and other racialized women.

Canada did not initially collect race-based data, which resulted in the omission of data on the economic, social, and housing impacts to Black people as well as the very lives of Black people. Black experiences, inclusive of pain and suffering, were hidden from the mainstream through the grouping of all non-white groups under the umbrella term of "racialized" groups. Canada's failure to break down racial disparities by racial groups impeded the development of effective and equitable policies and programs to address the specific issues faced by Black communities.

Understanding Black health, including as it pertains to COVID-19, requires examining race not as a risk factor for the contraction of, or death from, COVID-19, because Black people are not genetically inclined to acquiring chronic or infectious diseases, nor are they predisposed to illness because of adverse cultural traditions or ways of living. Racism and colonialism wielded by capitalist institutions are the causal factors that marginalize African/Black communities and increase their susceptibility to disease. African/Black people were most likely to experience the most severe consequences of the current economic recession because they were least likely to be employed, or have a high probability of being exposed to the virus because they work disproportionately in frontline occupations and were less likely to be able to work from home. COVID-19 is likely to spread in African/Black communities because Black people are more likely to live in crowded housing with limited access to PPE, running water, and nutritious food as a result of governmental neglect and abuse. Therefore, it is the system that sacrifices African/Black lives for colonial endeavours. It is not Black people who contribute to their institutionally engineered demise.

African/Black communities were reported to employ countless measures and initiatives to aid one another during a time when social support and substantial resources were important to combatting COVID-19. Moreover, Black people are battling multiple pandemics simultaneously. Resistance against COVID-19, police and authoritative brutality, transphobia, misogynoir, housing discrimination, anti-Black racism and poverty demonstrate that African/Black communities stand at the forefront of a movement in resistance for all Black lives.

Works Cited

Adusei, Alex. "COVID-19 Is Hitting Communities in Ghana Hard." *The British Medical Journal Opinion,* 7 May 2020, blogs.bmj.com/bmj/2020/05/07/covid-19-is-hitting-communities-in-ghana-hard/. Accessed 18 Aug. 2023.

Al Jazeera. "Coronavirus Pandemic Exposes South Africa's 'Brutal Inequality.'" *Al Jazeera*, 12 June 2020, bitly.ws/pFpV. Accessed 18 Aug. 2023.

Aldridge, Robert, et al. "Black, Asian and Minority Ethnic Groups in England Are at Increased Risk of Death from COVID-19: Indirect Standardisation of NHS Mortality Data." *Wellcome Open Research*, version 2, vol. 5, no. 88, 24 June 2020, https://doi.org/10.12688/wellcomeopenres.15922.2. Accessed 18 Aug. 2023.

Austrian, Karen, and Timothy Abuya. "We Wanted to Know How Coronavirus Affects Nairobi's Slum Residents. What We Found." *The Conversation*, 5 May 2020, theconversation.com/we-wanted-to-know-how-coronavirus-affects-nairobis-slum-residents-what-we-found-137621. Accessed 18 Aug. 2023.

Bain, Beverly, et. al. "COVID-19 Discriminates against Black Lives via Surveillance, Policing and Lack of Data: U of T experts." *The Conversation*, 21 Apr. 2020, theconversation.com/coronavirus-discriminates-against-black-lives-through-surveillance-policing-

and-the-absence-of-health-data-135906. Accessed 18 Aug. 2023.

Baker, Rafferty. "A Who's Who of the Wet'suwet'en Pipeline Conflict." *CBC News.* 26 Feb. 2020, www.cbc.ca/news/canada/british-columbia/wetsuweten-whos-who-guide-1.5471898. Accessed 18 Aug. 2023.

Bauck, Whitney. "Workers Who Form the Backbone of the Second-hand Market Are Especially Vulnerable in a Time of Pandemic." *Fashionista,* 6 May 2020, bitly.ws/pFqa. Accessed 18 Aug. 2023.

Black Lives Matter. "COVID-19 Black Emergency Support Fund." *GoFundMe,* 15 March 2020, www.gofundme.com/f/black-emergency-support-fund. Accessed 18 Aug. 2023.

Bowden, Olivia, and Patrick Cain. "Black Neighbourhoods in Toronto Are Hit Hardest by COVID-19—and It's 'Anchored in Racism': Experts." *Global News,* 2 June 2020, globalnews.ca/news/7015522/black-neighbourhoods-toronto-coronavirus-racism/.

CBC News. "Black People in Halifax 6 Times More Likely to Be Street Checked Than Whites." *CBC News,* 27 Mar. 2019, www.cbc.ca/news/canada/nova-scotia/street-checks-halifax-police-scot-wortley-racial-profiling-1.5073300. Accessed 18 Aug. 2023.

CBC News. "Unmarked Grave Findings in Canada Prompt Reckoning among U.S. Churches." *CBC News,* 22 July 2021. www.cbc.ca/news/canada/north/unmarked-graves-residential-schools-us-churches-1.6113448. Accessed 18 Aug. 2023.

Centers for Disease Control and Prevention (CDC). *COVID-19 in Racial and Ethnic Minority Groups.* 2020, stacks.cdc.gov/view/cdc/89820/cdc_89820_DS1.pdf. Accessed 18 Aug. 2023.

Cilluffo, Anthony, and Neil G. Ruiz. "World Population Growth Is Expected to Nearly Stop Growing by the End of the Century." Pew Research Centre, 17 June 2019, www.pewresearch.org/fact-tank/2019/06/17/worlds-population-is-projected-to-nearly-stop-growing-by-the-end-of-the-century/. Accessed 18 Aug. 2023.

Coleman, Colin. "This Region Will Be Worth $5.6 trillion within 5 Years—But Only If It Accelerates Its Policy Reforms." *World Economic Forum,* 11 Feb. 2020, www.weforum.org/agenda/2020/02/africa-global-growth-economics-worldwide-gdp/. Accessed 18 Aug. 2023.

Collins, Patricia Hill. "Intersectionality's Definitional Dilemmas." *Annual Review of Sociology,* vol. 41, no. 1, 2015, pp. 1-20.

Cooper, Afua. "Canada, COVID, and Police Brutality: The Experience of the Black Community." *Afua Cooper,* 9 June 2020, afuacooper.com/2020/06/10/canada-covid-and-police-brutality-the-experience-of-the-black-community/. Accessed 18 Aug. 2023.

Office of National Statistics (ONS). "Coronavirus (COVID-19) Related Deaths by Ethnic Group, England and Wales: 2 March 2020 to 10 April 2020." *Office for National Statistics,* 7 May 2020, www.ons.gov.uk/peoplepopulationandcommunity/birthsdeathsandmarriages/deaths/articles/coronavirusrelateddeathsbyethnicgroupengland andwales /2march2020to10april2020. Accessed 18 Aug. 2023.

Cousins, Sophie. "Indigenous Australians Avert an Outbreak—for Now." *Foreign Policy,* 19 May 2020, foreignpolicy.com/2020/05/19/indigenous-australians-avert-coronavirus-outbreak-for-now-aboriginal/. Accessed 18 Aug. 2023.

Crenshaw, Kimberlé. "Mapping the Margins: Intersectionality, Identity Politics, and Violence against Women of Color." *Stanford Law Review,* vol. 43, no. 6, July 1991, pp. 1241-99.

Czyzewski, Karina. "Colonialism as a Broader Social Determinant of Health." *International Indigenous Policy Journal: Health and Well-Being,* vol. 2, no. 1, 16 May 2011, https://doi:10.18584/iipj.2011.2.1.5.

Darity, William. "Revisiting the Debate on Race and Culture: The New (Incorrect) Harvard/Washington Consensus." *Du Bois Review: Social Science Research on Race,* vol. 8, no. 2, 2011, pp. 467-76.

Davis, Angela Y. *Women, Race, & Class.* First Vintage Books Editing, 1983.

De Oliveira Andrade, Rodrigo. "The Brazilian Slums Hiring Their Own Doctors to Fight Covid-19." *British Medical Journal,* vol. 369, 22 Apr. 2020, doi:10.1136/bmj.m1597.

Edwards, Neil. "Rwanda's Success and Challenges in Response to COVID-19." *AfricaSource,* 24 Mar. 2020, www.atlanticcouncil.org/blogs/africasource/rwandas-successes-and-challenges-in-response-to-covid-19/. Accessed 18 Aug. 2023.

Flanagan, Ryan. "Does COVID-19 Discriminate? This Is How Some Canadians Are Harder-Hit." *CTV News,* 15 Apr. 2020, www.

ctvnews.ca/health/coronavirus/does-covid-19-discriminate-this-is-how-some-canadians-are-harder-hit-1.4897298. Accessed 18 Aug. 2023.

Food and Agricultural Organization of the United Nations. *Food Systems and COVID-19 in Latin America and the Caribbean: A First Look at Impact, and Country Response.* Bulletin 1, Santiago FAO, 23 April 2020, https://doi.org/10.4060/ca8677en. Accessed 18 Aug. 2023.

Freeze, Colin. "More Than One-Third of People Shot to Death over a Decade by RCMP officers Were Indigenous." *The Globe and Mail,* 17 Nov. 2019, www.theglobeandmail.com/canada/article-more-than-one-third-of-people-shot-to-death-over-a-decade-by-rcmp/. Accessed 18 Aug. 2023.

Friedman, Uri. "Brazil's Pandemic Is Just Beginning: The Hardest-Hit Country in Latin America Is Facing a "Perfect Storm," as Inequality Collides with COVID-19." *The Atlantic,* 10 May 2020, www.theatlantic.com/politics/archive/2020/05/brazil-coronavirus-hot-spot-bolsonaro/611401/. Accessed 18 Aug. 2023.

Furman, Ellis, et al. "Activism, Intersectionality, and Community Psychology: The Way in which Black Lives Matter Toronto Helps Us to Examine White Supremacy in Canada's LGBTQ Community." *Community Psychology in Global Perspective,* vol. 4, no. 2, 2018, pp. 34-54.

Gannon, Megan. "Race Is a Social Construct, Scientists Argue: Racial Categories Are Weak Proxies for Genetic Diversity and Need to be Phased Out." *Scientific American,* 5 Feb. 2016, www.scientificamerican.com/article/race-is-a-social-construct-scientists-argue/. Accessed 18 Aug. 2023.

Gates, Henry Louis. *Black in Latin America.* New York University Press, 2011.

Green, Laura. *Stereotypes: Negative Racial Stereotypes and Their Effect on Attitudes Toward African-Americans.* Jim Crow Museum of Racist Memorabilia, Ferris State University. www.ferris.edu/htmls/news/jimcrow/links/essays/vcu.htm. Accessed 18 Aug. 2023.

Huaxia. "East African Leaders Agree on Joint Interventions to Tackle COVID-19." *Xinhua,* 12 May 2020, www.xinhuanet.com/english/2020-05/12/c_139051462.htm. Accessed 18 Aug. 2023.

Human Rights Watch. "China: Covid-19 Discrimination Against Africans—Forced Quarantines, Evictions, Refused Services in Guangzhou." *Human Rights Watch*, 5 May 2020, www.hrw.org/news/2020/05/05/china-covid-19-discrimination-against-africans. Accessed 18 Aug. 2023. Accessed 18 Aug. 2023.

Human Rights Watch. "Covid-19 Fueling Anti-Asian Racism and Xenophobia Worldwide: National Action Plans Needed to Counter Intolerance." *Human Rights Watch*, 12 May 2020, www.hrw.org/news/2020/05/12/covid-19-fueling-anti-asian-racism-and-xenophobia-worldwide. Accessed 18 Aug. 2023.

Hunte, Shelly-Ann, et al. "Health Systems' Resilience: COVID-19 Response in Trinidad and Tobago." *The American Journal of Tropical Medicine and Hygiene*, vol. 103, no. 2, Aug. 2020, pp. 590-92.

Iyayi, Mudia. "How Black Canadians Are Disproportionately Impacted by COVID-19." *The Gazzette*, 2 June 2020, westerngazette.ca/culture/how-black-canadians-are-disproportionately-impacted-by-covid-19/article_89293cc4-a033-11ea-ae15-631b3c049880.html. Accessed 18 Aug. 2023.

Jama, Subban, and Ayan Abdullahi. "'We Are Used to a Virus Called Bombs': The Coronavirus Will Ravage a Resilient Somalia—With Ripples Far beyond Its Borders." *Argument, Foreign Policy*, 20 May 2020, foreignpolicy.com/2020/05/12/coronavirus-pandemic-somalia-al-shabab/. Accessed 18 Aug. 2023.

Jones, El. "Black People Already Struggle to Breathe in Canada. Ignoring Us during this COVID-19 Crisis Will Only Make It Worse." *Halifax Examiner*. 3 Apr. 2020, www.halifaxexaminer.ca/commentary/black-people-already-struggle-to-breathe-in-canada-ignoring-us-during-this-covid-19-crisis-will-only-make-it-worse/. Accessed 18 Aug. 2023.

Kajunju, Amini. "Africa's Secret Weapon: The Diaspora." *CNN*, 1 Nov. 2013, www.cnn.com/2013/11/01/opinion/africas-secret-weapon-diaspora/index.html. Accessed 18 Aug. 2023.

Kelly, Kim. "Essential Workers Don't Need Our Praise. They Need Our Help." *The Washington Post*, 30 Apr. 2020, www.washingtonpost.com/outlook/2020/04/30/essential-workers-dont-need-our-praise-they-need-our-help/. Accessed 18 Aug. 2023.

King, Christopher J., and Yanique Redwood. "The Health Care Institution, Population Health and Black Lives." *Journal of the National Medical Association*, vol. 108, no. 2, Summer 2016, pp. 131-36.

Lampen, Claire. "How to Support the Struggle against Police Brutality." *The Cut*, 2 July 2020, www.thecut.com/article/george-floyd-protests-how-to-help-where-to-donate.html. Accessed 18 Aug. 2023.

Lapierre, Matthew. "Groups, Advocates Disappointed by Quebec's Decision Not to Collect COVID-19 Race Data." *Calgary Herald*, 22 May 2020, calgaryherald.com/news/groups-advocates-disappoint ed-by-quebecs-decision-not-to-collect-covid-19-race-data. Accessed 18 Aug. 2023.

Laurencin, Cato T., and Aneesah McClinton. "The COVID-19 Pandemic: A Call to Action to Identify and Address Racial and Ethnic Disparities." *Journal of Racial and Ethnic Health Disparities*, vol. 7, 2020, pp. 398-402.

Lee, Bruce. "Over 1700 Reports of Coronavirus-Related Discrimination Against Asian Americans Since March 19." *Forbes*, 26 May 2020, www.forbes.com/sites/brucelee/2020/05/26/covid-19-coronavirus -continues-to-expose-anti-asian-bigotry-how-to-stop-it/?sh=738b 6c0148a4. Accessed 18 Aug. 2023.

Lee, Jessica. "Chinese Canadians Share Their Experiences of Racism during COVID-19." *McLean's*, 12 Aug. 2020, macleans.ca/society/ chinese-canadians-share-their-experiences-of-racism-during-covid-19/. Accessed 18 Aug. 2023.

Lewis, Thomas. "Transatlantic Slave Trade." *Encyclopedia Britannica*, 18 Aug. 2021, www.britannica.com/topic/transatlantic-slave-trade. Accessed 18 Aug. 2023.

Lituchy, Terri R. "Journal of African Business—Special Issue on the Diaspora." *Journal of African Business*, vol. 20, no.1, 2019, pp. 1-5.

López, Nancy, and Vivian Gadsden. "Health Inequities, Social Determinants, and Intersectionality." *National Academy of Medicine*, Discussion Paper, 5 Dec. 2016, nam.edu/wp-content/uploads/2016 /12/Health-Inequities-Social-Determinants-and-Intersectionality. pdf. Accessed 18 Aug. 2023.

Lowrey, Annie. "Don't Blame Econ 101 for the Plight of Essential Workers." *The Atlantic*, 13 May 2020, www.theatlantic.com/ideas/archive/2020/05/why-are-americas-most-essential-workers-so-poorly-treated/611575/. Accessed 18 Aug. 2023.

Lujan, Heidi, and Stephen DiCarlo. "The 'African Gene' Theory: It Is Time to Stop Teaching and Promoting the Slavery Hypertension Hypothesis." *Advances in Physiology Education*, vol. 42, no. 3, Sept. 2018, pp. 412-16.

Mackintosh, Thomas. "Coronavirus: Ethnic Breakdown of London Deaths Revealed." *BBC News London*, 30 Apr. 2020, www.bbc.com/news/uk-england-london-52453782. Accessed 18 Aug. 2023.

Maheux, Hélène, and Deniz Do. "Diversity of the Black Population in Canada: An Overview." *Statistics Canada*, 27 Feb. 2019, www150.statcan.gc.ca/n1/en/pub/89-657-x/89-657-x2019002-eng.pdf?st=QuCasKmG. Accessed 18 Aug. 2023.

Martis, Eternity. "Why COVID-19 Is Even More Dangerous for Black Women." *Refinery 29*, 19 May 2020, www.bbc.com/news/uk-england-london-52453782. Accessed 18 Aug. 2023.

Maynard, Robyn. *Policing Black Lives: State Violence in Canada from Slavery to the Present*. Fernwood, 2017.

McCoy, Terrence, and Mary Sheridan. "Coronavirus Collides with Latin America's Maid Culture—With Sometimes Deadly Results." *The Washington Post*, 29 March 2020, www.washingtonpost.com/world/the_americas/coronavirus-collides-with-latin-americas-culture-of-domestic-help--with-sometimes-deadly-results/2020/03/29/c987d2f6-6f7a-11ea-a156-0048b62cdb51_story.html. Accessed 18 Aug. 2023.

McCue, Harvey A. "Reserves in Canada." *The Canadian Encyclopedia*, 12 July 2018, *Historica Canada*, www.thecanadianencyclopedia.ca/en/article/aboriginal-reserves. Accessed 31 August 2020. Accessed 18 Aug. 2023.

Meighoo, Kirk. "The Caribbean and Covid-19: Not a Health Crisis, but a Looming Economic One." *The Round Table*, vol. 109, no. 3, 2020, pp. 340-41.

Mera, Manuel. "Social and Economic Impact of the COVID-19 and Policy Options in Jamaica." *United Nations Development Program*,

Policy Document Series, May 2020, www.undp.org/latin-america/publications/social-and-economic-impact-covid-19-and-policy-options -jamaica.

Miller, Jason. "Why the Black Struggle in Canada Has All but Been Erased. Two Historians Explain Our Blind Spot." *The Toronto Star.* 5 June 2020, www.thestar.com/news/gta/2020/06/04/why-the-black-struggle-in-canada-has-all-but-been-erased-two-historians-explain-our-blind-spot.html. Accessed 18 Aug. 2023.

Moore, Nick. "Senator Concerned about Disproportionate Impact of COVID-19 on African Nova Scotian Communities." *CTV Atlantic News,* 13 April 2020, atlantic.ctvnews.ca/senator-concerned-about-disproportionate-impact-of-covid-19-on-african-nova-scotian-communities-1.4894790. Accessed 18 Aug. 2023.

Mulligan, Kate, et al. "Race-Based Health Data Urgently Needed during the Coronavirus Pandemic." *The Conversation,* 30 Apr. 2020, theconversation.com/race-based-health-data-urgently-needed-during-the-coronavirus-pandemic-136822. Accessed 18 Aug. 2023.

National Law Center on Homelessness and Poverty. "Racism, Homelessness, and COVID-19." *Homeless Law,* May 2020, homelesslaw.org/wp-content/uploads/2020/05/Racism-Homeless ness-and-COVID-19-Fact-Sheet-_Final_2.pdf. Accessed 18 Aug. 2023.

Native Women's Association of Canada. "Fact Sheet Missing and Murdered Aboriginal Women and Girls." *NWAC,* 24 July 2015. www.nwac.ca/assets-knowledge-centre/Fact_Sheet_Missing_and_Murdered_Aboriginal_Women_and_Girls.pdf. Accessed 18 Aug. 2023.

Noonan, Allan S., et al. "Improving the Health of African Americans in the USA: An Overdue Opportunity for Social Justice." *Public Health Reviews,* vol. 37, no. 12, 2016, pp. 1-12.

Okigbo, Patrick O. "Nigeria Must Not Forget Its Poor in the Covid-19 World." *Health Express,* 10 Apr. 2020, www.orfonline.org/expert-speak/nigeria-must-not-forget-its-poor-in-the-covid-19-world-64389/. Accessed 18 Aug. 2023.

Okome, Mojúbàolú Olúfúnké, and Olufemi Vaughan. "Transnational Africa and Globalization: Introduction." *West African Migrations Transnational and Global Pathways in a New Century,* edited by Mojúbàolú Olúfúnké Okome and Olufemi Vaughan, Palgrave

Macmillan, 2011, pp. 1-15.

Oliveira Sellmann, Mauricio. "In Brazil's Raging Pandemic, Domestic Workers Fear for Their Lives—And Their Jobs." *The Conversation*, 3 June 2020, theconversation.com/in-brazils-raging-pandemic-domestic-workers-fear-for-their-lives-and-their-jobs-138163. Accessed 18 Aug. 2023.

Orkin, Jessica. "Letter to the City of Toronto." Goldblatt Partners, 20 Apr. 2020, goldblattpartners.com/wp-content/uploads/COVID-19-and-Outbreaks-in-Toronto%E2%80%99s-Shelter-System.pdf. Accessed 18 Aug. 2023.

Osman, Laura. "Researchers Scramble to Inform Doctors of Barriers LGBTQ People Face in Getting COVID-19 Care." *CTV News*, 27 April 2020, www.ctvnews.ca/health/coronavirus/researchers-scramble-to-inform-doctors-of-barriers-lgbtq-people-face-in-getting-covid-19-care-1.4913848. Accessed 18 Aug. 2023.

Palmater, Pamela. "Genocide, Indian Policy, and Legislated Elimination of Indians in Canada." *Aboriginal Policy Studies*, vol. 3, no. 3, 26 June 2014, pp. 27-54.

Perreaux, Les. "Women make up over half of COVID-19 deaths in Canada, counter to trends in most of world." *The Globe and Mail*, 20 May 2020, www.theglobeandmail.com/canada/article-women-make-up-over-half-of-covid-19-deaths-in-canada-counter-to/. Accessed 18 Aug. 2023.

Platt, Lucinda, and Ross Warwick. "COVID-19 and Ethnic Inequalities in England and Wales." *Fiscal Studies*, vol. 41, no. 2, 3 June 2020, pp. 259-89.

Public Safety Canada. "Guidance on Essential Services and Functions in Canada During the COVID-19 Pandemic." *Public Safety Canada*, 25 Aug. 2020, www.publicsafety.gc.ca/cnt/ntnl-scrt/crtcl-nfrstrctr/esf-sfe-en.aspx. Accessed 18 Aug. 23.

Public Health Ontario. "Enhanced Epidemiological Summary: COVID-19 in Ontario—A Focus on Diversity", February 26, 2020 to December 13, 2021." *Public Health Ontario*, 14 May 2020, www.publichealthontario.ca/-/media/documents/ncov/epi/2020/06/covid-19-epi-diversity.pdf?la=en. Accessed 18 Aug. 2023.

Rocca, Ryan. "Coronavirus: 'Zero Tolerance' for Those Who Disobey Physical Distancing,' Toronto Police Chief Says." *Global News*, 11

Apr. 2020, globalnews.ca/news/6807347/coronavirus-toronto-mayor-physical-distancing/. Accessed 18 Aug. 2023.

Ryssdal, Kai, and Alli Fam. "GoFundMe CEO: 'We're Not Yet Seeing Much around Recovery.'" *Marketplace*, 28 April 2020, www.market place.org/2020/04/28/gofundme-unprecedented-use-during-covid19/. Accessed 18 Aug. 2023.

Sandoiu, Ana. "'A No-Win Situation'—Expert Weighs in on COVID -19 Racial Disparities." *Medical News Today*, 22 May 2020, www. medicalnewstoday.com/articles/a-no-win-situation-expert -weighs-in-on-covid-19-racial-disparities. Accessed 18 Aug. 2023.

Shadpour, Bahar. "City of Toronto Is Failing Those Experiencing Homelessness." *Advocacy Centre for Tenants Ontario*, 21 Apr. 2020, www.acto.ca/homelessnesscovid/. Accessed 18 Aug. 2023.

Siddiqi, Arjumand, et al. "A Lack of Data Hides the Unequal Burden of COVID-19." *The Toronto Star*, 16 Apr. 2020, www.thestar.com/opinion/contributors/2020/04/16/a-lack-of-data-hides-the-unequal-burden-of-covid-19.html. Accessed 18 Aug. 2023.

Siddiqi, Arjumand, et al. "Illustrating a 'Consequential' Shift in the Study of Health Inequalities: A Decomposition of Racial Differences in the Distribution of Body Mass." *Annals of Epidemiology*, vol. 28, no. 4, 2018, pp. 236-41.

Slattery, Gram, and Rodrigo Viga Gaier. "A Brazilian Woman Caught Coronavirus on Vacation. Her Maid Is Now Dead." *Reuters*, 24 Mar. 2020, www.reuters.com/article/us-health-coronavirus-rio/a-brazilian-woman-caught-coronavirus-on-vacation-her-maid-is-now-dead-idUSKBN21B1HT. Accessed 18 Aug. 2023.

Strings, Sabrina, and Lindo Bacon. "The Racist Roots of Fighting Obesity." *Scientific American*, 4 June 2020, www.scientificamerican.com/article/the-racist-roots-of-fighting-obesity2/. Accessed 18 Aug. 2023.

The Voice of Community. *Voice of Community*, 2020, https://www.tvocnetwork.org/. Accessed 18 Aug. 2023.

Thomson-DeVeaux, Amelia, and Likhitha Butchireddygari. "For Black Americans, Wearing a Mask Comes with Complicated Anxieties." *FiveThirtyEight*, 30 June 2020, fivethirtyeight.com/features/for-black-americans-wearing-a-mask-comes-with-complicated-anxieties/. Accessed 18 Aug. 2023.

Timothy, Roberta K. "Coronavirus Is Not the 'Great Equalizer'—Race Matters: U of T Expert." *U of T News*, 8 Apr. 2020, www.utoronto. ca/news/coronavirus-not-great-equalizer-race-matters-u-t-expert. Accessed 18 Aug. 2023.

Timothy, Roberta K. "Racism Impacts Your Health." *The Conversation*, 28 Feb. 2018. theconversation.com/racism-impacts-your-health-84112. Accessed 18 Aug. 2023.

Timothy, Roberta K. "Reparations for Slavery and Genocide Should Be Used to Address Health Inequities." *The Conversation*. 5 Dec. 2019. theconversation.com/reparations-for-slavery-and-genocide-should-be-used-to-address-health-inequities-111320. Accessed 18 Aug. 2023.

Timothy, Roberta K. "What Is Intersectionality? All of Who I Am." *The Conversation*, 7 Mar. 2019. theconversation.com/what-is-intersectionality-all-of-who-i-am-105639. Accessed 18 Aug. 2023.

Tuck, Eve, and K. Wayne Yang. "Decolonization Is Not a Metaphor." *Decolonization: Indigeneity, Education & Society*, vol. 1, no. 1, 2012, pp. 1-40.

UNDP Africa. "Government of Rwanda Deploy Smart Anti- Epidemic Robots to Fight qgainst COVID-19!" *UNDP Africa*, 21 May 2020, www.undp.org/africa/news/undp-and-government-rwanda-deploy-smart-anti-epidemic-robots-fight-against-covid-19. Accessed 18 Aug. 2023.

UNDP Africa. "In Nigeria, COVID-19 Threatens to Hit Three Fragile Northeastern States hardest, UNDP Studies Find." *UNDP Africa*, 5 June 2020, www.undp.org/press-releases/nigeria-covid-19-threatens-hit-three-fragile-northeastern-states-hardest-undp-studies-find. Accessed 18 Aug. 2023.

United Nations. "International Decade for People of African Descent: 2015–2024." *United Nations*, 2015, un.org/en/observances/decade-people-african-descent. Accessed 18 Aug. 2023.

United Nations. "The Impact of COVID-19 on Women." *United Nations*, 9 Apr. 2020, www.un.org/sexualviolenceinconflict/wp-content/uploads/2020/06/report/policy-brief-the-impact-of-covid-19-on-women/policy-brief-the-impact-of-covid-19-on-women-en-1.pdf. Accessed 18 Aug. 2023.

Vyas, Kirti. "This Is Where Face Masks Are Now Mandatory in Ontario and What You Need to Know." *blogTO*. 7 July 2020, www.blogto.com/city/2020/07/mandatory-masks-ontario/. Accessed 18 Aug. 2023.

Weaver, Matthew, and Vikram Dodd. "UK Rail Worker Dies of Coronavirus after Being Spat at while on Duty." *The Guardian*, 12 May 2020, www.theguardian.com/uk-news/2020/may/12/uk-rail-worker-dies-coronavirus-spat-belly-mujinga. Accessed 18 Aug. 2023.

Wherry, Aaron. "One Country, Two Pandemics: What COVID-19 Reveals about Inequality in Canada." *CBC News*, 13 Jun. 2020, www.cbc.ca/news/politics/pandemic-covid-coronavirus-cerb-unemployment-1.5610404. Accessed 18 Aug. 2023.

Williams, David R., and Selina A. Mohammed. "Racism and Health I: Pathways and Scientific Evidence." *American Behavioral Scientist*, vol. 57, no. 8, Aug. 2013, pp. 1152-1173.

Wyton, Moira. "Queer Canadians 'Particularly Vulnerable' to Effects of COVID-19: Being Discriminated against in the Health-Care System Is One Factor, but Not the Only One." *The Tyee*, 6 May 2020, thetyee.ca/News/2020/05/06/Queer-Canadians-Vulnerable-COVID19/. Accessed 18 Aug. 2023.

Yang, Jennifer, et al. "Toronto's COVID-19 Divide: The City's Northwest Corner Has Been 'Failed by the System.'" *Toronto Star*, 28 June 2020, www.thestar.com/news/gta/2020/06/28/torontos-covid-19-divide-the-citys-northwest-corner-has-been-failed-by-the-system.html. Accessed 18 Aug. 2023.

Chapter 16.

Dealing with Museum Educational Tours as Heritage Knowledge Sharing Practices in South Africa during the COVID-19 Pandemic

Daniel Rankadi Mosako

COVID-19 was labelled a dangerous disease and an international public health emergency concern by the director-general of the World Health Organization on January 30, 2020. The disease belongs to a group of viruses that cause the common cold. It is believed that the disease is caused by the SARS-CoV-2 pathogen, which causes a common influenza (flu) that infects the nose, sinuses, and upper throat, possibly leading to respiratory arrest and death (Wu et al.). This unique sickness rapidly affected people around the world, beginning with China, Italy, and the United States; COVID-19 them spread to the African continent, causing similar symptoms (Fang et al. 645). On May 25, 2020, Africans and others in the diaspora celebrated the fifty-seventh Africa Day through virtual connectivity while staying indoors, with the following theme: silencing the guns. For several days, numerous African countries were under siege, with some succumbing to the new global pandemic and threat. The president of South Africa, Cyril Matamela Ramaphosa, then delivered a declaration of support, saying, "Africa Day is commemorated beneath the shadow of the Coronavirus epidemic, which has swept the globe and left no portion of our continent unscathed" (qtd. in Western Cape Education). "The COVID-19 pandemic," he added, "will have a long-term impact on Africa's ability to achieve the African Union's Agenda 2063 vision of a peaceful, united, and wealthy continent" (qtd. in Western Cape Education). Simultaneously, he expressed considerable optimism that the epidemic will enable a new Africa to emerge, bridging the continent's significant divides.

President Ramaphosa subsequently invited citizens to look for great deeds of solidarity—such as cross-border collaboration and knowledge and resource sharing—to aid in the construction of a resilient Africa united by a common goal. During the Africa Day commemoration address in 2021, the African Union Development Agency-New Partnership for Africa's Development (AUDA-NEPAD) echoed this suggestion. The African Union's theme for 2021 became "Arts, Culture, and Heritage: Levers for Building the Africa We Want." Notably, the 2021 Africa Day was marked by the AUDA-NEPAD's promotion of youth-led projects to build a resilient Africa through arts, culture, heritage, innovation, and entrepreneurship. The commemoration of Africa Day in 2021, like the previous year, came at a tough time because of global pandemic difficulties. As a result, the event's message centred on the need to develop and promote new ideas aimed at resolving problems on the continent (AUDA-NEPAD). In terms of achieving these goals, museums are well positioned to foster cross-border collaboration and knowledge exchange through theme-based exhibitions.

COVID-19 was declared a national disaster and a public health emergency in South Africa in accordance with the global lockdown initiative (Perold et al.). To manage the spread of the disease, many countries opted to close their borders to incoming travellers, leading to disruption of economic activities. Governments also imposed curfews and other measures to keep people isolated, reducing physical contact as a technique to manage the spread of the disease (Kalish). Travel restrictions and bans, widespread quarantines, closure of nonessential national security venues and public facilities, and prohibitions on public gatherings, arts and cultural activities, national cultural site visitations, and leisure tourism were all part of the enforced lockdown. One of the most effective new-normal lifestyle conditions for limiting the transmission of infectious disease was social distancing (Kalish). Regulations enacted under the South African Disaster Management Act affected and restricted research visits to museums as well as the viewing of onsite displays. Contemporary museum curators, however, are obliged by their functional role to keep patrons informed about relevant museum information. As museum curators, they must inform the public about a variety of museum exhibitions that speak to everyday life experiences and cultural teachings.

A setback to the museum curator's role was the unprecedented reduction in tourist and leisure activities. Furthermore, would-be visitors were now forced to rely on virtual methods to interact with museums after being denied access to conduct onsite studies and view exhibits (Kahn). As a result of these imposed restrictions, many institutions, including South African museums, turned to alternative techniques to communicate with their patrons, since knowledge can be transmitted and consumed in a variety of ways, including online. This kind of education uses technology to help acquire knowledge from different remote locations and uses the internet as well as video/audio text communication software to create the learning environment (Basilaia and Kvavadze 2).

A significant amount of information sharing can be developed and made available through real-time and non-real-time operations thanks to the online availability of electronic sources, including video and live streaming. With this strategy, during the pandemic, learners of all ages and levels were mandated to switch from in-person learning to online alternatives (South African Government Disaster Management Act). More and more business-to-business and business-to-person relationships were made possible because of such a strategy. As a result, online connectivity and the availability of computers and/or smart-phones became essential; in communities, however, that were challenged by a digital divide, poverty, and socioeconomic inequities, access to online learning, not to mention enjoying remote museum programs, remains a challenge (Basilaia and Kvavadze).

Problem Statement

Since the start of the COVID-19 pandemic, many governments have implemented restrictive measures to reduce the infection rate. Many public institutions throughout the world, including museums and art galleries in South Africa, closed their doors and cancelled onsite visits indefinitely. As a result, art enthusiasts were unable to physically access the museum sites. Consequently, cultural institutions, such as museums, had to identify other ways to serve their customers amid COVID-19 while adhering to the lockdown laws.

Objectives and Theoretical Framework

The goal of this paper is to explore how cultural institutions, specifically museums, provide services to patrons during COVID-19. It is crucial to transmit knowledge and information to the general public. The use of online services can help fulfill the important role and obligation of information distribution. Paolo Spagnoletti, Andrea Resca, and Gwanhoo Lee emphasize the theoretical narrative and usage of the internet through virtual connectivity as the driving force for knowledge acquisition, arguing that connectivity supports online communities and effectively communicates casual and formal information in virtual spaces (364). Thus, online connectivity between the public and cultural institutions can provide a sense of place and an embedded user experience (Mason, Whitehead, and Graham) that goes beyond a physical space. As Nina Tura et al. argue, "Online services enable participants to be connected to resources across various sectors and markets. (881)" Roberto Moro-Visconti also affirms that an online technology-enabled infrastructure enables network connections between different stakeholders and further emphasizes that these platforms facilitate connectivity between cultural institution participants who cannot physically interact with one another or their knowledge base institutions.

Cultural institutions, such as museums and art galleries, offer a unique role in cultural sustainability and connection by maintaining their communities' heritage (United Nations). They offer their services to many citizens, regardless of religious affiliation, age, nationality, disabilities, race, or gender.

In the *Culture of Connectivity*, José van Dijck states that it is through the exploration of constructs of connectivity that most online and social media platforms facilitate user connectedness at a global scale. These online and social media platforms use constructs and features that are a measure of cultural connectedness, which is culturally appropriate content and language that has the ability to capture commonalities (i.e., processes, beliefs, and practices) within and between diverse communities of interest (Snowshoe 15).

These constructs are expanded by van Dijck in *Flickr and the Culture of Connectivity*, in which she perceives a culture of connectivity as a postbroadcast, networked culture where social interactions and cultural products are enmeshed in technological systems. Connectivity is an important concept, but it is also a complicated phenomenon, whose foundations are not fully understood. Nevertheless, the Oxera Consulting firm reports that connectivity is multidimensional in nature and that such dimensions are dependent on the strength of each link to explain what interconnectedness is. The strength of the connectivity network infrastructure determines the effectiveness of connectivity; as a result, the concept of interconnection can be experienced by individuals, corporations and the entire world. According to Fu, institutions can overcome structural segregation and build a connection with potential patrons through connectedness (2); nevertheless, this relationship may not be solid and trustworthy because of other factors. In a strict or flexible network, however, participants are inclined to trust and are required to assist some individuals while relying on connectedness and communication with others (Fu 2). Patricia Bromley, in contrast, takes a cosmopolitan approach to cultural connections. Her cosmopolitan definition fits with the concept of an integrated society and culture that is unbounded by political demarcations and geographical divisions. In this case, the concept of interconnectedness is explored beyond national borders, potentially creating global interconnection (Bromley 38).

Other procedures and alternatives to connectivity and interactions can regulate adversity and negative outcomes resulting from people who are skeptical of online connectivity (Van Breda 3). Cultural heritage is recreated in society through the application of such a theoretical framework. As a result, I agree with Magdalena Gertruide Calitz (118), who argues that learning is an important element of culture and that individuals can learn and acquire a cultural ethos by being exposed or connected to cultural institutions. As a result, online interconnectivity serves as a crucial link between cultural institutions and society, as it is via such connectedness that individuals engage with and study culture and history, which serves as a template for shaping society's awareness and behaviour.

Discussion

Elisabeth Holl et al. argue that there are direct benefits of online connectivity and other connectivity interventions because these can foster social interaction and give many people the impression of being united as a society, especially in a situation where movement restrictions are enforced under stringent curfew laws. The five lockdown levels devised by the Department of Corporate Governance and Traditional Affairs (CoGTA) and enacted by the South African government, with severe consequences for violators, are as follows (see Figure 1):

- Level 5 – Drastic measures are required.
- Level 4 – Some activity can be allowed, subject to requirements.
- Level 3 – Some restrictions on work and social activities are eased.
- Level 2 – Further easing of restrictions, but social distancing measures are maintained.
- Level 1 – Most normal activity can resume, with health guidelines always being followed.

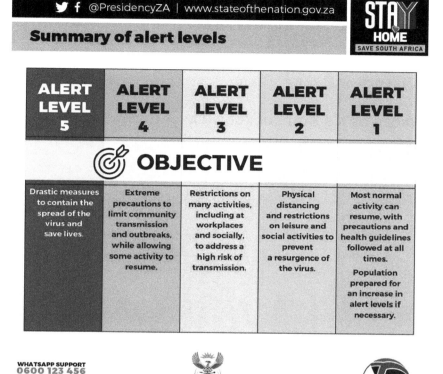

Figure 1: Summary of Alert Levels

The introduction of these levels, together with the government's strategy to deal with COVID-19, was met with some resistance from citizens, residents, and politicians. Some individuals described lock-down laws as irrational, arbitrary, and bizarre (Maseko). The Democratic Alliance political party took the matter further by proposing and circulating its own designed stages and Smart Lockdown Approach as follows (see Figure 2):

The Smart Lockdown is composed of four stages:

- Red (row 1): Stage 4 (hard lockdown)
- Orange (row 2): Stage 3 (soft lockdown)
- Yellow (row 3): Stage 2 (soft open)
- Green (row 4): Stage 1 (open)

STAGES OF A SMART LOCKDOWN APPROACH

	PUBLIC SECTOR	PRIVATE SECTOR	INDIVIDUALS	GOODS	TRANSPORT
Stage 4: Hard lockdown	Institutions necessary for provision of essential services.	Workplaces necessary for provision of essential goods and services.	Obtain/perform essential service or good. Funeral < 10. Seek emergency, chronic care.	Essential goods or services.	Private vehicles, limited public transport.
Stage 3: Soft lockdown	Institutions necessary for provision of essential services.	Primary, secondary sector firms, retail stores open. All subject to social distancing regs. Places of entertainment, leisure and lifestyle to remain closed.	Obtain any service or good available. Go to work if permitted. Funeral < 10. Seek emergency, chronic medical care.	Extended consumer goods, with some restrictions still in place.	Private vehicles, limited public transport within area of residence, all domestic travel for commercial vehicles.
Stage 2: Soft open	All public institutions subject to social distancing.	All business to open, subject to social distancing and use of PPE (incl. other health protocols). Restricted opening hours.	Obtain any good or service available. Travel domestically. Attend social gatherings < 100 with use of PPE. Seek medical care.	All consumer goods.	Private vehicles, all public transport incl. domestic air travel, commercial vehicles, air travel to be limited.
Stage 1: Open	All public institutions subject to social distancing.	All business to open, subject to social distancing and use of PPE (incl. other health protocols). Unrestricted opening hours.	Obtain any good or service available. Go to work. Domestic and international travel to low-risk countries. Attend social gatherings < 500 with use of PPE. Seek medical care.	All consumer goods.	Private vehicles, domestic transport, commercial vehicles, air travel to/from all but high-risk countries.

*The content in this table is purely for illustrative purposes to show a lockdown in different stages.
**South Africa will need to develop at a national level stages in consultation with stakeholders.
***Stages are non-linear, country could move from stage 2 back to stage 4 if situation warranted.

Figure 2: Stages of a Smart Lockdown Approach

Both strategies were intended to open the country to certain business transactions, including tourism, which directly and indirectly included onsite visits to cultural institutions. The opposing arguments concluded that the tourism industry had to be opened for business in Level 3 to save the sector from being eroded, as an estimated 1.2 million sector-based jobs had already been lost as a result of government's lockdown mandate (Steenhuisen). However, the alternative recommendation was not successful, as CoGTA reaffirmed its decision to keep cultural institutions closed for public visits on June 27, 2021:

(1) Any place or premises normally open to the public where re-ligious, cultural, entertainment, recreational, or similar activi-ties, which are prohibited in terms of these of these regulations,

take place, is closed. (2) The following places or premises normally open to the public or where people may gather, are closed,
and include (b) flea markets. (c) museums, libraries, archives,
and galleries.

The use of online connectivity has expanded globally, and its usage in
developing countries continues to reach new heights, granting many
individuals the ability to conduct a cross-border transaction (Manyika
et al. 37). In relation to this statement, Marco Furini et al. emphasize
that museums can create and use multiple hashtags for the same
exhibition to spread the message carried in the exhibition to audiences
of different ages to influence behavioural change. This statement is also
emphasized by Baylie Stillwell, who put exhibitions at the forefront of
social awareness strategies. Stillwell states that exhibitions explain the
message through interactive displays and it is through them that
societies can become interconnected.

Although opportunities exist to share museum exhibitions with the
public in a virtual manner, there are still challenges, hence museum
curators' hesitation to venture into new territory with copyrighted
collections, museums' ethical considerations, and tight budgets. The
audience might also be hesitant to trust content from the internet in a
world that is clouded by disinformation, such as fake news and
propaganda, which has the potential to wreak havoc (Jankowicz 2020).
This statement is supported by Michal Choraś et al. (5), who present
the European Union's plan of action to combat online disinformation:

> Raise awareness and improve societal resilience. This action aims
> to increase public awareness and resilience by activities related to
> "media literacy in order to empower EU citizens to better identify
> and deal with disinformation." In this sense, the development of
> critical thinking and the use of independent fact-checkers are
> highlighted to play a key role in "providing new and more effic-
> ient tools to the society in order to understand and combat online
> disinformation" (5).

As a result, content circulated through the internet and online
streaming channels has both beneficial and harmful qualities. Barriers—such as the digital divide, the cost of data, inexperience with
technology, poor quality smartphones or computer devices, online

platform hackers, and low awareness levels of museum archival hold-
ings—hampered attempts to make museum archives and exhibits
available to the public during the COVID-19 pandemic in South Africa
(Servon). In terms of the digital divide, Holl et al. argue that during
periods of high connectivity demand, the disadvantages faced by people
with poor online connection quality under normal circumstances may
become much more significant. During the lockdown, traditionally
disadvantaged groups faced even greater challenges. Students from socially disadvantaged families, for example, had less access to digital
infrastructure. While there is a fundamental need for a solid connection, access to hardware is also critical.

Conclusion and Limitations

Attracting museum visitors during the COVID-19 pandemic was a
major problem for museums across the world, and South Africa was
not an exception. The pandemic hampered core museum functions,
including offering educational tours. This chapter investigated online
connectivity as an alternative method for societies to stay connected to
their information and knowledge bases, such as educational museum
tours. These were done online in the lockdown period and could benefit
citizens beyond the pandemic, but only if more citizens trust online
platforms, thus fulfilling the cultural connectivity theory.

The COVID-19 pandemic clearly accelerated the demand for
extensive online connectivity and altered the behaviour of many
worldwide economic ecosystems, corporate relationships, and cultural
institutions that are part of the tourism and societal education sectors.
As a result, patrons and the public will benefit extensively if they
explore the benefits of online connectivity and learn from museum
exhibitions remotely. Culture is the way people make meaning of their
lives and defines the people's long-term viability. Cultural institutions
have expanded their functional obligations to show the public the
exhibitions in their possession through virtual content dissemination
thanks to web connectivity. As exhibitions shift from a single-entry
point to worldwide connectivity, this is a respectable new normal
approach. Many worldwide cultural institutions have been able to
widen the knowledge bases of their patrons and the public as a result of
this diversity. It would also benefit South Africans if the government

would speed up the installation of free Wi-Fi in urban and rural areas.

As a result of online connectivity, cultural institutions have expanded their functional responsibility to provide digital content. As a result of this diversity, many cultural organizations around the world have been able to broaden the knowledge bases of their patrons and the broader public. The rise of online communities, which opened new channels of communication and spawned networked learning groups, has aided in the spread of information (Lock).

The use of information communication technology and online platforms in international museums is redefining museum practices and enriching traditional museum responsibilities. Museums are in a better position to disseminate educational content through an array of new digital channels, technologies, and media, thanks to the deployment of online platforms (Pesce et al. 1884). It is thus advantageous for museums in South Africa to optimally implement the use of online platforms to attract new and retain existing clients, as well as to maintain an active online presence so that the public does not forget about physical exhibitions. Museums should share their exhibitions, such as theme-based temporary and permanent exhibitions, and market themselves through other institutions' web spaces by using materials that are already publicly available online. Museums can become more efficient and effective communicators in the tourism industry as a result of these connectivity methods.

This paper focussed on how the public can see and be exposed to exhibits at cultural institutions for the objective of cultural learning. Follow-up studies could expand and analyze the influence of the COVID-19 pandemic on how patrons evaluated their experience and relationship with cultural institutions during the pandemic.

Works Cited

Africa Day Celebration: "Building the Africa We Want with the Youth through Arts, Culture, Heritage, Innovation and Entrepreneurship."*African Union Development Agency-New Partnership for Africa's Development (AUDA-NEPAD),* 31 May 2021, www.nepad. org/news/building-africa-we-want-youth-through-arts-culture-heritage-innovation-and. Accessed 18 Aug. 2023.

Basilaia, Giorgi, and David Kvavadze. "Transition to Online Education in Schools during a SARS-CoV-2 Coronavirus (COVID-19) Pandemic in Georgia."*Pedagogical Research*, vol.5, no. 4, em0060. https://doi.org/10.29333/pr/7937.

Bromley, Patricia. "Cosmopolitanism in Civic Education: Exploring Cross-National Trends, 1970-2008."*Current Issues in Comparative Education*, vol. 12, no. 1, 2009, pp. 33-44.

Calitz, Magdalena Gertruide. "A Culturally Sensitive Therapeutic Approach to Enhance Emotional Intelligence in Primary School Children." *University of South Africa*, November 2005, uir.unisa.ac.za/bitstream/handle/10500/1648/00titlepage.pdf?sequence=4&isAllowed=y. Accessed 18 Aug. 2023.

Choraś, Michał, et al. "Advanced Machine Learning Techniques for Fake News (Online Disinformation) Detection: A Systematic Mapping Study." *Applied Soft Computing*, vol. 101, Mar. 2021, https://doi.org/10.1016/j.asoc.2020.107050.

Democratic Alliance. "Stages of a Smart Lockdown Approach." *Democratic Alliance,* 13 Apr. 2020, www.da.org.za/2020/04/da-proposes-smart-lockdown-as-a-sustainable-approach-to-save-lives. Accessed 18 Aug. 2023.

Department of Cooperate Governance and Traditional Affairs (CoGTA). *Disaster Management Act, 2022: Amendment of Regulations Issued in Terms of Section 27(2),* SA, Reg. 565/21, s.24.2(j). www.gov.za/sites/default/files/gcis_document/202106/44772rg11299gon565.pdf. Accessed 18 Aug. 2023.

Disaster Management Act: Regulations: Alert level 3 during coronavirus COVID-19 lockdown. South African Government, Department of Cooperative Government and Traditional Affairs, 28 May 2020, www.gov.za/documents/disaster-management-act-regulations-alert-level-3-during-coronavirus-covid-19-lockdown-28. Accessed 18 Aug. 2023.

Fang, Yaqing, et al. "Transmission Dynamics of the COVID-19 Outbreak and Effectiveness of Government Interventions: A Data-Driven Analysis." *Journal of Medical Virology*, vol. 92, no. 6, 16 Mar. 2020, pp. 645-59.

Fu, Ping. "The Strength of Interconnectedness between Structure and Culture: Market Development in the Presence of Over-embedded Social Structure in the Lime Market of Hui Town." *The Journal of*

Chinese Sociology, vol. 3, no. 25, 12 Aug. 2016, pp. 1-27.

Furini, Marco, et al. "The Use of Hashtags in the Promotion of Art Exhibitions." *Digital Libraries and Archives.* 13th Italian Research Conference on Digital Libraries IRCDL 2017, Modena, Italy, 26–27 January 2017, Revised Selected Papers. Edited by Constantino Grana and Lorenzo Baraldi. Springer International Publishing, 2017.

Holl, Elisabeth, et al. "Corona and the Media: Effects of the COVID-19 Pandemic and Curfew Regulations on Media Consumption." *Self and Society in the Corona Crisis: Perspectives from the Humanities and Social Sciences,* edited by George Mein and Johannes Pause, Melusina Press, July 2020, pp. 489-490.

Jankowicz, Nina. *How to Lose the Information War: Russia, Fake News, and the Future of Conflict.* Bloomsbury Publishing, 9 July 2020.

Kahn, Rebecca. "Locked Down Not Locked Out—Assessing the Digital Response of Museums to COVID-19." *LSE Impact of Social Sciences Blog,* 8 May 2020, blogs.lse.ac.uk/impactofsocialsciences /2020/05/08/locked-down-not-locked-out-assessing-the-digital-response-of-museums-to-covid-19/. Accessed 18 Aug. 2023.

Kalish, Ira. "Weekly Global Economic Update." *Deloitte Insights,* 2020, https://www2.deloitte.com/us/en/insights/economy/global-economic-outlook/weekly-update.html. Accessed 18 Aug. 2023.

Lock, Jennifer V. "A New Image: Online Communities to Facilitate Teacher Professional Development." *Journal of Technology and Teacher Education,* vol. 14, no. 4, 2006, pp. 663-78.

Manyika, James, et al. *Digital Globalization: The New Era Global Flows.* McKinsey Global Institute, 2016.

Moro-Visconti, Roberto. "Corporate Governance, Digital Platforms, and Network Theory: Information and Risk-Return Sharing of Connected Stakeholders." *Social Science Research Network,* 28 Aug. 2019, pp. 179-204.

Oxera Consulting Ltd. *Understanding the Theory of International Connectivity.* Prepared for Department of Transport, *Oxera,* April 2010. www.oxera.com/wp-content/uploads/2018/03/Theory-of-international-connectivity.pdf. Accessed 18 Aug. 2023.

Perold, Ilanza, et al. "The Forced Cancellation of Four Jewel Events amidst COVID-19 and Its Probable Influence on the Western Cape Economy: A Literature Review." *Social Science Research Network*, 18 May 2020, https://www.researchgate.net/publication/341528169_ The_Forced_Cancellation_of_Four_Jewel_Events_Amidst_ COVID-19_and_Its_Probable_Influence_on_the_Western_Cape_ Economy_a_Literature_Review. Accessed 18 Aug. 2023.

Pesce, Danilo, et al. "When Culture Meets Digital Platforms: Value Creation and Stakeholders' Alignment in Big Data Use." *Current Issues in Tourism*, vol. 22, no. 15, 19 Mar. 2019, pp. 1883-1903.

Ramaphosa, Cyril. "President Cyril Ramaphosa: 2020 Africa Day." Remarks by Chairperson of the African Union President Cyril Ramaphosa on the occasion of Africa Day, 25 May 2020, *South Africa*, www.gov.za/speeches/president-cyril-ramaphosa-2020-africa-day-25-may-2020-0000. Accessed 18 Aug. 2023.

Statistics South Africa. "SA Loses More Than 600K Formal Sector Jobs during COVID-19 Lockdown." *Statistics South Africa*, 15 Oct. 2020, www.statssa.gov.za/?p=13690. Accessed 18 Aug. 2023.

Servon, Lisa J. *Bridging the Digital Divide: Technology, Community and Public Policy*. John Wiley & Sons, 2008.

South African Government. "Summary of Alert Levels." *South Africa*, www.gov.za/covid-19/about/about-alert-system. Accessed 18 Aug. 2023.

Spagnoletti, Paolo, Andrea Resca, and Gwanhoo Lee. "A Design Theory for Digital Platforms Supporting Online Communities: A Multiple Case Study." *Journal of Information Technology*, vol. 30, 2015, pp. 364-380.

Steenhuisen, John. "DA Proposes Smart Lockdown as a Sustainable Approach to Save Lives." *Democratic Alliance*, 13 Apr. 2020, www. da.org.za/2020/04/da-proposes-smart-lockdown-as-a-sustainable-approach-to-save-lives. Accessed 18 Aug. 2023.

Stillwell, Baylie. *Putting the "Play" Back into Display: Interactive Exhibits in Small Museums*. Scholar's Bank, 1 June 2017.

Tura, Nina, et al. "Platform Design Framework: Conceptualisation and Application." *Technology Analysis & Strategic Management*, vol. 30, no. 8, 2018, pp. 881-94.

van Breda, Adrian D. "A Critical Review of Resilience Theory and Its

Relevance for Social Work." *Social Work*, vol. 54, no. 1, 2018, pp. 1-18.

van Dijck, José. "Flickr and the Culture of Connectivity: Sharing Views, Experiences, Memories." *Memory Studies*, vol. 4, no. 4, 2011, pp. 401-15.

van Dijck, José. *The Culture of Connectivity: A Critical History of Social Media*. Oxford University Press, 2013.

Wu, Di, et al. "The SARS-CoV-2 Outbreak: What We Know." *International Journal of Infectious Diseases*, vol. 94, 2020, pp. 44-48.

PART III

Poetry

Chapter 17.

Corona Reign

Roberta K. Timothy

Twisted twisting and turning in my bed,

Jumping up screaming,

Black people dead.

Shango, hear my cry,

How much of my peeps must die?

Shango, the thunder and lightning above,

Hold me, comfort me, show My people love...

My grief is forbidden, ridiculed, silenced,

Put on a lynching stool, mutilated, villainized.

Dissociative fools, detached, data-collecting fighting tools,

Inhumane rules.

Yet bodies float in my dreams,

My face distorted in endless Zoom meetings, numb to my PEOPLES'
realities,

My tearless streams.

Shame.

Supposed to be Happy for a job,

Yet forever feeling robbed,

Fame.

Black elites competing for the colonial light,

I am in a revolution, no time to fight.

Numbers on CNN, on the news

Dying outside, inside,

Yellow tape across murder scenes.

Jogging while Black,

You will also be dead.

Transatlantic ghosts float by my head,

Deep breathing, yoga, meditation?

Seeing through muffled colour red.

Eugenics media game, Nothing said.

Hospitals filled by us, Black workers dead.

Smelling Flambeau flame.

Saying it isn't happening, racism ain't to blame!

We need education, good food choices, better decisions?

Biomedical, unethical incisions.

No mention of anti-Black hate, racist, sexist,

heterosexist, white-supremacist, classist, ablest, colonial state.

Capitalist poison wrapped in a milkshake,

Wearing masks and no handshakes.

Social distancing doesn't stop police surveillance, CARDING persistence

Like Enslavement, trying to escape again and again.

I feel the loss,

From Toronto, Brooklyn, Halifax, Detroit, London, and through other nations,

While they keep talking about travel bans and future VACATIONS.

Sunshine prayers to leave Africa, Caribbean, Brazil, and Central America out of this mess,

Can't even imagine corona's reign on the rest.

Ancestors brewing juju-soup,

Jumping prayers, salutations,

Feeding and strengthening our guts,

Reminding us of the wars, once fought,

Seasoning with okra and pine nuts,

Stirring our strength through the blood of resistance!

Black faces,

Black bodies,

Black Pain,

Black TEARS,

Black Fears,

Black rain,

African reign,

Liberation, blue bathing, womb shaking,

Poetry making,

Sing song, African, soul food baking!

Womb aching,

Surviving waking,

Black, Afrikan, People Reign!

Chapter 18.

School during COVID-19

Amelia McFarlane

During COVID-19, my experience with school was very difficult.
In the beginning, my mom tried the home school program.
She worked hard with my brothers and me.
It was not a good experience because
I think my teacher didn't know how to teach online.
I was not getting the help I needed to do my work.
One day my teacher logged out and never came back.

When we went back to in-person school, it was better.
My teacher was there to help me understand my work.
She was also able to show me different ways to problem solve.
I don't really like to wear the mask all day.
It sometimes gets wet and uncomfortable.
In-school is much better than online learning.

Chapter 19.

A Caribbean Caregiver Speaks

Bernice Duncan

Out of a conscious Caribbean
Van Sertima, Rodney, Negritude
Holy black, wholly beautiful
My lighter shade seemed to exude
Such extrinsic kind of discomfort
That I often marvelled when my own
Saw me as anomaly, not quite real
How could you love your origin when
You're not half as Black as we feel?!
And so, to Canada I came
A mere seven years ago
As a respected professional
With one more star to follow
No doors welcomed experience:
"Too qualified!"
"Selling yourself too short!"
But if I wished to volunteer?
"My, what expertise you've brought!"
Social schizophrenia demanded I survive
Kill pride, a splintered self
Pay bills to stay alive!

I donned the garb, went back to school
With real humility
I knew my worth though life had thrown
A nuclear bomb at me
Typecast as Trini-Canadian
BIPOC and ACB
Mere acronyms for alien
Inside-outsiders just like me!
Starting from the ground up
Here you have to pay your dues
Postgrad a plus on applications
But once landed, forced to lose
What status you brought with you
Mired in the sands of time
If not well known or born Canadian
You'll catch your Commonwealth behind!

Grasping the straw of caregiving
Back to school; top of the class
Though that distinction could not placate
The culture gods
Who deemed me second class
Senior, foreign, woman of colour
All shibboleths, all branding
Brand new, this adopted land
In newfound understanding
Of being ignored and overlooked
Newbie customer? Invisible!
Until the day you bare your teeth
My being here? Irreversible!

I've been through circumstances
Where the common thread was me
Client upon client, after two weeks
Saying, "No thanks, it's not you
It's just your agency!"
So I opted out of long-term care
Choosing care at home, one bed
Respectful welcome awaiting
Laughter, affection in its stead
Though not for a moment presupposing
That I was irreplaceable at all
On guard, compassionate and caring
Quintessential professional
Such common ground which everyone
Has always understood
Racist, red-necked, anti-Asian
Your service had better be good!
Home care of an aged, sweet client
Occasional stints at an agency
However grateful or resilient
Service warred with servility

And then came COVID-19
Where those values were celebrated
Customer service at the cost of life
Touted and heralded
Suddenly PSW "Pooper Scoopers" grew fragrant
Angels without wings
Backbones of care
The world pivoted to make Maslow proud
Its hierarchy of needs so clear
At first my employers were terrified

"Take three weeks off with pay!"
But soon recalled me, mortified
Elder care was tough—no way!

COVID turned the tide
Of all who would deride
Hardworking souls
With jobs one, two, three
As virus spread to grave concern
For health worker security!
Who would have thought a virus could
Force a real appreciation
Of the caregiver workhorses
To whom the virus-stricken
Turned weary, hopeful eyes
Blinded at last to colour
Praising commitment to the skies
As survivor or at last hour.

I am today at crossroad point
Growing in understanding
Of colour shifts that make us
Heroes or villains notwithstanding
COVID-19 has come to see and perhaps to conquer
Our many concerns made petty
We are in charge no longer.
Dust we are in the wind
With challenges aplenty
But in that moment, all you have
And all you'll ever be
Is a soul who gives its best
For in service lies divinity.

Chapter 20.

Move Over Heartache

Louise Adongo

Move on over
Four leaf clovers
COVID griefs have taken over

So much heartache
Waves of heartbreak
Who knew there'd be
So many reasons to grieve?

And what's all this about stages
It hasn't quite been that way
Looking forward to a time again
Like back when
We could take a breath
Between each bout
Of tears and scarring
Of careening and jarring
Jolts and jabs

But maybe that's romanticizing
And what's true is
I'll get through
Like Black women do

By stable footing
And harnessing the power in lineage
Rooted in memories of past toils our ancestors overcame
With divine intervention and perhaps
A dogged intention to keep stepping forward
No matter what came

Move on over
Four leaf clovers
My magic toolbox
Of supports and navigators
In this haze
Includes remembrances
Of those before us
Who made it through
Whether or not
They truly knew at first what all to do

Chapter 21.

Black Lives Do Matter

Delores V. Mullings

I want to cry again today for the loss of my people
As we planned and organized at the Scarborough Charter meetings
News began to seep in that we were under attack again
For simply being Black

Our joy, happiness, peace of mind, and triumph
Dissipated with the news that the little white boy
Went into our neighbourhood with the intent
To hurt, murder, and erase our Black bodies

When we should have been celebrating our triumph
For the work accomplished before today
Success at taming those in the hallowed halls
We stood motionless, numb with fright and sadness

With a Sistah's help our Brotha stood at the podium
Broken bodied, shattered spirit and twisted peace
Tears flowing, shaken voice, hoping to fool time
Announced that our relations were under attack

Next door in Buffalo an unknown eighteen-year-old white boy
Executed the unthinkable he planned in silence
Driving hundreds of kilometers across state line
Away from home and into our people's backyard

Opened fire with a semi-automatic human destroyer
Against fourteen unsuspecting victims eleven Blacks, three whites
Shopping for food to sustain their basic human needs
Anti-Black racism hurts everyone, including white people

We are not meant to breath and live in this place
Fending off brutality and violence against all odds
Doing our best when the authorities fail us
And tirelessly watching our people burn

Could this carnage have been prevented beforehand?
What did the authorities know about this boy?
Why did they think the white boy was not a threat?
And left him unchecked to descend upon us

Now my brothers, sisters, mothers, and fathers are left
Mopping uncooperative tears that refuse to stop
But keep up the flow openly and silently
In public at the grocery stores and behind closed doors

And so, we ended our time together sadly
Feeling the destructive acts of white supremacy
Crying, hugging, holding hands, and singing
We shall overcome some day

Because BLACK LIVES DO MATTER
We don't care what anyone says or does
Our people are here to stay for eternity
Watch us as we march to victory trampling white supremacy

Chapter 22.

This Will End

Delores V. Mullings

Here we stand on the precipice
Of an experience that is foreign to all of us
We know and understand little
Except it is a virus that attacks unexpectedly
A silent killer that we call Rona.

Pandemic is on everyone's lips
Some mention the bubonic plague
How did a pandemic that decimated
Europe, Asia, and North Africa
Become the Black death?

Frantically glued to the information highway
We hear of Black pain, abandonment, and deaths
Black bodies literally dying in front of our eyes
Carnage at our back doors and front steps
Body bags insufficient to dignify our dead.

Sharing cures, remedies, and old-time treatments
To stave off Rona before it reach wi yard
Try as we might, Rona still killing us
Granny, pickney, mama, bredah all ah wi
Still feeling the pangs of anti-Black racism.

But our bloodlines are resilient
And we have each other
So regardless of Rona's fierceness
Together we are stronger than the pandemic
And we know this too shall pass.

Epilogue

Delores V. Mullings, Olasumbo Adelakun, and
Jennifer Clarke

Writing this book has been an incredible journey of sisterhood, joy, learning, and supporting each other through some very challenging times during the past two years of the COVID-19 and racial injustice pandemics. As Black women, mothers, daughters, sisters, and friends, we have experienced grief and loss and felt deep, emotional pain and rage at the racial injustice of police brutality and systemic anti-Black racism that continues to impact the lives of our people locally and globally. Through all these experiences, we never lost hope and never gave up on humanity and the possibility of justice and freedom for our people. As we discussed in the introduction, systemic anti-Black racism predates the pandemic, but as we saw in the chapters, the pandemic has made the pre-existing social inequities, violence, and exclusion far worse, with no ideas or actions in sight to help our people from government and decision makers. One thing is for certain: ACBs have proven again that we know how to act in partnership for the betterment of our people. We are not waiting on the government to suggest mediocre Band-aid treatments that do little to impact institutional racial injustices.

We could not have produced this book without the incredible authors and poets who contributed to the collection. Their writings on giving birth, experiencing personal and professional loss because of death from COVID-19, job loss following the economic shutdown, education interruptions, mental health inequity, and other barriers produced by systemic anti-Black racism highlight the strength and resilience of ACB peoples under challenging circumstances and the way they work to navigate and overcome them. To understand resilience and strength among Black people, it is necessary to acknowledge their experiences and recognize the fact that the legacy of anti-Black racism and discrimination that affects their daily lives continues globally even today. The book concludes with two questions. The first explores the essence of resilience as it relates to ACB peoples, including debunking its premise by looking at the manifestation of harm and racial trauma on mental health and wellbeing. The second discusses how the negativity of social deprivation that has impacted ACB peoples in relation to education, employment, and health can be transformed.

Debunking the Myth of the Strong, Black Woman, and Black People in General

Q1. Does the narrative "Black people are so resilient" minimize the detrimental effects that pandemic-related racial trauma has on Black people's mental wellbeing?

The super-humanization of Black people goes all the way back to slavery and to physicians, who in the early 1900s characterized Blacks as having bodies that could withstand pain and surgical procedures without anaesthesia or pain relief. This strong and resilient Black person syndrome is a dangerous ideology that makes many Black people, especially women, susceptible to diseases, such as stroke, heart attacks, diabetes, and high blood pressure.

Black women are expected to solve problems, to be caretakers for everyone in their lives, and to constantly "hold it down." They are not expected to buckle, to be vulnerable, or to feel pain, physical or emotional. If we all think about the Black women we know, we will find similarities in how often they rest, if at all; how they cry in private, hiding their tears for fear of being viewed as weak; and how they carry the burden of their own pain on their shoulders, never seeking help.

The same applies to men. Boys are raised not to cry because "real men don't cry." Black boys and men are perceived as hypersexual and physically strong. They are depicted as violent regardless of age and therefore are believed to be more capable of physical harm than their white counterparts. Social constructs and prejudice have created these narratives, and this burden has left many of them deeply fragile.

In addition, the popular saying "Black don't crack" is not a compliment.

Rather, it is a stereotype that marginalizes Black people and absolves others from their responsibility to see a Black person as a human being who can feel pain and who is capable of weakness and worthy of support. Indeed, Black does crack because these constructs, subjugations, and prejudices have resulted in a hidden mental health crisis of depression, suicidal tendencies, and anxiety within many Black communities across the globe. This has been exacerbated by the COVID-19 pandemic and the lack of access to the required healthcare professionals to diagnose and treat health problems. Even though it is important to encourage people to persist through life's challenges, it is unfair to expect them to overcome structural barriers and injustices unscathed and to endure the trauma that comes with trying to be resilient through these experiences.

COVID-19-Related Harm

The myths of the strong, Black woman, Black men not needing counselling, and Black children being tough are caricatures of the resilience theme evidenced throughout this edited book and discussed in the section that debunks the term earlier in this chapter. Except for within ACB communities and countries predominated by Black leaders, the violence and harm that Black people endured globally during the pandemic has been largely ignored. Black people—including children in K-to-12, postsecondary institutions, frontline and professional workers, entrepreneurs, as well as the underemployed and unemployed—have been mostly erased in the mental health and mental wellness discussions around the pandemic. By the end of the first wave of the COVID-19 pandemic, experts were beginning to talk more about mental health resilience, especially in relation to people's response to public health mandates of isolation and social distancing. Almost everyone knows someone who has been affected by COVID-19 through food insecurity (Clarke), illness (Iroanyah), death (Adongo), birth (Clarke et al.), loss of business and employment (Adelakun and Aishida), and education (Mullings; Williams et al.), as authors in this edited book discussed. Like other communities, ACB peoples have been unable to grieve their losses, but they have found different ways of grieving and honouring their dead (Fearon), supporting one another through time and space (Deachman), and adjusting to virtual mental healthcare to support those dealing with the harms caused to Black life (Clarke et al.) both in the diaspora and continental Africa. We could interpret these adjustments as resilience, but, in line with Alyson Renaldo's arguments in this book, the question remains: Where do Black health and mental health end and resilience begin? In response, we suggest that resilience, as it is embraced by ACB peoples, is harmful and a form of anti-Blackness that emerged out of, and is still connected to, white people's superiority and economic greed.

The onslaught of prepandemic racial violence on the Black body has been exacerbated during the pandemic: public execution; killing; police home invasions; beatings; harassment; loss of jobs, careers, homes, livelihoods, and relationships; and death. These stressors have caused more anxiety, sadness, and loneliness and has increased exposure to intimate partner violence and transphobic violence. Pandemic health measures, lack of staff, and low supplies does impact access to mental health services. However, ACB people cannot access mental health services, or when they do, they frequently experience violence through a white service delivery model, so these individuals who are trying to access support often leave before receiving proper care. Therefore, the availability of racially and culturally relevant mental health and wellness programs and support services continues to lag behind the increasing needs and demands of an already underserviced population. This gap further forces Black people into accepting the myth of resilience, which plays on the notion that only those who are unmotivated, weak, or spiritually cursed experience mental health and wellness challenges. The resilience theme continues to cause significant harm to ACB people globally and must be addressed.

Racial Trauma

The narrative that "Black people are so resilient" is a contradiction. On the one hand, it acknowledges our resilience as a people given our survival of colonization both in the African diaspora and continental Africa. This violence and brutality include the arbitrary dividing up of Africa, the occupation of our lands, the legacy of chattel slavery, and the intergenerational trauma they have caused. Our ancestors resisted colonization, enslavement, and Jim Crow and continue to fight other structural and systemic forms of current anti-Black racism. The narrative can also be used to offer hope to our people, especially our young people, who have and continue to experience insurmountable grief, loss, joblessness, poor education outcomes, and lack of opportunities.

On the other hand, we need to be aware of how thinking of resilience as a way of offering hope and empowerment might also minimize the negative effects of racial trauma that Black people experience. We were traumatized in the workplace prior to and during the pandemic. When we tried to gain access to health and mental healthcare services, housing, mortgages, and small business loans, we were denied for lack of eligibility. This narrative can also cause young people to feel as though they are not enough if they ask for help—not strong enough, not smart enough, and not working hard enough, especially if their peers are achieving and accomplishing goals, and they are not. It can set up young people for self-blame and feelings of powerlessness, hopelessness, and helplessness.

A further detrimental effect of this narrative is that it normalizes Black pain and the dehumanization of Black bodies in all domains of life from birth to death. This was evident in the murder of George Floyd in the early days of the pandemic in 2020. The sheer lack of empathy for Black pain and the failure to implement systemic change to address racist police violence not only compounded but also complicated our collective grief and minimized the racial trauma of watching the public killing of a Black man.

Finally, this narrative has been used to let white supremacist capitalist patriarchy off the hook for failing to provide equitable access to healthcare and other services for Black people, historically and present day, and it ignores racial trauma as part of mental healthcare. The insidiousness of systemic anti-Black racism and the cumulative racial trauma it produces in Black life must be acknowledged, and institutions must be held accountable for intergenerational harms in ACB communities.

Education Deprivation

Q2. How can social deprivation, which negatively impacts Black people, as seen in this COVID era, be transformed?

COVID-19 has set back the education of all children, but it has had a far greater and more devastating impact on Black children because of pre-existing social deprivation in the schools, communities, and neighbourhoods where Black families live that predates the pandemic. Prior to the pandemic, Black children experienced poor educational outcomes because of underinvestment in Black communities and under-resourced schools with majority Black student populations. Black children's reality of family poverty and vulnerability to teacher bias and anti-Black racism created more disadvantages. They were also deprived of valuable education instruction, materials, and experience because of their parents' lack of access to high-speed internet connection. As schools and educators struggled to provide online learning for students, ACB parents were also challenged to support their children because of their limited education, income, and language skills, and a lack of literacy in technology. Many could not access the educational materials their children needed for homework or adequately support them to succeed academically. In addition, many ACB children did not have adequate access to the technology (e.g., computer, laptop, or smartphone) required to participate fully in remote online learning, and their parents could not afford to hire a private tutor to supplement their education with extra lessons. The result is that Black children missed important milestones, social skills development, cultural activities for positive racial identity development, and they were isolated from friends, peers, and teachers.

Education Transformation

K-to-12 education in the province of Ontario needs a radical transformation. It needs to be reimagined and uprooted from its foundation, as too many Black children were unable to access or benefit from online learning during the pandemic, which will lead to further disparity and poor educational outcomes. Education transformation means challenging the structural inequality and persistent anti-Black racism that widen the educational divide and keep Black children from receiving quality education opportunities and economic advancement in adulthood. Government responses to education must reflect the needs of Black children, including investments in high-speed internet and access to devices for online learning, culturally relevant programming, access to free online tutors and Black teacher representation to strengthen under-resourced schools and communities. In addition, teacher education programs must prepare teachers with technology skills and digital literacy to create and deliver innovative curricula, and they must instruct them on how to engage Black students in face-to-face and online learning, and other culturally relevant programming. Government and education institutions must innovate and build recovery plans that address educational inequities, bridge the digital divide, and take the lessons that the pandemic highlighted and implement policies, provide resources, and improve infrastructure to create a fully inclusive, quality online learning environment for all students, including ACB students.

Employment Deprivation

The term "double pandemic" surfaced early in the first wave of COVID-19 and describes how the pandemic intersects with racism and impacts Black, Indigenous, and racialized people. Not all racialized groups are experiencing a double pandemic, but ACB people certainly are. Many Black small businesses—such as hair salons, office cleaning services, barbershops, and restaurants—lost their businesses because they could not weather the loss of income from government-imposed measures to reduce the spread of the coronavirus. While some ACBs were closing their businesses, low-skilled workers were getting extended hours, as they were suddenly part of the essential workforce for the crisis.

In the Global North, many Black people, particularly women, work in the low-skilled labour market service sector as cooks, maids, cleaners, servers, cashiers, personal care workers, and orderlies. The work is often low paying, on-call, temporary, seasonal, or short term, where vacation and extended benefits (e.g., dental) are nonexistent. The work is physically demanding and labour intensive with a lot of heavy lifting. During the pandemic, these jobs (e.g., cleaners, personal support workers, and orderlies) were deemed essential to society, and ACBs were hired as temporary workers at exhaustingly extended hours with no additional benefits or recognition of their contribution to fighting the pandemic. Although these workers were deemed essential, they were not accorded the respect similar to those in the medical profession who were called heroes even at the onset of the pandemic. Black women's roles as frontline workers and a lack of private transportation caused these workers to be more exposed and at risk of contracting COVID-19 than those who did not have to take public transportation or who worked from home. Despite these hurdles, ACB people made gains in rebuilding and transforming their lives to address the social deprivation and negative impact of the pandemic.

Employment Transformation

Many new Black small businesses opened during the pandemic; they are now providing digital services, counselling, delivering goods and groceries, making face coverings and masks, as well as growing and cooking food. During the government-imposed lockdowns, some hairdressers and barbers tried working from their homes but were penalized with warnings and hefty fines. Some shifted to providing in-home services to customers who wanted haircare and were able to save their businesses from closing permanently through creativity. These self-employment activities helped reduce systemic employment discrimination, put money back into Black communities, and create access to employment for ACB people who otherwise would be dependent on others for their livelihood. Employment discrimination shows up in wage gaps, unemployment and under-employment, and a high concentration in the service sector. Western governments continue to suggest that vaccines are the only option to deal with the pandemic, but we also need equitable access to good jobs with benefits, housing, and daycare so that these essential workers can have sustainable employment to provide for their families and thrive. The impact of the pandemic will be with us for a long time, but as we move forwards after the immediate crisis, it is important to implement strategies and policies to deal with anti-Black racism.

Health System Deprivation

It is a well-known fact that race, racial prejudice, and race discrimination have shaped the experiences of Black people globally and that these social factors are directly responsible for the continuing legacy of poor health in ACB populations. In comparison to other racial groups, the health inequities experienced by Black people mainly result from discrepancies in access and differences in socioeconomic standing and lifestyle.

Many Black communities have survived for centuries on the philosophy of Ubuntu—"I am because you are," a philosophy that has enabled them to face and survive adversities by relying on one another and supporting one another through community living. However, when individuals who are already faced with personal trauma are further exposed to mass traumas as seen during this COVID-19 pandemic—such as loneliness, grief from inability to carry out cultural funeral practices, inability to support loved ones, not being able to visit and care for families in long-term care homes, and fear of seeking life-saving healthcare)—it becomes extremely difficult to manage these complex layers without help. The myriad of disparities that Black people experience continues to adversely affect their mental health and wellbeing.

Health System Transformation

Lifestyles of Black people have been influenced by a history of injustices, which has shaped their worldview of health and illness. To transform the negative health outcome mechanisms of race-based discrimination, the health-seeking behaviours and choices of Black community members must be examined. However, Black healthcare providers who historically have given effective and more appropriate care to Black service recipients make up only a small percentage of professionals in the healthcare workforce. For this reason, many turn to faith-based organizations when seeking help. For change to happen, emphasis should be placed on providing access to high-quality care for all and strengthening preventative healthcare approaches in underserved communities. It is also crucial to diversify the healthcare workforce to reflect the demographic composition of the population. Moreover, adequate income has been shown to help achieve improved health. Therefore, access to employment opportunities is important to provide the income needed by families to support health.

When considering intervention efforts to reduce racial prejudice, racial beliefs, and stereotypes, initiatives to raise awareness on the prevalence of inequities in healthcare and support for addressing these health inequities are needed. The urgency of these intervention efforts can be communicated to affected communities so that they can be empowered to actively participate and propose social, political, and policy changes that will improve their overall health outcomes.

Looking Towards the Next Chapter

Black people's trauma and resilience are historical and will not end anytime soon. We have seen stories and narratives in this book that describe love, grief and loss, pain, support, surprise, happiness, perseverance, determination, and yes—resilience. We do not know what the future brings, but we are hopeful for our people and the promise to ourselves to create a brighter tomorrow for future generations. As we complete this book, yet a different variant of COVID-19 (Omicron) is settling in bodies around the globe. We are not prepared for what will come next, but one thing is for sure: We will continue to fight, resist, and challenge whatever is coming, just as our ancestors before us had done. There is an unsettling feeling that we are sitting on top of an iceberg unprepared for the inevitable. What gives us hope is the possibility of creating something new, a chance to uproot systemic anti-Black racism, and give our children a chance for a better future. Perhaps as a next step, we can begin to document life after COVID-19 for ACB peoples globally.

Notes on Contributors

Olasumbo Adelakun is an adjunct professor at St. Bonaventure University teaching global leadership; she is an independent consultant, author, and has served as an assistant editor for various academic books and book chapters. Having lived on three continents, her penchant for improving the life experiences of others is reflected in her work as an educator, her commitment to studying challenging human conditions and her desire to create opportunities to provide a voice and hope for change.

Oladele Aishida is a financial analyst, stockbroker, and an entrepreneur with an MBA. He is a passionate businessman who has participated in the incubation of many businesses in West Africa. Presently, he is involved with data analytics and developing trading algorithms to monitor the global financial markets. He is married to his beautiful wife, Melissa.

Louise Adongo is a bold and grounded leader with ten-plus years of experience in systems change, policy and evaluation. She brings care and intention to uncovering the roots of tangled problems, thus enabling shifts to greater resilience, sustainability, and impact.

Falan Bennett is an MD-PhD candidate at the University of Toronto's medical school. She holds a master's degree in public health from the University of Toronto. Her interests span the structural determinants of health, health equity, Black reproductive justice, and social policy as a fundamental causative of reproductive health disparities.

Denessia Blake-Hepburn is a public health professional who holds a master's degree in public health from the University of Toronto. Her interests include Black health, health equity, the social determinants of health, and examining the intersection between social policy and inequitable health outcomes among Black populations.

Jennifer Clarke is a mother, social worker, psychotherapist, clinical anti-racist trainer, consultant, and author. She is the founder and CEO of Advancing Racial Trauma Care (ART Care). She has published widely in the areas of child welfare, youth mental health, gun violence loss and trauma, school safety, violence against women and girls, with a focus on cybersexual violence, and Africentric social work education and practice. She is co-editor of two books: *Today's Youth and Mental Health* and *Africentric Social Work*.

Preeyaah Clarke is a registered dietitian, Master of Health Science graduate from Toronto Metropolitan University and the founder of the Prenourish Wellness and Weight loss Clinic. She has worked in a variety of health settings across the Greater Toronto Area, such as at Southlake Regional Health Centre, York Region Public Health and Wharton Medical Clinic. She utilizes her unique skill set and knowledge in health science and nutrition to be a health advocate and a credible source of information to Black and racialized communities on a variety of nutrition issues, including chronic diseases, weight management and diabetes prevention

Wesley Crichlow is an African/Black Canadian critical race theorist intersectional decolonial queer scholar. His work critically connects theories of anti-Black racism, intersectionality, and decoloniality as the signature praxis and framing for research, teaching and service. His work aims to provide measures to alleviate anti-Black racism, hetero-cisnormativity, transmisogyny, structural, and systemic inequalities. Dr. Crichlow teaches at Ontario Tech University (2003–present) within the youth and criminal justice discipline with over twenty-five years of critical race theory approaches to intersectionality university community mobilization and development.

Bruce Deachman has been a reporter, senior writer, and columnist with *The Ottawa Citizen for* close to thirty years. Over that time, he has covered a wide variety of topics, including health issues, politics, arts and entertainment, sports, and municipal affairs.

Stacy Diedrick is the proud mother of two beautiful children who lights up her world daily. She is an Early Childhood Educator who is passionate about working with children and helping them to bring out their best. She enjoys interacting with and supporting children who others have written off because of the challenges they have experienced in their lives.

Bernice Duncan wears several hats as a social engagement consultant, health promoter and caregiver. Her Caribbean background in HIV and sexual and reproductive health training has given her a wide context for viewing the deepening impact of viruses like Covid 19 on all aspects of our lives. Her lived experience in Canada continues to be so heart-felt that she periodically pours out its rewards and challenges through poetry.

Bo Ebuehi is an avid adventurer, nature enthusiast, and lover of the arts. Her passion for exploration is matched only by her zest for life. Whether it's embarking on scenic hikes in the mountains or strolling through bustling city streets, savouring a good cup of coffee, Bo finds solace in the rhythm of her footsteps. Traveling has become her gate-way to discovering diverse cultures, capturing breathtaking landscapes, and forging lifelong memories.

Rachel Ewan is the first person in her family to complete post-secondary education and earn a PhD. She is an instructor in the Social Work Diploma Program at Red Deer Polytechnic. Born and raised in Toronto, Dr. Ewan is of Jamaican descent. She is focussed on creating equitable perinatal mental health and maternal health service and care for Black women.

Stephanie Fearon is the inaugural assistant professor of Black thriving and education at York University. Stephanie's work uses literary and visual arts to communicate in a structured, creative, and accessible form insights gleaned from stories shared by Black mothers and their families. Her recently published article, "At Mummy's Feet: A Black Motherwork Approach to Arts-Informed Inquiry" (*Canadian Review of Sociology/Revue canadienne de sociologies*) advances an arts-informed research methodology grounded in Black motherwork theory.

Sydney Henry holds a Bachelor of Science degree in sociology and a Master of Science degree in social policy from the University of the West Indies, Mona, Jamaica. His main area of focus has been on housing for the indigent, children, and young people as well as community development, specializing in social policy implementation and the management of social projects. His work in community development has been in both the private and public sector, delivering projects in communities in the USA, Jamaica, St. Lucia, Haiti, and other Caribbean islands.

Tamar Hewitt is a wife and mother of two wonderful children living in Toronto, Ontario. She enjoys reading different genre especially those that bring light and love into her life. She prioritizes and enjoys spending time with her family and for down times, she watches family movies, comedies, dramas and documentaries.

Tina Hewitt is a loving and involved sister, daughter, aunt, and avid reader. Tina is the loving mother of a still-born child surrounded by love. She has demonstrated resilience in the face of this loss and trauma. Her grieving and healing processes have been firmly rooted in family and sharing with women who have also lost a child. Now a Quality Control professional, she is deliberately being gentle with her soul and learning to live fully in the moment.

Ngozi Iroanyah MA, is a PhD student investigating the experiences and perspectives of Black Canadians living with dementia and their care partners in the GTA. She is a health equity specialist working in the field of dementia, and primary care. She is an anti-racism strategist, policy analyst, community engagement practitioner, and public speaker. She implements an intersectional lens as the foundation of her work to support meaningful change. Her heart lies with racially and culturally diverse older adults living with dementia and their carers and seeks to inform policies, strategies, and programs that affect them to ensure better access to health and social care. She is a caregiver to her father Felix, who currently lives with end-stage dementia and is her inspiration

Gregory King (he/him) received his MFA in choreographic practice and theory from Southern Methodist University and has performed with the Washington Ballet, Metropolitan Opera, and *The Lion King* on

Broadway. An artist, educator, and activist, King has served as director for the Decolonizing Dance Writing: International Exchange Project, which brought together artists from Peru, Columbia, Sri Lanka, New Zealand, and Ghana to share their practices and to discourse about teaching and learning dance through a non-Western lens.

Amelia McFarlane is a twelve-year-old student who aspires to be a writer and teacher when she grows up. She lives with family in a neighbourhood surrounded by many things she likes. She enjoys spending time with her grandparents.

Daniel Rankadi Mosako is a renowned artist, archivist, and heritage practitioner who has acquired the following degrees: Bachelor of Arts in Fine Arts in Education, Bachelor of Arts with Honors with specialization in Art History, Bachelor of Information Science Honors, Postgraduate Diploma in Heritage and Museum Studies, Master of Historical and Cultural Science in Heritage and Museum Studies, Master of Arts in Fine Arts, and Doctor of Philosophy in Art.

Delores V. Mullings rests on the shoulders of her African ancestors who have paved the way, enabling her to be the first among many firsts. She is the first Black person, and only Black woman and mother, to be hired in the School of Social Work and appointed to a senior administrative position at Memorial University. Her scholarship explores mothering and parenting using critical pedagogies, including anti-Black racism, Africentric theory, and critical race theory.

Eboni-Rai Mullings is a graduate of Toronto Metropolitan University, a writer, and an editor raised primarily in Southern Ontario. Her writing focuses on her experiences as a Black child and youth in white spaces and the personal evolution that took place as she moved to a culturally and racially diverse city. She hopes to use these experiences to uplift young Black readers by publishing Afrocentric fiction for current and future generations.

Joyce Mullings is a God-fearing elder residing in a long-term care home. She gets joy in reading her Bible everyday, and spending time with her family. She loves to do word puzzles. She is the mother of six children, 13 grand children and 11 great grand children.

Marcia Mullings is a retired health care professional who spent twenty-five years on the frontlines at Sunny Brook Hospital in various departments, including emergency and recovery. She is an avid baker, gardener, and tailor. She is a favoured church mother in her congregation and grandmother to three beautiful girls.

Alyson Renaldo is a professor of English and critical thinking at Humber College. She is also an actor, producer, and writer for film and theatre, as well as a freelance journalist. Her published work can be found in *The Huffington Post*, *The Root*, and *NOW Magazine*. Alyson holds BFA and MA degrees from the University of Southern California and Columbia University, respectively.

Bukolah Salami is a professor at the Cumming School of Medicine, University of Calgary. Her research focusses on Black people's health, immigrant health, and racialized people's health. She is a Faculty of Nursing fellow, Canadian Academy of Nursing Killam Laureate for 2021 to 2024. She is the founder and lead of several organizations and programs, including Black Youth Mentorship and Leadership Program and African Child and Youth Migration Network.

Vinnette Thompson is a retired red shield chef who has worked at several well-known establishments, including Holiday Inn, Red Lobster, and Chartwell. She walks steadfastly in the footsteps of God, the creator of all things. She has embarked on new learnings as a seasonal fisher and knitter.

Roberta K. Timothy's work addresses key areas of concern in anticolonial, antioppression, and community-responsive health promotion, policy, and practice. She is the Black health lead, and the program developer and inaugural program director of the first MPH in the field of Black health. She is an assistant professor, a political scientist, therapist, and community health leader. She prioritizes critical and creative approaches to knowledge production that reflect the experiences and aspirations of African/Black diasporic, migrant, refugee, and transnational Indigenous communities.

Khadijah Williams is an educator, researcher and consultant with a PhD in Applied Social Sciences from Lancaster University, UK, with other qualifications from the University of the West Indies, St.

Augustine, Trinidad and the Vocational Training Development Institute, Jamaica. She is the Director/Principal of a postsecondary residential school in rural Jamaica and has over 28 years' experience in her field of study. Her current interests include young people transitioning from state care, international social work, social work education, community violence prevention work, children and young people's participation in decision making processes and child and youth justice issues.

Deepest appreciation to
Demeter's monthly Donors

DEMETER

Daughters
Tatjana Takseva
Debbie Byrd
Fiona Green
Tanya Cassidy
Vicki Noble
Myrel Chernick

Sisters
Amber Kinser
Nicole Willey

Grandmother
Tina Powell